CAMBRIDGE

active GRAMMAR

LEVEL 3

Without answers

Mark Lloyd and Jeremy Day
Series editor: Penny Ur

CAMBRIDGE
UNIVERSITY PRESS

University Printing House, Cambridge CB2 8BS, United Kingdom

One Liberty Plaza, 20th Floor, New York, NY 10006, USA

477 Williamstown Road, Port Melbourne, VIC 3207, Australia

314–321, 3rd Floor, Plot 3, Splendor Forum, Jasola District Centre, New Delhi – 110025, India

103 Penang Road, #05-06/07, Visioncrest Commercial, Singapore 238467

Cambridge University Press is part of the University of Cambridge.

It furthers the University's mission by disseminating knowledge in the pursuit of education, learning and research at the highest international levels of excellence.

www.cambridge.org
Information on this title: www.cambridge.org/9780521152471

First published 2011

20 19 18 17 16 15 14 13 12

Printed in Great Britain by CPI Group (UK) Ltd, Croydon CR0 4YY

A catalogue record for this publication is available from the British Library

ISBN 978-0-521-15250-1 Paperback with answers and CD-ROM
ISBN 978-0-521-15247-1 Paperback without answers and CD-ROM

Introduction

What is Active Grammar?

Active Grammar is a grammar reference and practice series for secondary students and university students. It is divided into three levels, corresponding to the levels of *The Common European Framework of Reference for Languages* (CEF). Level 1 corresponds to A1–A2, Level 2 to B1–B2, and Level 3 to C1–C2. The books give comprehensive coverage of grammar at each level, while also covering reading, composition and discussion. The books are suitable for students who are preparing for Cambridge ESOL exams.

How are the books organised?

Each unit includes

- a short **presentation** text which shows the grammar in context and provides authentic content in areas such as geography, history, social studies and science.
- easy-to-understand **grammar explanations** with plenty of examples.
- **Tip** boxes which highlight common errors or other interesting facts about the grammar.
- graded grammar **practice exercises**, many of which are in the style of Cambridge ESOL exams, aimed at building students' confidence.
- a **My Turn** activity, where students can actively apply the grammar to their own experiences, opinions and personal preferences.
- a **My Test** section which allows students to check their understanding of key points.

Also included in the book

- regular **Review** units which provide contrastive practice of previous units.
- the **Appendices**, which include a **Glossary** with definitions for all highlighted words in the units.

The CD-ROM includes

- extra activities for all the grammar covered in the book.
- printable progress tests.

How do I use the book?

You can work through the book unit by unit from Unit 1. Alternatively, you can use any unit or group of units separately if you want to focus on a particular area of grammar.

The book can be used for self-study, or in the classroom. For teachers, a comprehensive online teacher's guide gives practical tips on how to use the material in class.

www.cambridge.org/elt/activegrammar

Contents

Verb structures

Word formation

Conditionals, clauses, questions, indirect speech

Sentences and varieties of English

Appendices

1 Present simple and present continuous

Why is the girl in the photo smiling?

A bowler **smiles** at her friends after a good shot.

Why **is** the girl in the photo **smiling**? It **sounds** like an easy question: she'**s having** a good time with friends and she'**s feeling** good after a good shot. But psychologists **are** forever **arguing** about this question.

Some **believe** that smiling **is** an individual act: we **smile** because we **feel** happy ... unless we'**re trying** to hide our emotions. Others **claim** that we **smile** to build social relationships. Some animals **use** a grin to show that they **don't want** to fight, for example, so perhaps our smile **serves** the same function.

So who'**s** right? In one study, researchers filmed people bowling. If you **watch** people doing a very social activity like this, it **looks** as if they'**re always smiling**. They **stop** smiling only when they **are concentrating** on their next shot. But when **do** they **start** smiling again? After each good shot, the researchers took photographs to identify when the smile **starts** – while the player **is** still **looking** down the alley or a few seconds later when they **turn** round to share their happiness with the group?

And the results? Only around 4% of bowlers **smile** with their backs to their friends. Far more – 42% – **smile** as soon as they **turn** round. The conclusion: we usually **smile** not because we'**re** happy, but because we'**re** friendly.

?
1 What are the two theories of smiling?
2 Why did the researchers choose a bowling alley?

Answers: 1 We smile because we feel happy; we smile to build social relationships. 2 Because bowling is a very social activity.

Present simple and present continuous

Present simple

1 Use the present simple to refer to facts and specific routines or habits, and with adverbs of frequency.
   *We **smile** because we **feel** happy.*
   *We usually **smile** because we'**re** friendly.*

2 We usually use the present simple with state verbs such as ***think, feel, believe, know, seem, appear, like, consist, have*** and ***belong.***
   *Some **believe** that smiling is an individual act.*

3 We also often use the present simple to describe events shown in a picture, to make them seem more immediate and alive. For the same reason, we usually use the present simple in news headlines and in television or radio commentaries on sports or other ongoing events.

A bowler ***smiles*** *at her friends.*

And Jake ***heads*** *the ball to Gallant – who* ***kicks*** *... and it's a goal!*

Prince William visits local hospital.

4 Use the present simple in the expressions *Here come(s)* ... and *There go(es)* ... .

There ***goes*** *Mike, looking as cheerful as usual.*

NOT ~~*There is going Mike, ...*~~

Use the present simple with verbs like ***promise, agree, assure*** and ***demand***, which are used to perform the act they describe.

I promise *I won't be late.* (I am using these words to make a promise.)

Present continuous

5 Use the present continuous to refer to activities, situations and changes happening now / around now.

... while the player ***is*** *still* ***looking*** *down the alley ...*

6 We can use the present continuous with indefinite adverbs of frequency (e.g. *always, constantly, forever*) to refer to regular behaviour which is typical, habitual and predictable.

Psychologists ***are forever arguing*** *about this question.*

We sometimes use the present continuous in this way to criticise or express disapproval.

Sally's ***always losing*** *things. She should be more careful.*

7 When we describe an action or event with the present simple, we can use the present continuous to refer to activities, situations and changes happening around the same time.

If you ***watch*** *a group of friends bowling, it* ***looks*** *as if they****'re always smiling****.*

Present simple or present continuous

The present simple is much more common than the present continuous, and it is the best form to use if you are not sure.

8 We usually use the present simple to refer to situations which we see as permanent, and the present continuous to refer to situations which we see as temporary. Note the difference:

Tom ***lives*** *in Rome. He* ***works*** *as a lawyer for a big Italian company.* (Rome is his permanent base.)

Jane ***is living*** *in Rome at the moment. She* ***is working*** *as an English teacher.* (She is in Rome temporarily, e.g. for one year.)

9 When we tell stories or to give instructions, we use the present simple to describe the shorter actions and events and the present continuous to describe the longer situations or background activity.

Gavin and his wife ***are sitting*** *at home one evening when the telephone* ***rings*** *and their lives* ***change*** *for ever.*

First, you ***fry*** *the onion in a little oil. While the onion's* ***cooking****, you* ***chop*** *the vegetables.*

10 Although we usually use the present simple with state verbs (see 2 above), we can use the present continuous if we are talking about an ongoing present process rather than a fact.

She's ***feeling*** *good after a good shot.*

Some verbs (e.g. ***hear, see, think, appear***) can be state verbs or action verbs, but with a different meaning.

What ***do*** *you* ***think*** *of Jan's new hairstyle?*
(= What's your opinion about it?)

I'm thinking *of taking a few days off.*
(= I'm considering the possibility of doing it.)

In the present simple, ***see*** and ***hear*** have different meanings.

I ***see*** *him every day.* (= I see)
I ***see*** *what you mean.* (= I understand)
I ***hear*** *you loud and clear.* (= I hear)
I ***hear*** *you're coming to stay.* (= I have been told)

11 We use the present simple with verbs like ***hope*** and ***look forward to*** in formal situations, and we use the present continuous if we want to sound more informal and less direct.

We very much ***hope*** *you will be able to attend.*
*We****'re*** *really* ***hoping*** *you'll be able to come.*

I ***look forward to*** *hearing from you in the near future.*
I'm looking forward to *hearing from you soon.*

Practice

A **Underline the correct option.**

1 Ice <u>*melts*</u> / *is melting* above 0°C.
2 Have you got an umbrella? It *starts* / *is starting* to rain.
3 Gabriela looks lovely today – she *wears* / *is wearing* her new dress.
4 Paul's daughter lives in Spain – he *visits* / *is visiting* her two or three times a year.
5 There *goes* / *is going* Maggie, on her way to work, I suppose.
6 Don't worry, I *promise* / *am promising* I won't tell anyone your secret.
7 This carpet *gets* / *is getting* very dirty – maybe we should wash it.
8 That's great tennis from Thompson as he *hits* / *is hitting* another winning shot into the corner!

B **Complete the sentences, using the present simple or present continuous form of the verb given.**

1 always go
a Sue and I ......always go...... to the cinema on Thursdays.
b I saw Mary in the travel agent's this afternoon – she ......'s always going...... on holiday!
2 play
a Giovanni .... football for a local team.
b Anthony .... in goal today because our normal goalkeeper is injured.
3 have
a I .... lunch at the moment. Can I phone you back in half an hour?
b The hotel .... 14 double rooms, all with bathrooms.
4 wonder
a We .... whether we should buy a birthday present for Lucie.
b I .... what time the next train is.
5 come
a Look – here .... the bus, at last!
b More and more people .... to live here these days.
6 (you) think
a You look worried – what .... about?
b Why .... Jim is so happy today? Is it his birthday or something?
7 stand
a St Thomas's Tower .... at the entrance to the harbour.
b A strange woman .... outside the house. Do you know her?
8 work
a It's 8.30 on a hot July evening. Gordon Stevens .... late in his office, when suddenly ...
b These tablets .... better if you take them with food.

C **Underline the correct option. Sometimes both options are possible.**

1 John <u>*regrets* / *is regretting*</u> the way he behaved yesterday.
2 Mistakes like that *cost* / *are costing* the company a lot of money.
3 Sue *has* / *is having* the flu, so she's off work today.
4 It's a very simple camera. You *just press* / *are just pressing* the button and that's it!
5 My neighbours are really noisy – they *always play* / *are always playing* loud music late at night.
6 Annie's car *doesn't sound* / *isn't sounding* very good. She should take it to a garage.
7 I *don't have* / *am not having* much time right now. Can we talk tomorrow instead?
8 The company *hopes* / *is hoping* to expand into Europe in the next few years.

D **Complete the sentences with the present simple or present continuous form of the verbs in brackets.**

1 I ......understand...... a little Italian, but I can't speak it. (understand)
2 My cousins .... skiing nearly every winter. (usually go)
3 Here .... Michelle. Maybe she wants to talk to me. (come)
4 I invited Jill to the party – she .... to it. (look forward)
5 .... what time the bank opens? (you know)
6 This bed .... 180 centimetres by 210 centimetres – I think it's too big. (measure)
7 A: What ....?
B: My homework. Don't interrupt me. (do)
8 I just heard Wendy's news – she .... a baby. (expect)
9 The first thing to do is peel the potatoes. Then you .... them in salted water for about 20 minutes. (boil)
10 And at the line ... Powell .... – in 9.64 seconds – a new personal best! (win)

E **Complete the news story, using the present simple or continuous form of the verbs in the box.**

~~ask~~ be consider follow look forward to love play score think want

JOHNSON [1] ....ASKS........ FOR NEW CONTRACT

City striker Simon Johnson [2] .... a new contract, and the club [3] .... the possibility of offering him a five-year deal, according to Johnson's website. The news [4] .... Johnson's winning goal in last Saturday's game against their rivals United. Johnson's agent told reporters: 'Simon [5] .... the best football of his career, and the fans [6] .... him. He [7] .... a lot of goals at the moment, and he [8] .... he can help the club to win the league. Simon [9] .... one of the best players at the club, and right now he [10] .... scoring lots more goals for them in the next twelve months.'

MY TURN!

Write three things that you are doing at this minute, three things that you are doing these days but only temporarily, and three things that you always do.

Examples: *I'm wearing black jeans. I'm reading War and Peace. I always go to bed early.*

MY TEST!

Circle the correct option.

1 I .... there are going to be a lot of people at the match tonight. **a** am hearing **b** can hear **c** hear
2 Hey, look. Here .... Robert. I wonder why he's smiling. **a** goes **b** comes **c** is coming
3 .... for money. It's really annoying. **a** She forever asks **b** She asks forever **c** She's forever asking
4 .... getting a new camera. This one is getting really old now. **a** I'm thinking of **b** I think of **c** I think about
5 Do we have to go home now? .... so much fun! **a** I've got **b** I have **c** I'm having

My Test! answers: 1c 2b 3c 4a 5c

2 Past simple and past continuous; *used to* and *would*

Musicians sang and threw flowers.

Arjumand Banu Begam **was working** in her shop when Prince Khurram **saw** her for the first time as he **was walking** through the market. He immediately **decided** this was the woman he **wanted** to marry. Indian princes, however, **didn't use to marry** for love but for political reasons, so marriage between Khurram and Arjumand **was** impossible. It **was** six years before the prince **could** marry the woman he **loved**, but when it finally **happened** the wedding **was** magnificent. A long procession **travelled** to Arjumand's house, and musicians **sang** and **threw** flowers to the hundreds of people who **were watching**. At the wedding, the prince's father **gave** Arjumand the name of Mumtaz, or 'Chosen One', as a present.

When Khurram's father **died**, he **became** Emperor Shah Jahan, or 'King of the World'. He **had** many responsibilities and **was frequently leading** his army off to fight in different parts of the empire. Mumtaz **would always travel** with him and sometimes she even **used to go** with him into battle. Sadly, while her husband **was fighting** one of these battles, Mumtaz **fell** ill. As she **was dying**, Shah Jahan **promised** to build a beautiful monument in her memory. After Mumtaz **died**, Shah Jahan quickly **began** to turn his promise into reality, and twenty years later the Taj Mahal, perhaps the greatest symbol of love the world has ever seen, **was** finally completed.

?

1 Why was it difficult for Prince Khurram to marry Arjumand at first?
2 What did Shah Jahan decide to do in memory of his wife?

Answers: 1 Because she wasn't an important person 2 Build a beautiful monument

Past simple and past continuous; *used to* and *would*

Past simple

1 **We usually use the past simple to refer to events or states in the past, or to repeated past actions.**

*He **had** many responsibilities.*
*I **went** to the cinema three times last week.*

Past continuous

2 **We use the past continuous to refer to events which were unfinished or in progress at or around a definite time in the past.**

*At 7 o'clock this morning I **was having** a shower.*

3 **We often use the past continuous to refer to background activities or situations in a story.**

*He looked through the window. Rain **was falling** steadily on the city's streets.*

Don't use the past continuous to refer to general habits and routines in the past.

*Every summer my grandparents **came** to stay with us.* NOT *~~... were coming to stay with us.~~*

4 We sometimes use the past continuous with words like *always, constantly* and *forever* to refer to repeated past actions if we want to emphasise or criticise.

*When my dad worked in a bakery he **was always bringing** home cakes and biscuits.*

*My old neighbours **were forever having** parties and **playing** loud music.*

5 We sometimes use the past continuous instead of the present continuous with *hope, plan, think about* (+ *-ing*), and *wonder about* (+ *-ing*) to show uncertainty.

*Sally and I **were hoping** to meet up this afternoon. If we do, would you like to come too?* (less definite than *We're hoping to ...*)

We can use the past continuous with *wonder* to make very polite suggestions and requests.

*I **was wondering** if you could help me.*

Past simple or past continuous

6 We often use the past simple and the past continuous to talk about two events or situations which happened at or around the same time.

The past continuous shows that two continuing activities were in progress at the same time.

*Arjumand **was working** in her shop as the prince **was walking** through the market.*

The past simple shows that two or more events happened at or around the same time.

*A long procession **travelled** to Mumtaz's house, and musicians **sang** and **threw** flowers.*

Use the past simple to refer to events which happened during a longer activity, shown by the past continuous.

*Musicians **sang** and **threw** flowers to people who **were watching**.*

7 We sometimes use the past simple or the past continuous with verbs like *hope, mean, plan, think about* (+ *-ing*) and *want* to refer to things we intended to do but didn't or can't.

*I **hoped** / **was hoping** to get there on time but the traffic is really heavy, so I'm going to be late.*

The past simple is much more common than the past continuous when we refer to the past, and it is the best form to use if you are not sure.

Used to and *would*

8 We often use *used to* (+ infinitive) instead of the past simple to refer to past habits, routines and states, especially when the habit or routine does not happen any more or when the state is no longer true.

*She even **used to go** with him into battle.*

*Jackie **used to have** three rabbits, but one died.*

9 The negative and question forms are usually *didn't use to* and *Did ... use to ...?*

*Indian princes, however, **didn't use to marry** for love but for political reasons.*

Nowadays we often form the negative and question forms with *used* instead of *use*.

*Amanda **didn't used to like** school, but now she loves it.* OR *Amanda **didn't use to like** ...*

10 We sometimes use *would* (+ infinitive) instead of *used to* to refer to past habits or routines if the time reference is clear.

*Mumtaz **would** always **travel** with him.*

OR *Mumtaz always **used to travel** with him.*

We don't use *would* to refer to past states or if the time reference is not clear.

*I **used to love** dance music.* NOT *~~I would love dance music.~~*

*I **used to go** to the cinema a lot.* NOT *~~I would go to the cinema a lot.~~*

Be / *Get used to* (+ noun or *-ing*) is not connected with *used to* (+ infinitive). *Used to* (+ noun or *-ing*) means *accustomed to*.

*I don't really like the food here. I'**m not used to eating** so much meat.*

The past simple, *used to* and *would*

11 Use the past simple, not *used to* or *would* (+ infinitive), to say exactly how many times something happened in total. Note the difference:

*I **read** six books last month!*

*I **read** / **used to read** / **would read** a lot when I was a child.*

Practice

A **Underline the correct option. Sometimes both options are possible.**

1 The police arrested three men who *robbed* / *were robbing* a bank in the High Street.
2 They *planned* / *were planning* to get up early, but they overslept.
3 I saw Jon in the park today – he *read* / *was reading* a book.
4 When she *ate* / *was eating* her sandwich, the sun came out.
5 After the film *finished* / *was finishing*, I turned the TV off and went to bed.
6 Vanessa's really shy because everyone *constantly criticised* / *was constantly criticising* her when she was a child.
7 Do you like my watch? My wife *gave* / *was giving* it to me for my birthday.
8 My sister's really happy – she *passed* / *was passing* all her exams.

B **Complete the sentences with the past simple or past continuous form of the verbs in brackets.**

1 ......Did you see...... that film on TV last night? (you / see)
2 A: What was that terrible noise last night? B: Sorry, it was me. I .... my singing. (practise)
3 I .... in the bath last night when suddenly there was a loud bang in the kitchen. (lie)
4 James .... to visit me every single day when I was in hospital. (came)
5 A: How was the game? B: Terrible! We .... 6–0. (lose)
6 After he ...., my dad took up golf as a hobby. (retire)
7 I ...., why don't you come round for dinner at the weekend? (think)
8 The kids .... when I left for work this morning. (still / sleep)
9 A: What happened to you? Did you cut yourself? B: Yes, when I .... in the garden this morning. (work)
10 Simon got a job in a factory when he .... school last year. (leave)

C **Circle the TWO correct options. All the sentences are about the past.**

1 In the past, people ... married at a younger age than they do now.
a are used to getting (b) would get (c) used to get d were getting
2 I ... playing computer games when I was younger, but now I love them.
a wasn't liking b didn't use to like c wouldn't like d didn't like
3 In the past, my friends and I ... each other much more regularly than we do now.
a saw b used to seeing c used to see d were seeing
4 I think I know you. ... in Forest Lane?
a Didn't you use to live b Wouldn't you live c Weren't you living d Didn't you live
5 When I first moved to London, I ... in a big city.
a didn't use to live b wasn't used to living c didn't live d quickly got used to living
6 Dave ... to work every day until he had an accident.
a use to cycle b was cycling c used to cycle d cycled
7 I ... a lot more when I was younger.
a read b was used to read c was reading d used to read
8 My next-door neighbours ... in South Africa.
a were living b lived c used to live d would live

D **Complete the sentences by putting the words and phrases in the correct order.**

1 as / flowers and rice / they / came out of / threw / at the bride and groom
People ...threw flowers and rice at the bride and groom as they came out of... the church.
2 to invite us / were / they / meaning / but
They .... kept forgetting.
3 when he / about / stories / was always / was / telling us
Our grandfather .... a boy.
4 was / eat / when I / anything / would
I .... a child.
5 side of the road / to / isn't / to drive on the other / getting / but / strange / I'm / used
It's .... it.
6 thinking about / having a barbecue / were / at the weekend / the weather's / if
We .... nice.
7 from the south of / was constantly / by armies / invaded / being
The city .... the country.
8 was / your plates / while / one of / she / doing / dropped
Suzie .... the washing up.
9 heard / as soon as / phoned / I / her
I .... the news.
10 what I said / listening / hear / know you / didn't / because / you weren't
I .... to me.

E Complete another famous love story using the past simple, the past continuous, *used to* or *would* with the verbs in brackets. Sometimes more than one form may be possible.

Victoria was born in 1819, and became Queen in 1837, at the age of 18. In 1840 she [1] married (marry) her cousin, Albert of Saxe-Coburg Gotha, and for the next 20 years they [2] .... (be) inseparable. Around that time, Britain [3] .... (change) into a constitutional monarchy, in which the monarch had very little real power, but Victoria [4] .... (not be) afraid to express her views about political matters. However, she [5] .... (always ask) Albert for his opinion first. When Albert died of typhoid in 1861, Victoria was devastated. Although she [6] .... (reign) for another 40 years she never recovered from her husband's death and [7] .... (wear) black for the rest of her life as a sign of her grief. The British Empire [8] .... (still expand) at that time, and in 1877 Victoria acquired the title of Empress of India as well as Queen of Great Britain and Ireland, but while people across the Empire [9] .... (celebrate) her Golden and Diamond Jubilees (in 1877 and 1897), she [10] .... (remain) largely in the background, and was even too upset to speak at the opening of the Royal Albert Hall, the London concert hall which carries her husband's name.

MY TURN!

How much do you remember about your life's 'magic moments'? Choose two events and write what you remember about them, using the past simple, the past continuous, and *used to* or *would* when appropriate.

1 Your earliest memory
2 The day you met your best friend
3 Your first day at school
4 The first time you travelled in a plane
5 Your first holiday
6 The first time you went to a party
7 Your first visit to a different country
8 Your first English lesson

Example: I was about six when I went to my first party. I was staying with my cousin and . . . .

MY TEST!

Circle the correct option.

1 When I .... romantic stories, but now I love them.
a didn't use to like b wasn't liking c wouldn't like

2 When I .... reading about Shah Jahan and Mumtaz, I wanted to see the Taj Mahal for myself.
a was finishing b used to finish c finished

3 It was a dark, stormy night. The wind .... and the moon was hidden behind clouds.
a was blowing b used to blow c would blow

4 Excuse me. I .... if you might have a spare ticket. I've lost mine.
a would wonder b was wondering c used to wonder

5 That's strange ... she .... so friendly. Is she trying to trick us, perhaps?
a isn't used to being b didn't use to be c doesn't use to be

My Test! answers: 1a 2c 3a 4b 5b

3 Present perfect simple and present perfect continuous

The higher temperatures have had dramatic effects.

A new report on climate change **has shown** that other reports were wrong about the effect of human activity on the Earth's temperature. The planet's temperature **has been rising since** the beginning of the 20th century, and **has increased** by nearly 0.8°C in that time. Earlier reports said this increase was the result of natural changes, but the new report says the main cause **has been** a rise in the levels of greenhouse gases because of increased industrial activity.

The higher temperatures **have already had** dramatic effects. In the Arctic, the area covered by ice **has been getting** smaller **for** more than 30 years, and average sea levels **have risen** by 3 mm each year **since** the beginning of this century, increasing the danger of flooding in many areas. So far this century many parts of the world, including South-East Asia, Africa, Central Europe and the Caribbean, **have already had** the worst floods anyone can remember. If the new report is correct, it seems that we are now seeing the cost to the environment of the growth that the developed world **has been enjoying** over the last two hundred years.

?

1 How is the new report different from older reports?
2 What does the new report suggest about the recent floods in many parts of the world?

Answers: 1 It says that the increased temperature of the Earth is mainly caused by industrial activity. 2 That they are the result of growth in the developed world.

Present perfect simple and present perfect continuous

Present perfect simple

1 **We use the present perfect simple to refer to events at an unspecified time in the past which are relevant and important now.**

*The higher temperatures **have** already **had** dramatic effects on the planet.*

We often use this form to talk about experiences in life up to now or to talk about recent events (including events which are in the news).

*She **has won** two Oscars.*
*A new report on climate change **has shown** ...*

We often use the adverbs *just, already, yet, not yet, ever* and *never* with the present perfect.

*Sorry, Sarah isn't here. She **has just left**.*

> **TIP**
> **Use the present perfect after *It's / This is the first / second / third* / etc. *time*.**
> ***This is the third time** someone **has told** me this.*
> NOT ~~This is the third time someone is telling ...~~

2 We use the present perfect simple (often with *since* and *for*) to refer to **facts:** states or developments that began in the past and are still going on or ended a short time ago.

... average global sea levels ***have risen*** *by 3 mm* ***each year since*** *the beginning of this century.*

Present perfect simple or past simple

3 We use the present perfect simple to refer to past events which we feel are relevant / important now. We use the past simple to refer to past events with no particular relevance to the present.

So far this century many parts of the world ... ***have*** *already* ***had*** *the worst floods anyone can remember.*
I saw Janet ***yesterday***.

In American English, the past simple is sometimes used instead of the present perfect, especially with time expressions like *already, yet, not yet, ever, never* and *just*.

They ***already finished*** *their assignments.* OR *They* ***have already finished*** *their assignments.*

Present perfect continuous

4 We use the present perfect continuous to refer to **activities:** active processes that began in the past and are still going on or ended a short time ago, particularly when we say how long they have been going on.

The planet's temperature ***has been rising since the beginning of the 20th century.***

We often use the present perfect continuous in this way to express a complaint or criticism.

I've been waiting *here for you* ***since three o'clock!***

5 We can use the present perfect continuous to focus on the activity itself, without saying how long it has been going on.

A: What ***have*** *you* ***been doing****?*
*B: I****'ve been working*** *in the garden.*

We sometimes use the present perfect continuous to explain present evidence, give an excuse, or with verbs like *mean, want, think* and *wonder* to express a vague intention / idea.

Your face is red. ***Have*** *you* ***been sunbathing****?*
*Sorry I'm late. I****'ve been writing*** *an urgent email.*
*I****'ve been meaning*** *to email Julie.*

Present perfect simple or present perfect continuous

6 We can often use either the present perfect simple or continuous to refer to past events or situations which we feel are relevant or important now, with little or no difference in meaning.

... the economic growth that the developed world ***has been enjoying*** */* ***has enjoyed*** *since the start of ...*

7 We usually use the present perfect continuous, not simple, if we want to express the feeling that a situation is temporary and incomplete.

*I****'ve been staying*** *with a friend while my house is being redecorated.* NOT ~~*I've stayed with a friend ...*~~

8 We use the present perfect simple, not continuous, when we want to imply that the activity was completed at some time in the past. Note the difference:

He ***has written*** *his report.* (It is complete.)
He ***has been writing*** *his report.* (It may or may not be complete.)

9 We normally use the present perfect simple, not continuous, with *for* or *since* with verbs that describe unchanging states (e.g. *like, hate, know*).

Jill and I ***have known*** *each other since we were children.*
NOT ~~*Jill and I have been knowing ...*~~

But we can use the present perfect continuous with *want*.

*We****'ve been wanting*** *to meet you for years.*
OR *We****'ve wanted*** *...*

Don't use the present simple or continuous with *for* or *since* to refer to states or activities which began in the past and continue up to the present.

They ***have been*** *married* ***for*** *20 years.*
NOT ~~*They are married for 20 years.*~~

10 We use the present perfect simple, not continuous, to refer to a single completed activity.

*Have you heard? Jim****'s passed*** *his driving test.*
NOT ~~*Jim's been passing ...*~~

11 We use the present perfect simple to refer to a series of actions when we mention or ask about the number of these actions. We use the present perfect continuous if the number of actions is not important.

*I****'ve walked*** *to work three times this week.*
My bike's broken so I've ***been walking*** *to work this week.*

Practice

A Circle the correct option.

1 The average temperature in Europe has increased by more than 1.5 °C ...
ⓐ since 1900. b from 1900–2005.
2 Half the world's tropical rainforest disappeared ...
a between 1960 and 1990. b since 1960.
3 Flooding has been a serious problem in many parts of the UK ...
a in 2007. b in the last few years.
4 In Australia, dry weather has caused a big increase in the number of forest fires ...
a in 2000. b since 2000.
5 The levels of carbon dioxide produced by human activity rose by 30% ...
a between 1800 and 2000. b since 1800.
6 Extreme weather events have become more frequent ...
a recently. b last year.
7 In the Arctic, the area covered by ice has fallen by nearly 10% every ten years ...
a for the last fifty years. b fifty years ago.
8 Climate change became a major political issue ...
a for the last 20 years. b in the last century.

B Circle option a (if only the present perfect simple is possible) or option b (if both present perfect simple and continuous are possible).

1 You can't have any more sweets. ... two already.
ⓐ You've had b You've had / You've been having
2 How many times ... you? Don't cross the road without looking!
a have I told b have I told / have I been telling
3 ... a curry – can you smell it?
a Mum's made b Mum's made / Mum's been making
4 Katie just phoned from the hospital – ... her arm!
a She's broken b She's broken / She's been breaking
5 My cousin's an actress. ... in three films.
a She's already appeared
b She's already appeared / She's already been appearing
6 ... a lot of headaches recently.
a I've had b I've had / I've been having
7 Inflation ... gradually since this time last year.
a has gone up b has gone up / has been going up
8 My father ... spicy food ever since he was a child.
a has hated b has hated / has been hating
9 ... the news? Jo's pregnant!
a Have you heard
b Have you heard / Have you been hearing
10 Look at that! ... such a beautiful view.
a I've never seen
b I've never seen / I've never been seeing

C Complete the sentences with the past simple or present perfect simple form of the verbs in brackets.

1 My grandmother ....has lived.... in this house for nearly fifty years. She loves it here. (live)
2 The price of petrol .... by nearly 2% last year. (go up)
3 You and I .... best friends since we were children. (be)
4 Do you like my watch? My grandmother .... it to me for my birthday last year. (give)
5 .... Anita's new hairstyle? Isn't it great? (see)
6 We .... the kids to Disneyland last Christmas – they loved it! (take)
7 My grandparents celebrate their Golden Wedding Anniversary next year – they .... together since they were at school. (be)
8 Tony Blair .... Prime Minister of the United Kingdom between 1997 and 2007. (be)
9 .... your homework yet? (do)
10 How was the food at that Italian restaurant you went to? .... it? (like)

D Make sentences by putting the words in the correct order.

1 has / The / going up / few years. / average temperature / been / in the last
The average temperature has been going up in the last few years.
2 hasn't / very much / It / recent years. / rained / in
....
3 been / have / the environment / doing / People / to protect / recently. / a lot more
....
4 and paper. / has now / Everyone / the importance / realised / bottles / of recycling
....
5 a lot / climate / changed / I / was / has / since / The / a child.
....

6 milder / have / winters / getting / been / every year. / The

....

....

7 appearing / about / reports / in the news. / climate change / More / been / have

....

....

8 been / government / more seriously. / taking / has / The / climate change

....

....

E Complete each sentence b so that it means the same as sentence a. Use two to six words, including the word in brackets.

1 a Stephen King is the author of more than 60 books. (has)
  b Stephen King ..has written.. more than 60 books.
2 a It's two years since I started working here. (for)
  b I .... two years.
3 a I spoke to Maggie a moment ago and she said she can't come to the party. (just)
  b Maggie .... that she can't come to the party.
4 a The country's demands for independence began in the 1950s. (since)
  b The country .... the 1950s.
5 a Jim hasn't missed any of United's games since he was a teenager. (seen)
  b Jim .... United game since he was a teenager.
6 a Sally doesn't have any more Christmas presents to buy. (has)
  b Sally .... all her Christmas presents.
7 a Sheila and Tom met when they were at college together. (have)
  b Sheila and Tom .... they were at college together.
8 a Andy has spent most of the day painting his kitchen. (for)
  b Andy .... most of the day.

MY TURN!

Complete the sentences so that they are true for you. Use the present perfect continuous instead of the present perfect simple where appropriate.

1 I've never ..ridden a horse.. .
2 I'm proud of the fact that I've ....
3 I haven't .... since ....
4 I've .... for ....
5 In the last few weeks I've ....
6 Recently I've been thinking of ....
7 I don't know anyone who has ....
8 I've .... but I haven't finished yet.

MY TEST!

Circle the correct option.

1 Scientists .... to identify the causes of climate change for many years. a are trying b try c have been trying
2 I can't believe you're still using the same old computer! How long .... it? a have you had b do you have c have you been having
3 I'm exhausted – .... football all morning. a I've been playing b I'm playing c I've played
4 We .... many examples of the effects of climate change. a have been seeing b are seen c have seen
5 I'm so pleased to see you – .... to talk to you since the weekend. a I'm wanting b I've been wanting c I want

My Test! answers: 1c 2a 3a 4c 5b

4 Past perfect simple and past perfect continuous

He'd been expecting an easy climb.

How far would you go to save your own life? That was the question facing Aron Ralston on 26 April 2003, when he was trapped behind a 360-kilogram rock in Utah, USA. The 27-year-old **had been climbing** alone in the Blue John Canyon when the rock moved suddenly and trapped his arm against the canyon wall. Aron **had always known** the importance of telling people where he was going when he went climbing, but unfortunately he**'d forgotten** to mention his plans to anyone – a mistake which might cost him his life.

Six days later, on 1 May, Aron was still alive, but he**'d started** losing energy and had nothing left to eat or drink – he**'d just drunk** the last drop of water in his water bottle. Expecting to die, he**'d** even **cut** his name into the wall and **recorded** a short film with his video camera, saying goodbye to his family. Then Aron made the biggest decision of his life: he decided to try and cut off his own arm.

Five hours later, now with only one arm and covered in blood, Aron was a strange sight for the three tourists who found him after he finally **left** the canyon. They**'d been walking** in the area for the day and were now on their way home. After they **had given** Aron some food and water they radioed for a helicopter to take him to hospital. At last, Aron was safe.

?

1 What mistake did Aron make when he went climbing in the Blue John Canyon?
2 What did Aron have to do in order to escape from the canyon?

Answers: 1 He forgot to mention his plans to anyone. 2 He had to cut his own arm off.

Past perfect simple and past perfect continuous

Past perfect simple or past simple

1 **Use the past perfect simple to describe events or situations which happened before another event or situation in the past which we describe using the past simple.**

*On 1 May, Aron was still alive, but he**'d started** losing energy.* (= He started losing energy before 1 May.)

*On 1 May, Aron was still alive, but he **started** losing energy.* (= He started losing energy on 1 May.)

2 **We often use the adverbs *before, just, already, yet, not yet, ever, never, for* and *since* with the past perfect.**

*Jan thought Susana was amazing – he'**d never met** anyone like her before.*

We use the past perfect, not the past simple, when we say *It was the first / second / third* / etc. *time* … .

*I was scared because **it was the first time I had tried** to climb a mountain.*

3 **When we join verbs in the past perfect with *and, or* and *but*, we often leave out *had*.**

*He'**d** even **cut** his name into the wall **and** (**had**) **recorded** a short film with his video camera.*

▶ See Unit 43 for more information on ellipsis (leaving out words).

4 **If the sequence of events is clear because of the context or a time expression, we can choose either the past perfect or the past simple to refer to the earlier event.**

*Aron was a strange sight after he finally **left** the canyon.* OR *… after he **had** finally **left** …*

When we use time expressions like *when, as soon as, after, until* and *by the time*, we sometimes use the past perfect instead of the past simple to emphasise the idea of waiting for something to happen. Both versions are correct.

*When she **arrived**, we started the meal.* (= First she arrived, then we started.)
*When she **had arrived**, we started the meal.* (= We waited for her to arrive and then we started.)

Past perfect simple or past perfect continuous

TIP

The rules for choosing between past perfect simple and past perfect continuous are similar to the rules for choosing between present perfect simple and present perfect continuous.

*I'm tired because I'**ve been working** all day and I still **haven't finished**.*
*I remember I was tired because I'**d been working** all day and I still **hadn't finished**.*

5 **We can often use either the past perfect simple or the past perfect continuous to refer to past events or situations which happened before another time in the past, with little or no difference in meaning.**

*Jill **had been doing** / **had done** a lot of exercise in the last few weeks, so she was very fit.*

6 **We usually use the past perfect continuous to describe an activity that was interrupted or followed by another event in the past.**

*He **had been climbing** alone when the rock moved suddenly and **trapped** his arm.*
*They'**d been walking** in the area and **were** now on their way home.*

7 **We use the past perfect simple, not the past perfect continuous, to emphasise that an action was completed before another time in the past.**

*He had nothing left to eat or drink – he'**d** just **drunk** the last drop of water.* NOT ~~*… he'd just been drinking …*~~

8 **We use the past perfect simple, not the past perfect continuous, to refer to the number of times something happened before another time in the past.**

*By the time she died she'**d written** more than 200 books.*

9 **We use the past perfect simple, not the past perfect continuous, with verbs that describe unchanging states, e.g. *like, hate, know, have*.**

*Aron **had** always **known** the importance of telling people where he was going.* NOT ~~*… had always been knowing …*~~

10 **We sometimes use the past perfect simple or the past perfect continuous instead of the past simple or past continuous with verbs like *hope, mean, plan, think about* (+ *-ing*) and *want* to refer to things we intended to do but didn't.**

***I'd meant** / **'d been meaning** to phone you but in the end I forgot.* OR *I **meant** / **was meaning** …*

TIP

We sometimes stress the word *had* with verbs like *hope* and *think* to emphasise a change from our expectations, especially if we are not happy with the change.

*A: I'm afraid I'm going to be late. B: That's not good. I **had hoped** we'd get this finished tonight.*

Past perfect continuous or past continuous

11 **To describe an activity that was interrupted, we can use either the past continuous or the past perfect continuous. We don't use the past continuous to say how long the interrupted activity lasted.**

*He'**d been sleeping** when the fire started.* OR *He **was sleeping** when the fire started.*
*He'**d been sleeping** for about an hour when the fire started.* NOT ~~*He was sleeping for about an hour …*~~

Practice

A **Underline the correct option.**

1 The party *almost finished* / *had almost finished* by the time we arrived.
2 As soon as I saw her, I knew I *met* / *had met* the woman I wanted to marry.
3 After he bought his ticket he *sat down* / *had sat down* to wait for the train to arrive.
4 The police arrived quickly, but it was too late – the robbers *went* / *had gone*.
5 Mrs Latimer *just shut* / *had just shut* the door when she realised her key was inside.
6 When she got paid, Julie realised that her boss *gave* / *had given* her a pay rise.
7 Sorry, I didn't catch that – what *did you say* / *had you said*?
8 We were very excited to meet again because we *didn't see* / *hadn't seen* each other for five years.

B **Circle option a (if only the past perfect simple is possible) or option b (if both past perfect simple and continuous are possible).**

1 I worked very hard all morning and by lunchtime ... all my jobs for the day.
   a I'd done   b I'd done / I'd been doing
2 They were tired when they arrived because ... all through the night.
   a they'd driven
   b they'd driven / they'd been driving
3 Stuart ... that he was expected to attend the meeting.
   a hadn't realised
   b hadn't realised / hadn't been realising
4 Jim and Sally ... to see us but we were all too busy.
   a had hoped   b had hoped / had been hoping
5 I knew about the accident because ... the news the night before and there was a report about it.
   a I'd watched
   b I'd watched / I'd been watching
6 Terry ... Serena, but he didn't know she felt the same way about him.
   a had always liked
   b had always liked / had always been liking
7 By the time they were rescued, ... nearly three days without food or water.
   a they'd spent
   b they'd spent / they'd been spending
8 By the age of 10, Mozart ... three operas and 25 symphonies.
   a had composed
   b had composed / had been composing

C **Complete each sentence, using an appropriate past form of the verb in brackets. Sometimes more than one form is possible.**

1 Before I bought my flat I *shared / was sharing / had shared / had been sharing* a house with friends. (share)
2 .... they were going away for the weekend? (you know)
3 Although he loves football, my brother .... to see a live match until last weekend. (not go)
4 I can't believe you didn't realise you .... to turn the oven off. (forget)
5 Recently he .... of taking a year off and travelling round the world. (think)
6 Henry .... for a couple of hours when he stopped to have some lunch. (write)
7 The speech was so boring people started to leave even before she .... speaking. (stop)
8 When I went back to my home town, I was sad to see that my favourite café .... (close down)

D **Rewrite each sentence, putting ONE missing word in the correct place.**

1 I didn't want to see the film because I seen it already.
   I didn't want to see the film because I had seen it already.
2 Rosie and Lewis weren't at the party because we invited them.
   ....
3 Sam had feeling sick all day, so we took him to the doctor's.
   ....
4 They been thinking of going out, but in the end they decided not to.
   ....
5 At that time I'd never been overseas because I'd never the opportunity.
   ....
6 Mike had the feeling that he been there before, but he didn't remember when.
   ....
7 We hadn't waiting very long when someone told us the train had been cancelled.
   ....
8 Tracey had known anyone like Matt before – he was very strange.
   ....

E Underline the correct option.

Born in 1919 in Auckland, New Zealand, Edmund Hillary [1]*became / had been becoming* interested in climbing as a schoolboy, and by the age of 30 he [2]*was climbing / had climbed* several 6,000-metre mountains. People [3]*tried / had been trying* to climb Mount Everest, the world's highest mountain, for years, and since 1920 seven major expeditions [4]*failed / had failed*. In 1924, George Mallory [5]*had died / had been dying* during one climb, then, in 1952, some Swiss climbers almost reached the top before bad weather forced them to give up. When Hillary [6]*heard / had heard* that a British climber was planning a new expedition for the following year, he joined it, and in March 1953 they [7]*set up / had set up* base camp. By 28 May, 398 of the original 400 expedition members [8]*were giving up / had given up*, exhausted by the high altitude. The last two – Hillary and the Nepalese climber Tenzing Norgay – [9]*had continued / had been continuing* to climb, however, and the next day they [10]*became / had become* the first humans to stand on the summit of Everest, more than 8,840 metres above sea level.

MY TURN!

How much have you done in your life? Write sentences about the things you had done by the time you were these ages: 8, 10, 12, 14, 16, 18.

Example: *By the age of 8, I had lived in three different houses and I'd been going to school for three years.*

....

....

....

....

....

....

....

....

....

....

MY TEST!

Circle the correct option.

1 I was shocked, even though it was the third time .... Aron's story. **a** I had heard **b** I heard **c** I'd been hearing

2 They didn't let us go home until .... tidying up. **a** we'd finished **b** we were finishing **c** we'd been finishing

3 I didn't want to watch the film because .... it five times.
a I've already been seeing **b** I'd already seen **c** I'd already been seeing

4 When we finally reached the top, it was wonderful – .... for eight hours.
a we climbed **b** we've been climbing **c** we'd been climbing

5 She was angry when I phoned because .... to get the baby to sleep for an hour.
a she'd tried **b** she was trying **c** she'd been trying

My Test! answers: 1a 2a 3b 4c 5c

5 The future 1: *will, be going to*, present continuous, present simple

I'm going to ask her to marry me.

Tim: How are things with Jo?
Dan: Great! Actually, I've decided I'**m going to ask** her to marry me.

Tim: Congratulations!
Dan: Thanks. But what if ...?
Tim: Don't worry! She **won't say** no! Not to a good-looking guy like you!

Mike: **Are** you **going** to Dan's wedding?
Tim: Of course – I'm the best man!
Mike: Oh yes! **Are** you **giving** a speech? What **are** you **going to say**? I hope it'**s going to be** funny!
Tim: Well, there'**ll be** some jokes, so I **hope** it'**s** funny.
Mike: How **are** you **getting** there? **Are** you **going to drive**?
Tim: Yes. I'**ll give** you a lift if you like.

Mike: OK. Great. What time **are** you **going to leave**?
Tim: Well, the wedding **is** at 2 and it'**ll take** a couple of hours to get there, so ... I think I'**ll set** off about 11.30.
Mike: Great! I'**ll come** round to your house at about 11.15, then.

Mike: Look, it's Tim. It looks like he'**s going to give** his speech.
Sally: Great! This'**ll be** interesting.

Mike: Why?
Sally: Because we'**ll find** out what Dan's really like. All his secrets. Isn't that what a best man's speech is for?

?

1 Who is getting married, and what time is the wedding?
2 Who is the best man, and what does he have to do?

Answers: 1 Dan (and Jo); 2 o'clock 2 Tim; he has to give a speech about Dan.

The future 1

Will

Will is the most common way to refer to future time.

1 We use ***will*** / ***won't*** + infinitive to make confident predictions about future events or situations.
*This'**ll be** interesting.*
*She **won't say** no! Not to a good-looking guy like you!*

2 We use ***will*** / ***won't*** + infinitive for things we decide quickly at the moment of speaking.
*I'**ll come round** to your house at about 11.15, then.*

3 We use ***will*** / ***won't*** + infinitive to make offers or promises.
*I'**ll let you know** as soon as it's ready.*

▶ See Units 9 and 10 for other uses of *will*.

Be going to

4 We use ***be going to*** + infinitive for the future when there is present evidence that something is going to happen, when the event is already starting / starting very soon, and (particularly in informal style) for present plans / intentions for the future.
*It looks like he's **going to give** his speech.*
*I'**m going to ask** her to marry me.*

Present continuous

5 Use the present continuous to talk about already fixed plans / arrangements.
***Are** you **giving** a speech?* (asking if this has already been arranged)

Use ***will*** or ***be going to*** + infinitive, not the present continuous, for predictions about events which are out of your control.

*It'**ll** take / '**s going to** take a couple of hours to get there.* NOT ~~*It's taking ...*~~

Present simple

6 We usually use the present simple for known facts about the future or future events which are part of a fixed timetable.
*The wedding **is** at 2.*
*What time **does** your train **leave** tomorrow?*

Will or *be going to*

7 We can often use either ***will*** or ***be going to*** + infinitive for facts / predictions about the future.
*Christmas Day **will be** / **is going to be** on a Friday next year.*

8 We usually use ***will*** (or ***won't***) + infinitive to say things about the future based on personal opinions / beliefs. We usually use ***be going to*** + infinitive to make predictions when there is clear outside evidence.
*She'**ll have** lots of children.* (= I know she wants to have lots.)
*She'**s going to have** a baby.* (= She's already pregnant.)

▶ See Unit 9 for *might*, *may* and *could* to indicate different levels of certainty when making predictions.

We often use ***expect, hope, imagine, think, wonder if, be sure*** and (in more informal situations) ***bet, reckon*** before ***will*** or ***be going to*** when we make predictions.

*I hope it'**s going to be** funny.*

Will, *be going to* or present continuous

9 We can often use either ***be going to*** + infinitive or the present continuous, not ***will***, for present plans / intentions / expectations for the future.
*I can't meet you after work tonight. I'**m going to see** / I'**m seeing** a film with Kath.* NOT ~~*I'll see a film ...*~~

If we are only considering a plan and are still not sure, we sometimes use ***will*** after ***I think***.
***I think I'll leave** about 11.30.*

▶ See Unit 34 for more information on the use of present forms with future time reference.

With the verb ***go***, we usually use the present continuous instead of ***be going to go***.

***Are** you **going** to Dan's wedding?* (instead of ***Are** you **going to go** ...?*)

10 After words like ***when, after, before, as soon as, if, unless*** and ***until*** we use the present simple (or the present perfect), not a future form, although we are talking about future time.
***When** you **arrive** home, you can tell me about your journey.* NOT ~~*When you will arrive ...*~~

Will, *be going to*, present continuous or present simple

11 We can sometimes use either ***will, be going to***, the present continuous or the present simple with little or no difference in meaning. This is usually for official future events which we see as out of our control.
*The new boss **will start** / **is going to start** / **is starting** / **starts** / tomorrow.*

We usually use ***will*** in a more formal style, e.g. in invitations, public notices, etc.
*The wedding reception **will begin** at 8.30.*

Practice

A Cross out the ONE incorrect option.

1 I *am going to cycle / am cycling / ~~cycle~~* into town. Can I get you anything?
2 We believe the company *will create / is going to create / is creating* more jobs in the area in the next year.
3 According to the weather forecast it *snows / is going to snow / will snow* later.
4 Now is a good time to buy a house, because prices *will definitely go up / definitely go up / are definitely going to go up* soon.
5 Chris *isn't going to come out / doesn't come out / isn't coming out* with us next Saturday.
6 *Do you watch / Are you watching / Are you going to watch* the match tomorrow?
7 Hi Jon, it's Trevor. Listen, we *will have / are having / are going to have* a barbecue on Sunday – do you want to come?
8 These flowers *aren't lasting / won't last / aren't going to last* very long without water.

B Complete the dialogues, using appropriate future forms of the verbs in brackets.

1 A: It's going to be a really boring party.
B: No it's not. Graeme *'s going / 's going to go* and he's always good fun. (go)
2 A: I'm sorry, we've run out of beef.
B: Oh, OK. I .... chicken then, please. (have)
3 A: Why do you need a new laptop?
B: My old one's very old and it .... working one of these days. (stop)
4 A: Do you need a babysitter to look after the children tonight?
B: No, it's OK. They .... with my mum. (stay)
5 A: It's a bit hot in here, isn't it?
B: Just a second. I .... the window. (open)
6 A: Have you got a hammer I can borrow?
B: No, sorry. Ask Terry. I bet he .... you one. (lend)
7 A: Do you want to play tennis this afternoon?
B: I can't. I .... my sister and her husband to the airport. (take)
8 A: I've got an appointment with Doctor Patel.
B: That's fine. Take a seat and we .... you when she's free. (call)

C Complete each sentence b so that it has a similar meaning to sentence a. Use two to six words, including the word in brackets.

1 a What are your holiday plans for next summer? (you)
b *Where are you going* on holiday next summer?
2 a It's Gary's 21st birthday on Thursday. (be)
b Gary .... 21 on Thursday.
3 a It's going to be impossible for us to come on Friday. (able)
b We .... on Friday.
4 a I've got an appointment with a new client this afternoon. (meeting)
b I .... this afternoon.
5 a The departure time of your flight is 19.25. (at)
b Your .... 19.25.
6 a There's no chance of the situation improving in the next few years. (definitely)
b The situation .... in the next few years.
7 a I haven't seen Ellie for years. I don't think I'll recognise her. (bet)
b I haven't seen Ellie for years. .... recognise her.
8 a The Bank of England has announced an increase in interest rates for the end of the month. (is)
b The Bank of England .... at the end of the month.

D Complete the dialogues, using the words in brackets and correct future verb forms.

1 A: There's no milk left.
B: OK. I *'ll go and get some. I'll be back* in five minutes.
(go / get / some. I / be / back)
2 A: How are Sam's exams going?
B: OK, I think. His last one .... when it's over.
(be / next Tuesday. He / be / very happy)
3 A: I have to go now, but I'll probably see you at Helen's party on Saturday.
B: Actually, I ....
(go / away / for the weekend / so I / not / be able to go)
4 A: We should get together soon. I haven't seen you for ages.
B: Good idea! In fact, what .... Would you like to come?
(you / do / next weekend? I / have / a barbecue on Sunday)
5 A: What kinds of new inventions can you imagine in the next 100 years?
B: I don't know, but .... a machine for going back in time!
(I / not / think / anyone / invent)

6 A: When will I know the results of the interview?
B: Well, we ....
....
early next week.
(interview / more people this week, / then we / let you know / our decision)

7 A: Where shall I meet you tonight? At the cinema?
B: No, the film ....
....
....
in the Blue Café from about 7.
(start / at 8 but / we / have a coffee first. / We / be)

8 A: What's the matter with Sue? She seems worried about something.
B: Yes, she is! She ....
.... too difficult for her!
(start / her new / job tomorrow. / She / think / it / be)

E Complete the dialogues, using appropriate future forms of the verbs in brackets.

1 A: *When is Elena's birthday?* ? (be)
B: On 22 April. She'll be 17.
2 A: .... ? (arrive)
B: Half past three. As long as it's on time.
3 A: .... ? (snow)
B: No, I don't think so. It hardly ever snows here.
4 A: .... ? (do)
B: I'm going to have dinner with some friends.
5 A: .... ? (have)
B: Probably pasta or something like that.
6 A: ....
.... ? (win)
B: The next election? No idea! I hate politics!
7 A: ....
.... ? (buy)
B: I'm not sure. Maybe a book, because I know she likes reading.
8 A: .... ? (stay)
B: No, with some friends actually. They live right next to the beach.

MY TURN!

In your notebook, write replies to these people which are true for you. Use the future forms from this unit.

1

2

3

4

5

6

7

8

9

10

Example: 1 *I'm probably going to stay at home.*

MY TEST!

Circle the correct option.

1 I'm feeling tired. I think .... to bed. a I go b I'll go c I would go
2 How long .... you to drive to our house next Tuesday? a does it take b is it taking c will it take
3 I hope she .... no tomorrow when I ask her to marry me. a isn't saying b won't say c hasn't said
4 I reckon .... their wedding present when they open it. a they'll love b they love c they're loving
5 I can't go out with you tomorrow. .... my sister move into her new flat. a I help b I'll help c I'm helping

My Test! answers: 1b 2c 3b 4a 5c

6 The future 2: other ways to refer to the future, the future in the past

They will be lying on the sofa.

CAMP 4TEENS

Life today is less active than at any time in our history, particularly for our children. If you have typical teenage children, when you arrive home tonight they **will** probably **be lying** on the sofa watching TV or chatting on the Internet rather than playing outside in the fresh air. And, with current trends, the situation **is set to get** even worse in the future. The facts speak for themselves:

By the time they've reached 20, today's average 12-year-olds:
... **will have watched** more than 15,000 hours of television!
... **will have eaten** in a fast-food restaurant more than 700 times!
... **will have drunk** over 700 cans of cola or similar drinks!

By the age of 20 a large number of today's teenagers **will be suffering** from diseases caused by being too fat. In other words, we **are on the verge of** a health disaster.

But if you **were about to give up** all hope of a stress-free future surrounded by happy, healthy teenage children, don't worry ... it's not too late!

Camp4Teens organises two-week summer courses for teenagers. Your kids **will be enjoying** sports, adventure games and survival activities from morning to evening!

Send your teenagers on one of our courses and we promise that when they return home, their TV-watching, fast-food eating habits **will have changed** for ever!

For details, contact Camp4Teens: info@camp4teens.com!

?
1 What is the problem with the lifestyle of the average 12-year-old?
2 What solution does Camp4Teens offer?

Answers: 1 It's not active or healthy. 2 It offers summer courses with lots of sports, games and activities.

The future 2

Future continuous

1 Use the future continuous to talk about an activity that will be in progress at a point or period in the future.
When you arrive home tonight they ***will be lying*** *on the sofa.*

2 We sometimes use the future continuous to talk about organised or official future events.
Local band The Elements ***will be appearing*** *at The Corn Exchange on Thursday evening.*

3 We sometimes use the future continuous to make polite enquiries about people's plans.
Will *you* ***be having dinner*** *before you go out tonight?*
(= I want to know your plans for dinner tonight.)

4 We sometimes use the future continuous to emphasise how long an activity will last.
Your kids ***will be enjoying*** *sports, adventure games and survival activities* ***from morning to evening.***

Future perfect simple and future perfect continuous

5 Use the future perfect simple to focus on the results of events that will happen or finish before a time in the future.
By the time they've reached 20, they ***will have watched*** *more than 15,000 hours of television!*

6 Use the future perfect to measure lengths of time (usually with *for*) before a point in the future. Use the future perfect simple for states and future perfect continuous for activities. With some verbs (*live, work, study*), both versions are possible.
*In October she'****ll have been working*** *here for 30 years.* OR *In October she'****ll have worked*** *...*

We often use *by* or *by the time* with the future continuous, the future perfect simple and the future perfect continuous.

By *the age of 20 a large number of today's teenagers* ***will be suffering*** *from diseases ...*
By the time *we arrive, the match* ***will have started****.*

Other ways to refer to the future

7 We sometimes use expressions like *be (just) about to* (+ infinitive), *be on the point of* (+ noun / *-ing*), and *be on the verge of* (+ noun / *-ing*) to talk about things that are going to happen in the very near future.
I'm just about to have dinner *– can you call back in about an hour?* (= I'm going to have dinner now.)
We ***are on the verge of*** *a health catastrophe.*

8 We sometimes use *be to* + infinitive to talk about official plans, particularly in news reports.
The Prime Minister ***is to give*** *a press conference at 3 this afternoon.*

9 News headlines usually use the infinitive to refer to the future in order to save space.
CAR COMPANY ***TO CUT*** *200 JOBS* (= A car company is going to cut 200 jobs.)

10 We can use *be bound to* (+ infinitive) to refer to events that are certain to happen.
I don't know why Jackie is so worried about her exam – she's ***bound to pass*** *easily.*

11 We use *be due to* (+ infinitive) to refer to events which are expected to happen at a particular time.
The next train from London ***is due to arrive*** *at 5.35.*

Due to + noun does not refer to the future. It is used in a formal style to mean *because of*.

Flight LN603 to Athens has been cancelled ***due to bad weather****.*

12 We use *be set to* (+ infinitive) if everything is ready or prepared for something to happen.
Is everybody ***set to leave****? OK, so let's go.*

We often use *be set to* (+ infinitive) to describe trends that we expect will continue.

The situation ***is set to get even worse*** *in the future.* (Current trends suggest this is likely to happen.)

The future in the past

13 Use *was / were going to* + infinitive to refer to planned events in the past. Often these are events which in fact didn't happen.
We ***were going to have a picnic*** *but it started raining, so we decided to stay at home.*

14 We sometimes use *was / were* with *(just) about to, on the point of*, and *on the verge of* to talk about events or situations which nearly happened or happened soon afterwards (but often in fact didn't).
Donna and Carl ***were just about to leave without me*** *when I got there.*

We can use *was / were* with *due to* and *set to* to refer to past events which were expected or ready to happen.
The meeting ***was due to start*** *at 2 but in the end it didn't start until 2.30.*
Smith ***was set to make*** *his debut in yesterday's match but he injured himself during training.*

15 We sometimes use *was / were bound to* to refer to past events or situations which we think were predictable or obvious.
I don't know why you're surprised – it ***was bound to happen****.*

Practice

A Complete the sentences with the verb forms from the box.

have arrived ~~be eating~~ be holding be playing football have left have lost be repairing have written

1. You won't ...be eating... here tonight, I assume.
2. Make sure you get here before 7, because if it's later than that we'll ....
3. There's no point ringing Alan between 2 and 4 – he'll .... then, so he won't be able to answer the phone.
4. The Lansdown Social Club will .... its annual members' meeting next Thursday (27th November), at 8.30 pm.
5. I don't know why she bought this game – she'll .... interest in it by next week.
6. I need your report by 5 o'clock at the latest. I hope you will .... it by then.
7. They definitely won't .... by then – it'll take them at least another hour to get here.
8. They'll .... the bridge next week, so the road is going to be closed.

B Complete the sentences, using one phrase from box A and one from box B.

A	B
~~hates his job so much~~	visit the city in the future
director of the company is	just about to start
country is on the verge of	there's bound to be a big queue
was about to	to retire at the end of the year
people are set to	an economic crisis
should get there early because	but it was delayed by two hours
was due to arrive at 3.40	~~I think he's on the point of resigning~~
the film is	call the police

1. Joe ...hates his job so much I think he's on the point of resigning... .
2. Hurry up, ...
3. Some experts think the ....
4. At last you're here! I ....
5. More ....
6. We ....
7. Her flight ....
8. The ....

C Cross out ONE wrong word in each sentence to make it correct.

1. I'll ~~have~~ be seeing Simon at college today – shall I invite him to your party?
2. Rovers were bound to be win the match last night – they've got a much better team.
3. The leaders of the two countries are go to meet in Washington next month.
4. Do you think Susan will have been left home yet?
5. We're on to the point of signing a new contract with a big Italian company.
6. NASA scientists are be set to announce a new space mission for next year.
7. She was so pleased to find her cat that she was going on the verge of tears.
8. My new secretary is just due to start work next Monday.

D Tick the sentence, a or b, which means the same as the sentence given.

1. One of our sales team will be calling you this afternoon.
   - a One of the sales team will call you later today. ✓
   - b I'm sure one of our sales team has already called you this afternoon.
2. Annie will be lying on a beach in Spain soon.
   - a I imagine Annie is lying on a beach in Spain.
   - b Before long Annie is going to be lying on a beach in Spain.
3. Ten years from now, many of our endangered species will have died out.
   - a Many of our endangered species will become extinct within the next ten years.
   - b In ten years' time, many of our endangered species will be dying out.
4. Bring an umbrella – it'll probably be raining by the time we get there.
   - a Bring an umbrella – it'll probably start raining when we get there.
   - b Bring an umbrella – it'll probably have started raining by the time we get there.
5. I knew it was a mistake to let Alice borrow your car. She was bound to have an accident.
   - a It isn't a good idea to let Alice borrow your car. She'll definitely have an accident.
   - b Lending your car to Alice was a bad idea because it was obvious she was going to have an accident.

6 By next June my grandfather will have been working for the company for 50 years.
   a It's nearly 50 years since my grandfather started working for the company.
   b My grandfather is going to stop working for the company next June.
7 Will you be paying your bill by credit card?
   a Do you intend to use your credit card to pay your bill?
   b I would prefer it if you paid your bill using your credit card.
8 They were just about to phone for a taxi when their neighbour offered to take them.
   a Their neighbour offered to take them but they had already phoned for a taxi.
   b They didn't need to phone for a taxi because at the last minute their neighbour offered to take them.

E Complete the dialogue, using appropriate future forms of the verbs in brackets. Sometimes more than one form is possible.

Anna: Have you decided where to go for your holidays this year?
Jane: Yes, we [1] 're going / 're going to go (go) camping.
Anna: Camping? Where?
Jane: We're not sure yet. We think we [2] …………………… (try) France for a change.
Anna: France? Really? What happened? I thought you [3] …………………… (book) a cruise?
Jane: We were. In fact, we [4] …………………… (pay) a deposit for one when Steve found out he'd lost his job.
Anna: Oh, I see. So you didn't want to spend so much money, is that it?
Jane: Exactly. We're a bit worried because there aren't many jobs around, and nobody knows when the situation [5] …………………… (get better). We can't even be sure that Steve [6] …………………… (find) another job by this time next year!
Anna: Don't be so pessimistic! He [7] …………………… (work) again within the next couple of months, I'm sure.
Jane: I hope you're right! Anyway, we [8] …………………… (be able) to afford a cruise for a while! What about you? What are you doing for your holidays?
Anna: Er, well, er, it's a bit embarrassing. Do you remember that Philip got a promotion recently? Well, er, now that he's earning more money we've decided we [9] …………………… (do) something we've always wanted to do.
Jane: Really? What's that?
Anna: Er ... we're going on a cruise! In the Mediterranean! I [10] …………………… (send) you a postcard, if you like!

MY TURN!

Copy the sentences into your notebook, making changes so that all the sentences are true for you.

1 Five years from now, I will still be living in my country.
   Five years from now I will be living in France.
2 By the time I am 30, I will have bought a big house.
3 Before my next birthday, I will have visited at least two more countries.
4 In ten years' time, I will have been working for at least five years.
5 At 7 o'clock tomorrow morning, I'll still be sleeping.
6 I'm on the verge of making some important changes in my life.
7 I'm just about to stop studying for the day.
8 My country is bound to change a lot in the next few years.
9 I was going to study more English today, but now I've changed my mind!

Now write three more sentences about yourself, using the future forms from this unit.

MY TEST!

Circle the correct option.

1 A: I don't know what she looks like. B: You'll know her when you see her. …………… a red sweater.
   a She's due to wear   b She'll be wearing   c She's about to wear
2 …………… the time I get back from the camp, I'll be feeling much fitter.   a At   b Until   c By
3 I'm sorry but I can't help you now. I was …………… to leave.   a just about   b on the point   c on the verge
4 The world's population …………… reach 10 billion in the year 2200.   a is set to   b is about to   c will have
5 I …………… at home and watch TV, but my dad said I needed to get some exercise.
   a will have stayed   b was going to stay   c will have been staying

My Test! answers: 1b 2c 3a 4a 5b

7 The passive 1: basic passive forms

Borders between countries are being broken down.

home | login | search

How globalisation might affect the English language **has** already been widely **written about**. But how do *you* think it will change the way people speak and learn English? Send your opinions to our 'Global Language' website! Here is one opinion:

Today thousands of languages **are spoken** around the world, but the everyday speech of over half the world's population **is made up of** only eleven. English is one, but it's unique because **it's spoken by** so many as a second language. Nearly two billion people **are now being taught** English – they understand the advantages of **being seen** to communicate effectively with people around the world. In the past, people **were worried** that someone with a clearer accent than them **would be considered** better. But as more people from developing countries become confident in English, they can use it to communicate with each other without needing to sound like native speakers. They can communicate in their own language too if necessary, giving them an advantage over most native English speakers. Borders between countries **are being broken down by** communication technology. One effect of this is that global languages like English **are no longer owned by** their native speakers. And for people with detailed knowledge of a local culture and language AND knowledge of English, the sky's the limit! (Tina, Manchester)

?

1 In what way is English different from the other most widely-spoken languages in the world?
2 What advantage do people learning English as a second language have over native English speakers?

Answers: 1 It's spoken by many people as a second language.
2 They can communicate in their own language too.

The passive 1

1 **Use the passive form *be* + past participle of the verb to emphasise what happens to, or what is done to, the subject of the sentence, rather than what the subject of the sentence does.**

*Borders between countries **are being broken down**.*

2 **We usually use the passive form if the person or thing that does the action (the agent) is unknown, unimportant or obvious.**

*6,500 languages **are spoken** around the world.*

3 **We sometimes use the passive if we want to be impersonal and avoid mentioning a specific agent.**

***It is thought** the accident was caused by dangerous driving.*

▶ See Unit 8 for more information on the use of passive forms in reporting opinions and beliefs.

4 If we mention the person / thing that does the action it is usually to emphasise who / what this is.

*... because it's **spoken by so many people** as a second language.* (highlighting that a lot of people speak English as a second language)

We usually use *by* to show the agent. To show what the agent uses to do the action, we usually use *with*.

*He **was hit by** a piece of wood.* (= It fell and hit him.)
*He **was hit with** a piece of wood.* (= Someone hit him using it.)

English uses the passive more often than many other languages.

*This house **was built** by my grandfather.*
In Spanish: *Esta casa la construyó mi abuelo.*
(= This house, he built it my grandfather.)

Passive forms after modals

5 **Passive forms after modal verbs are formed with *be* or *have been* + the past participle of the verb.**

*Further details **can be obtained** by writing to info@easytrips.com.*
*It's important for me to know things like that – I **should have been told**.*

▶ See Units 9 and 10 for more information on the different meanings of modal verbs.

Passive forms with *be being* or *been being* are possible but very rare.

*The room **might be being used** at the moment but it **can't have been being used** for very long.* (rare)
*Somebody **might be using** the room at the moment but they **can't have been using** it for very long.* (more common)

Verbs with two objects

6 **Verbs which can have two objects in active sentences, e.g. *give, bring, send, teach, lend, sell, tell, pass* and *show,* have two passive forms.**

*Two billion people **are** currently **being taught English**. / English **is** currently **being taught** to two billion people.*

▶ See Unit 28 for more information on verbs with two objects.

We often use reporting verbs in the passive to report something without saying who said it.

*We've **been asked** not to use our work computers to send personal emails.*

Verbs with an object and a complement

7 **Verbs such as *name, call, appoint, consider, elect, declare* and *vote* in the passive form can be followed by an adjective or noun phrase (without *as*).**

*... someone with a clearer accent would **be considered better**.* NOT ~~*... would be considered as better.*~~
*She **was appointed President** in 1962.* NOT ~~*She was appointed as President ...*~~

▶ See Unit 27 for more information on these verbs.

Verbs with prepositions

8 **We can make passive forms of verbs which are followed by prepositions.**

*The way globalisation might affect the English language **has** already **been widely written about**.*
*Our house **was broken into** while we were away on holiday.*

Verbs which usually take the infinitive without *to*

9 **Verbs such as *make, feel, help, see* and *hear* are sometimes followed by a *to*-infinitive in the passive form. Note the difference:**

*They **made me wait** for two hours.*
*I **was made to wait** for two hours.*

The *-ing* form of the passive

10 **Verbs such as *love, remember, deny, avoid, describe, hate, like, don't mind* and *imagine* can be followed by *being* + the past participle of the verb in the passive form.**

*I **love being given** presents.*
*In his book, he **describes being attacked** by a crocodile.*

Adjectival forms

11 **Many adjectives are formed from the past participle and are used in a way similar to the passive.**

*People **were worried** that someone with a better accent ...*
*I'**m** not really **interested** in politics.*

Practice

A Make sentences by putting the words in the correct order.

1 named / A 24-year-old woman / been / Young Writer of the Year. / has / from London
A 24-year-old woman from London has been named Young Writer of the Year.

2 is / English / the international language of business. / generally considered

3 being / English / taught / In some countries, / are / from the age of two. / children

4 founded / was / The company / in 1922.

5 a job / has / in New York. / My husband / offered / been

6 was / my grandmother. / taught / I / the piano / by / to play

7 decorated / For the wedding, / was / with beautiful yellow and white flowers. / the room

8 being / My office / last week. / repainted / was

9 you ever / Have / been / by a snake? / bitten

10 of the accident / not / At the moment / known. / the cause / is

B Write ONE missing word in the correct place in each sentence.

1 All our bread ^is made with natural ingredients using a traditional recipe.

2 The first programmable computer was invented Charles Babbage.

3 The theft of three valuable paintings from a museum in Paris is investigated by police.

4 Philip Majors, 56, been elected Mayor of Wallbridge.

5 We have been made feel extremely welcome throughout our holiday.

6 A baby tiger which escaped from a zoo yesterday found in a local park this morning.

7 I really hate asked to work at the weekend.

8 Free tickets will given away to the first 200 callers after the lines open at 7 pm.

9 It's better to leave early to avoid caught in the rush-hour traffic.

10 Her new book has read by nearly a million people.

C Complete the news report with appropriate passive forms of the verbs in brackets.

The large number of new words which [1] have been added (add) to dictionaries this year shows how the English language [2] .... (change) by the effects of the Internet and globalisation. A list [3] .... (publish) last week by one company, and includes many new words as well as some which [4] .... (know) for many years but which [5] .... (adopt) by more people and [6] .... (use) more and more on Internet blogs and in chat rooms. In fact, *blog* and *chat room* are two expressions which [7] .... (see) increasingly frequently in the media in recent years, whilst new inventions include *vlog* [a video blog], *staycation* [a vacation at home] and *frenemy* [a person who acts like your friend but is really your enemy]. Meanwhile, the ethnic diversity of English [8] .... (demonstrate) by the fact that many words and phrases from other languages, like *tapas*, *karaoke* and *feng shui*, [9] .... (accept) into many English-language dictionaries and [10] .... (use) in everyday speech.

D Rewrite each sentence, using a passive form of the underlined verb. Leave out the agent where possible.

1 The police <u>have arrested</u> a woman on suspicion of murder.
A woman has been arrested on suspicion of murder.

2 People <u>write</u> more than two billion emails every day.

3 Someone's <u>sent</u> Sarah a telephone bill for more than £200.

4 Culverton High School <u>has appointed</u> Graeme Turner, 42, from Banford, headteacher.

5 The manager spoke to me in a very rude way, which made me quite angry.

....

....

6 We won't allow the children to come inside with their shoes on because they'll get the carpet dirty.

....

....

7 The minister was criticised after people heard him swear during a live TV debate.

....

....

8 Someone caught a thief trying to steal a car.

....

....

9 They haven't decided the best way to deal with the situation yet.

....

....

10 You can easily walk up the mountain in less than two hours.

....

....

E Complete the sentences, using the words in brackets and an appropriate form of the verb.

1 I can't accept this assignment because it *has been copied from the Internet* .
(copy / the Internet)

2 Nearly 1,000 people have entered the competition and the winner ....
.... (choose / Friday)

3 We really enjoyed working on this project because we
....
(interest / the subject matter)

4 I'll have my phone with me, so I ....
....
(contact / any time)

5 You should have received the tickets by now because they ....
(send / two weeks ago)

6 The directors decided not to offer her the job because it ....
(feel / too inexperienced)

7 It's a very safe area because it ....
....
(patrol / security guards)

8 The company records all phone calls because they
....
(use / training purposes)

9 Three people are in hospital after they
....
(injure / car accident)

10 The city centre is more attractive now because a large amount of money ....
.... (invest / shops and facilities)

MY TURN!

Think about any changes in your town / city at different times in your life. Write at least two passive sentences describing the changes.

1 Changes when you were a child
The old paint factory was knocked down. The shopping centre was built.

2 Recent changes
....
....

3 Changes taking place at the moment
....
....

4 Likely or possible future changes
....
....

MY TEST!

Circle the correct option.

1 The picture was drawn .... a pencil. **a** through **b** by **c** with
2 This house is really old – it must .... hundreds of years ago. **a** have been built **b** be built **c** have built
3 English is .... by almost two billion people around the world. **a** learning **b** being learning **c** being learned
4 .... taught English at primary school. **a** I did **b** To me was **c** I was
5 They were seen .... the building. **a** to enter **b** enter **c** to be entered

My Test! answers: 1c 2a 3c 4c 5a

8 The passive 2: complex passive forms

It has been suggested that it was caused by secret experiments.

Shortly after 7 o'clock on the morning of 30 June 1908, the world ended. At least, that was what the people living near Siberia's Stony Tunguska River believed at the time, when an enormous explosion lit up the sky. More than 80 million trees were destroyed and although **there were no people killed**, many **had their houses damaged** or **their windows broken**. An explosion like that obviously **needs explaining** and the 'Tunguska Event' has been under investigation ever since. It **has been suggested** that it was caused by secret experiments or by an underground gas explosion. But there have also been more mysterious explanations. At the time, the explosion **was said by some people to** have been the result of a UFO crashing to the ground, and in 2004 **it was reported that** the remains of an alien spaceship had been found. After scientific tests, however, the truth is **now believed to** be a little less exciting: the explosion **is thought to** have been caused by a comet entering our atmosphere.

?
1 What was the 'Tunguska Event'?
2 What caused it, according to scientists?

Answers: 1 An enormous explosion which destroyed 80 million trees 2 A comet

The passive 2

Reporting with the passive

1 We often use *It* and a passive form of a reporting verb (e.g. ***suggest, say, believe, think, report, rumour***) with a *that*-clause, in formal situations, to report opinions and beliefs.

It has been suggested that it was caused by secret experiments.
It was reported that the remains of an alien spaceship had been found.

▶ See Unit 15 for more information on *it + be*.

To rumour is only possible in the passive.
***It was rumoured** that a UFO had been found.*
NOT ~~*People rumoured that a UFO had been found.*~~

2 We can also use a passive form of many reporting verbs (e.g. ***believe, say, think, rumour, understand, expect***) with the *to*-infinitive.

*The truth **is** now **believed to be** a little less exciting.*
*She **was thought to know** the truth.*

To report earlier events in this way, use *to + have* + past participle.

*A UFO was said **to have crashed** to the ground.*
*The explosion is thought **to have been** caused by a comet entering our atmosphere.*

A few verbs (e.g. ***suggest, decide, recommend*** and ***announce***) cannot be used in this way.

It was announced that the company is going to close.
NOT ~~*The company was announced to be going to close.*~~

▶ See Unit 39 for more information on reporting verbs.

There + be + subject + past participle

3 We sometimes use *There* at the start of a passive sentence to emphasise an indefinite subject.

***There were** no people **killed**. OR No people were killed.*
***There has been** a lot of money **invested** in alternative energy in the last few years. OR A lot of money has been invested in ...*

We don't use *There* in this way when there is a definite subject.
The Eiffel Tower was built in the nineteenth century.
NOT ~~*There was the Eiffel Tower built ...*~~

▶ See Unit 15 for more information on *there + be*.

Shortened passive structures

4 We sometimes use the past participle by itself as an adjective with a passive meaning.

*a **known** criminal, the **reported** crash*

When this type of passive structure is more than one word, it must come after the noun.
An explosion caused by a comet.
NOT ~~*A caused by a comet explosion.*~~

▶ See Unit 36 for shortened passive forms in relative clauses.

5 We often use the past participle by itself in newspaper headlines.

80 MILLION TREES DESTROYED (= 80 million trees have been destroyed.)

Have something done and *get something done*

6 We often use *have* + object + past participle to describe a service which someone does for us.

*I'm going to **have my hair cut** this afternoon.*

7 We sometimes use *have* + object + past participle when unpleasant things happen to us.

*Many **had their houses damaged**.*

8 We often use *get* instead of *have* in informal situations.

*Do you know anywhere where I can **get my car washed**?*
*Susana's upset because she **got her bag stolen** on the bus this morning.*

We usually use *have*, not *get*, with the present perfect.
*My neighbours **have** just **had their house painted**.*
NOT ~~*My neighbours have just got their house painted.*~~

9 We sometimes use *get* + object + past participle when an activity was difficult to complete for some reason.

*Doing all the reports took ages but we **got them all written** in the end. (= ... we managed to write them all ...)*

Verbs with passive meaning

10 We sometimes use the verbs ***need, want, deserve*** and ***require + -ing*** with a passive meaning.

*An explosion like that obviously **needs explaining**.*

When we use *want* in this way, it is very informal.
*That computer **wants looking at**.* (= The computer needs to be looked at.)

Practice

A Match the sentence beginnings to the correct endings.

1 It is hoped that the injured man
2 The car was reported
3 There will be new safety laws
4 It has been suggested that 400 workers
5 There were more than 20 people
6 This kind of monkey was believed
7 It was claimed that the fire
8 The robbers are thought

a made in order to prevent accidents in the future.
b injured in the explosion.
c will be able to leave hospital in a couple of days.
d to be extinct.
e to have escaped with more than $1 million.
f are likely to lose their jobs.
g to have been moving very fast when it hit the tree.
h had been started by some children.

1 ...c... 2 ...... 3 ...... 4 ...... 5 ...... 6 ...... 7 ...... 8 ......

B Complete the sentences, using the words in the boxes and *have / get something done.*

car eyes ~~nails~~ picture teeth wedding dress

check draw make ~~paint~~ service test

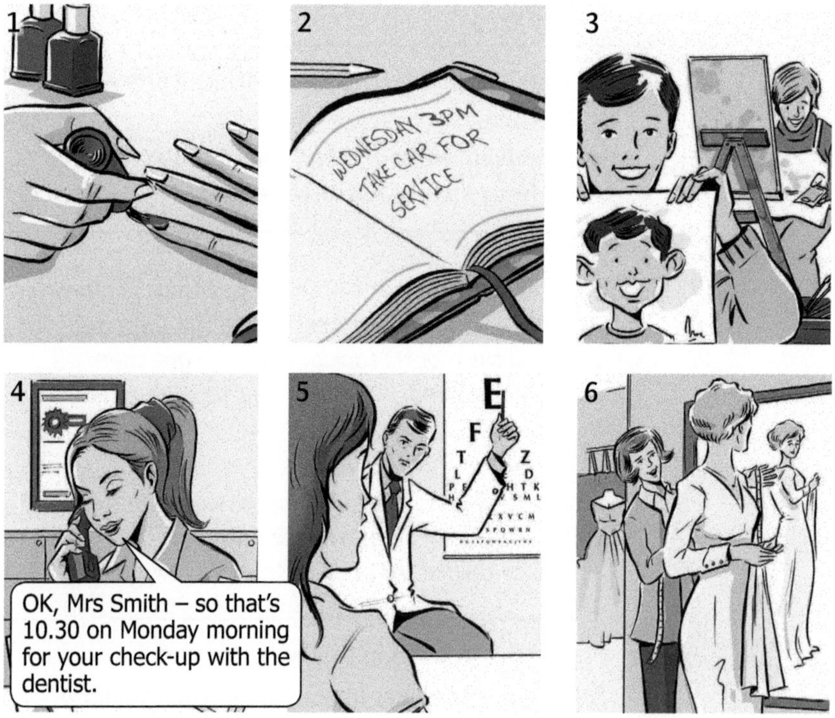

1

2

WEDNESDAY 3PM
TAKE CAR FOR
SERVICE

3

4

OK, Mrs Smith – so that's 10.30 on Monday morning for your check-up with the dentist.

5

E
F
T Z
L D

6

1 She's ...having her nails painted... .
2 He ....
....
3 He ....
4 She ....
....
5 She ....
6 She ....

C Complete each sentence b so that it means the same as sentence a, using a passive form. Write one word in each space.

1 a Did you manage to submit your assignment on time?
  b Did ...you get... your assignment ...submitted... on time?
2 a Someone needs to empty the rubbish bins.
  b The rubbish bins ....
  ....
3 a They thought the diamonds had been stolen during the night.
  b The diamonds ....
  ....
  ....
  .... during the night .
4 a They are going to take our local bus service away from us.
  b We ....
  .... our local bus service ....
  .... from us.
5 a Police arrested about 20 people after the riots.
  b There .... about 20 people
  .... after the riots.
6 a It took ages to plan the trip but we organised everything eventually.
  b It took ages to plan the trip but we
  ....
  .... eventually.
7 a Someone has repainted my neighbours' house recently.
  b My neighbours ....
  .... their house ....
  recently.
8 a People assume the damage was caused by wild animals.
  b The damage ....
  ....
  .... caused by wild animals.

D Complete the reporting sentences, using passive forms of the verbs in brackets.

1 'They broke the car window and stole the stereo.' (think)
The boys *are thought to have broken the car window and stolen the stereo*.

2 'We are worried that the missing woman may be in danger.' (fear)
It ....

3 'He was of medium height with long blond hair and a beard.' (report)
The suspect ....

4 'The opinion of many people was that it was a secret government experiment.' (believe)
It ....

5 'Could the hot summer be the result of climate change?' (suggest)
It ....

6 'People say she is one of the best young players in the country.' (say)
She ....

7 'Everyone agreed that the situation was very complicated.' (accept)
It ....

8 'The assumption now is that the planes crashed during a storm.' (assume)
The planes ....

E Use the words to write full passive sentences from news stories.

1 the thieves / report / carry / guns
The thieves are reported to have been carrying guns.

2 at the time, / the victim / believe / fall / from his balcony
....

3 there / a number of people / trap / by the fire
....

4 it / suggest / an election will take place next year
....

5 there / many complaints / make / about last week's decision
....

6 it / expect / the new statistics will show an improvement
....

7 the actor, 85, / say / be / in a serious condition in hospital
....

8 during yesterday's meeting, / it / explain / a new airport is to be built outside the city
....

MY TURN!

1 What have been the main news stories in your town / country recently? In your notebook, write five sentences using the passive forms from the unit. If you prefer, you can invent your own news stories.

Example: *A fire was thought to have been started by vandals.*

2 Write about five things you have had done for / to you in the past.

Example: *I had my hair cut about a month ago.*

MY TEST!

Circle the correct option.

1 The story about the alien spaceship was .... to have been invented by journalists.
a believed b suggested c announced

2 There were .... destroyed. a Siberia's oldest forests b millions of trees c the Tunguska bridge

3 I need to .... They're too long.
a get shortened my trousers b have shortened my trousers c have my trousers shortened

4 I was late because my dad couldn't .... his car started. a get b have c have got

5 Your bedroom needs .... a to clean b cleaned c cleaning

My Test! answers: 1a 2b 3c 4a 5c

9 Modal verbs 1

There must be something else.

Three friends each paid €100 for a hotel room. Later, the manager remembered the special offer: 3 rooms for €250. So she gave the receptionist €50 to return to the friends. The receptionist had an idea – he gave them €10 each and kept the other €20. So each friend had paid €90, making €270 in total. Adding the €20 that the receptionist took, we get €290. What happened to the other €10?

Lucy: I suppose the receptionist **will have kept** it too.

Emma: No, that **can't be** right. He had €50 and gave the friends €30, so he **can't have kept** more than €20.

Lucy: I give up. What's the answer?

Emma: Come on – you **might have tried** a bit harder before giving up! Let's think ...

Lucy: What about the manager? **Could** it **be** something to do with her? **Could** she **have taken** the money? Or one of the friends **might have found** it on the floor and **could have taken** it, perhaps.

Emma: No, it **won't be** that. There **has to be** a simple answer. When people make puzzles like this, they'**ll** always leave a clue in the story. And they'**ll have done** the same with this one. There **must be** something else. But what **could** it **be**? Wait ... yes, that's it! **How could I have been** so stupid?

?
1 How much did the three friends pay in total?
2 What's the answer to the puzzle?

1 €270 2 We shouldn't add the receptionist's €20 to the €270, because the €20 is part of the money the friends paid. Instead we should add the €30 which the friends got back to the €270 that they paid, making €300.

Modal verbs 1

Can / can't and *could / couldn't* for factual (im)possibility

1 We use *can* / *can't* to say what is generally possible / impossible in fact.

*It **can get** very hot at this time of year.*
*Plants **can't survive** without sunlight.*

2 We use *could* / *couldn't* to say what was / wasn't generally possible in fact in the past.

Before planes were invented it ***could take*** *three months to travel from Europe to Australia.*

Women ***couldn't vote*** *in Britain before 1918.*

We sometimes use *How could I / you?* when we are angry with our mistake or with someone's behaviour.

How could I *have been so stupid?*

Will / *won't* for factual certainty and habitual behaviour

3 *Will* / *won't* are not always about the future. We can use *will* / *won't* to refer to habitual present behaviour.

*They'****ll*** *always* ***leave*** *a clue in the story.*

Jake's so lazy – often he ***won't leave*** *his house all weekend!*

▶ See Unit 2 for the use of *would* to talk about habitual behaviour in the past.

We use *will* / *won't* when we are certain that something is always true.

*At this time of the year there'****ll be*** *a storm nearly every afternoon.*

Will / *won't*, *will* / *won't have* + past participle; *will* / *won't be* + *-ing* for assumptions

4 We sometimes use *will* / *won't* or *will* / *won't be* + *-ing* to assume things about now, and *will have* + past participle to assume things about the past.

No, it ***won't be*** *that.* (= I'm sure it isn't that.)

*Geoff'****ll be playing*** *tennis – he always plays on Sunday afternoons.*

The receptionist ***will have kept*** *the money.*

*I've got six missed calls from Steve. He'****ll have been ringing*** *about his exam result.*

Might (*not*), *may* (*not*), *could*(*n't*) and *can't* for theoretical (im)possibility

5 We use *might* (*not*) / *may* (*not*) or *could* to say we think something is possible now or in the future.

He ***may be*** *too busy.*

He ***might not be busy.*** NOT ~~*He could not be busy.*~~

TIP

We sometimes add *well* (to emphasise a possibility) or *just* (to emphasise that although unlikely, something is still possible) between *might*, *may* or *could* and the infinitive.

Tom thinks it's going to rain, and he ***may well be*** *right.*

I know it sounds like a stupid idea, but it ***might just work.***

When we ask questions about theoretical possibility now or in the future we use *could* / *might* (not *may*).

Could *it* ***be*** *something to do with her?*

NOT ~~*May it be ...?*~~

6 We use *can't* / *couldn't* to say we think something is impossible.

That ***can't be*** *right.*

Might (*not*) *have*, *may* (*not*) *have*, *could have* and *can't have* + past participle for theoretical possibility in the past

7 We use *might* (*not*) / *may* (*not*) *have* or *could have* + past participle, to say we think a past event / situation was possible.

One of the friends ***might have found*** *it on the floor.*

TIP

We usually prefer *may* in more formal situations and when we are a little more confident about something.

You ***may*** *know that Matt and I were very good friends.*

I ***may*** *come with you if I have time. I* ***might*** *come, but it's not very likely.*

We use *might* / *could have* + past participle to ask if something was theoretically possible in the past.

Could *she* ***have taken*** *the money?*

8 We use *can't* / *couldn't have* + participle to say we think a past event or action was impossible.

He ***can't have kept*** *more than €20.*

We ***couldn't have got*** *here any earlier.*

▶ See Unit 10 for the use of *can* and *could* for ability, permission, requests and suggestions.

Must and *must have* + past participle for theoretical certainty

9 We use *must* (or *have* [*got*] *to*) in more informal situations when we have reason to believe something is true in the present.

There ***must be*** *something else.*

There ***has to be*** *a simple answer.*

10 We use *must have* + past participle when we have reason to believe something happened / was true in the past.

The receptionist ***must have kept*** *the money.*

Practice

A Match the sentence beginnings to the correct endings.

1	When the traffic's bad, the journey	a	could easily die from any infection.
2	The world's biggest football stadium	b	can reach speeds of more than 100 km/h.
3	Some dinosaurs	c	could be uncomfortable and dangerous.
4	The cheetah, the fastest animal,	d	can seat more than 150,000 people.
5	The human brain	e	can't breathe if they're not in water.
6	Some kinds of camel	f	can last as little as five minutes.
7	The lives of some insects	g	can take up to 3 hours.
8	Before antibiotics, people	h	could grow to nearly 20 metres tall.
9	Fish	i	can go for days without food or drink.
10	In the Middle Ages, travelling	j	can't survive more than four minutes without blood.

1 ...g... 2 ...... 3 ...... 4 ...... 5 ...... 6 ...... 7 ...... 8 ...... 9 ...... 10 ......

B Circle the correct option. Sometimes both options are possible.

A: Try this puzzle. A man lives on floor 12 of a building. Every morning he takes the lift to the ground floor and walks to work. In the evening, he [1]... usually get into the lift and go to floor 10, then get out and walk up the stairs to floor 12. But if it's raining, he [2]... go straight to floor 12 in the lift. Why?

B: He [3]... not like lifts very much.

A: That [4]... be right – he uses the lift every morning.

B: That's true. Well, he [5]... be afraid of heights.

A: He lives on floor 12!

B: Oh yes ... . Wait! The rain – [6]... it be something to do with that?

A: Yes!

B: OK, so there [7]... be a reason why he can only go up to floor 12 in the lift when it's raining.

A: Exactly! Now, if it was raining in the morning, what [8]... he have taken with him when he left for work?

B: Er ... an umbrella? Now why [9]... he use an umbrella in the lift? Ah, I've got it! He [10]... be really short. So he [11]... use the umbrella to reach the button for floor 12 on a rainy day! On other days he [12]... only reach up to the button for floor 10!

1	(a) 'll	b might
2	a could	b 'll
3	a might	b could
4	a mustn't	b can't
5	a must	b may
6	a may	b might
7	a must	b can
8	a will	b must
9	a might	b will
10	a can	b must
11	a can	b can't
12	a must	b can

C Complete the sentences, using the verbs in brackets and *will / will (won't) have / will be + -ing.*

1 The train was due to leave at 10.30. It's now 10.40. (leave)
The train ...will have left...... .

2 Tina's favourite TV programme is on from 8.00 to 8.30. It's 8.20. (watch)
Tina ....

3 Your parents always go to bed before 11.00 and it's now 11.30. (be)
Don't phone them now. They ....
....

4 Sue's baby was due to be born on 3 September. It's now 25 September. (have a baby)
Sue ....

5 John said he was going to phone at 6.00. It's now 6.00, and the phone is ringing. (be)
That ....

6 Your colleague is 10 minutes late for a meeting and is worried. You know the meetings always start late. (start)
Don't worry, the meeting ....
....

7 You heard a lot of shouting from your neighbours' house last night. Your neighbours often have arguments. (argue)
They ....

8 The new James Bond film came out six weeks ago. Your friend loves James Bond films. (see)
He ....

9 Your grandparents always have dinner at 8.00. It's 8.00 now. (have dinner)
Don't phone them now. They ....

10 Your one-year-old nephew is crying. He hasn't eaten anything all day. (be)
He ....

D **Write two sentences about each picture, using modal verbs from this unit.**

1

2

3

4

5

6

1 *He might be late for school. / He must have missed the bus.*
2 ....
3 ....
4 ....
5 ....
6 ....

MY TURN!

Choose at least five of these situations and write possible explanations for them. Use different modal verbs in your answers where possible.

1 Your neighbour starts banging on your door at 3.00 in the morning.
Example: *There might be a fire.*
2 You receive a text message on your mobile saying 'Outside the post office. 2.30. Come alone.'
3 When you arrive home one night, you notice there is a light on in your bedroom.
4 When your washing comes out of the washing machine, all your clothes have turned pink.
5 You receive an email which tells you that you have won €1 million.
6 You turn on the television and everyone is speaking a language you don't understand.
7 Your photograph is on the front page of today's newspaper.
8 You arrive home and find that your key won't open the door.
9 After being missing for a month, your cat comes home looking much fatter than before.
10 You check your bank account and discover that it is completely empty.

MY TEST!

Circle the correct option.

1 I feel really stupid – how .... I not guess the answer to that puzzle? **a** might **b** can **c** could
2 She's locked herself in her room and she says she .... come out. She refuses! **a** might **b** won't **c** mustn't
3 He won't be at home at this time of the morning – .... to work.
a he'll have gone **b** he'll go **c** he'll have been going
4 You should keep that ticket somewhere safe – you .... well need it later. **a** must **b** will **c** may
5 Let's think about this puzzle again – there .... an obvious answer.
a has to have been **b** has to be **c** must have been

My Test! answers: 1c 2b 3a 4c 5b

Modal and non-modal verbs 2

I must admit, my first films were terrible.

Jimmy Fantoni's tips for up-and-coming film directors

1 Learn from mistakes

As a director, you **can** spend too much time trying to copy others' styles. But you **mustn't** try to make your own versions of their films – you **have to** find your own style. You **should** also realise you **need to** experience failure. I **must** admit, my first films were terrible, but making bad films teaches you how to make better ones. Fortunately, that's what I **managed to** do.

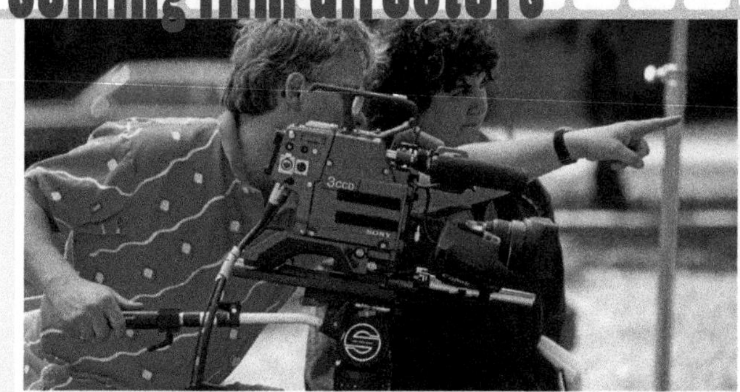

2 Don't dictate – direct!

A director **must** understand people. You **shouldn't** be a dictator – actors respond better to requests like: '**Do you mind if** we do that again?' or '**Would you mind** standing there?'. In the past, I **could have** benefited from listening to my actors, rather than always doing things my way. My advice to young directors is that they **should** exploit other people's experience whenever possible.

3 Know when to stop

When you're making a film, time is very expensive. So you **have to** know when to stop filming one scene and start the next one. I wasted a lot of time re-doing scenes when I really **needn't have** worried. I **ought to have** just stuck with the first version and moved on. Now I **won't** waste time trying to film a perfect scene – something I'll never **be able to** do anyway.

?

1 What were Jimmy Fantoni's first films like?
2 Why is it important not to spend too long filming one scene?

Answers: 1 Terrible 2 It's a waste of time and money.

Modal and non-modal verbs 2

Permission

1 We use *may* or *can* when we ask for or give permission. We use *may not* or *can't* to refuse permission. *May* is more formal.

*A: **May** / **Can** we leave? B: No, you **may** not / **can't**.*

We use *be allowed to* to talk about rules made by someone else.

*The teacher says we**'re** not **allowed to** use a calculator.*

We use *Do you mind if* ... + present tense to ask for permission. *Would you mind if* ... + past means the same but is more polite.

***Do you mind if** we do that again? / **Would you mind if** we did that again?*

Suggestions and expectations

2 We use *should* or *shouldn't* to make and ask for suggestions.

*You **shouldn't** be a dictator.*
*They **should** try to learn from their mistakes.*

Ought to means the same as *should*, but is less common.

*You **oughtn't to** stay out too late.* OR *You **shouldn't** stay out too late.*

We use *be supposed to* to talk about someone else's expectations.

*You**'re supposed to** be directing, not dictating.*

Criticism

3 We use *should* / *ought to* and *should have* / *ought to have* to criticise.

*You **should** try a bit harder.*
*I **ought to have** just stuck with the first version.*

We use statements or questions with ***be supposed to*** to make mild criticisms.

*You **were supposed to** be here an hour ago!*
*What's that **supposed to** mean?*

> **TIP**
> We use *could have* and *might have* to criticise someone for not doing something.
>
> *You **could** / **might have** told me you were having a party!* (= Why didn't you?)

Obligations

4 We use *must* / *mustn't* for strong obligations or prohibitions.

*A director **must** understand people.*
*You **mustn't** try to make your own versions of their films.*

We use *have to* or *need to* to talk about obligation or necessity. We use *don't have to, needn't* or *don't need to* when there is no obligation or necessity.

*You **have to** find your own style.*
*You **needn't** wait if you don't want to.*

> **TIP**
> *Have got to* means the same as *have to* and *need to*, but is less formal. *Gotta* is very informal.
>
> *I **have to** go* ➜ *I've **got to** go* ➜ *I've **gotta** go* ➜ ***Gotta** go.*

We usually use *must* for personal obligations and *have to* for rules made by someone else.

*I'm tired. I really **must** go home soon.*
*You **have to** use seatbelts, even if you're only driving a short way.*

> **TIP**
> Questions with *have to* or *should* are more common than questions with *must*.
>
> *What time **should** we / **do** we **have to** be here tomorrow?*
> (Less common: *What time **must** we be here?*)

Must and *mustn't* only refer to present obligations. For past and future obligations, we use *have to, need to* or *not be allowed to*.

*I used to **have to** practise a lot.*
*I **won't be allowed to** go out until I've finished.*

We use *needn't have*, not *didn't need to*, to show that an event or emotion was unnecessary.

*I really **needn't have** worried.* (= I worried unnecessarily.)

Ability

5 We use *can* and *can't* to talk about present abilities.

*I **can't** hear you.* (at the moment)
*You **can** spend too much time trying to copy others' styles.* (in general)

We use *be (un)able to* in more formal situations.

*I regret to inform you that we **are unable to** offer you a job.*

To talk about future abilities, we usually use *be able to*. We sometimes use *can* / *can't* when we make a decision or plan now about a future action.

*... something I'll never **be able** to do anyway.*
*I **can't** go out tomorrow night – I'm too busy.* OR *I **won't be able** to go out ...*

> We normally don't use *could* to talk about solving a specific problem in the past. Use a non-modal verb such as *managed to*.
>
> *That's what I **managed to** do.* NOT ~~*That's what I could do.*~~

▶ See Unit 11 for *manage to*.

We use *could* and *could have* when talking about hypothetical situations.

*If I had more time I **could** write a book.*
*I **could have** benefited from listening to my actors.*

We use *be able to* after other modals (e.g. *might*) and in infinitives.

*I might **be able to** leave early.*
*I used to **be able to** swim 50 lengths.*

Requests

6 We use modals and similar verbs for polite requests. In general, longer structures are more formal and polite.

Could you tell me ...?
Would you mind standing over there?
Do you think you might be able to ...?

Offers and refusals

7 We use *Shall I* / *we ...?* or *I'll* / *We'll* to make offers.

***Shall I** bring some sandwiches? **We'll** pay for the meal.*

We use *will not* or *won't* to talk about refusal to do something. This does not have a future meaning.

*I **won't** waste time trying to film a perfect scene.*
(= I refuse to do this.)

Practice

A Match the sentence beginnings to the correct endings.

1 May
2 I managed
3 I could
4 I used to be
5 Do you mind
6 Could I ask
7 Shall
8 She's not allowed
9 You ought to
10 I will not

a you to speak more quietly, please?
b sing beautifully as a child.
c get a new phone. Yours is really old.
d I phone you when I arrive?
e I leave early, please?
f let you speak to me like that!
g helping me to lift this box?
h to stay out late. Her parents get worried.
i able to say the alphabet backwards.
j to get tickets for tonight's match. It's going to be great.

1 ..e.. 2 ...... 3 ...... 4 ...... 5 ......
6 ...... 7 ...... 8 ...... 9 ...... 10 ......

B Rewrite each sentence so that it has a similar meaning, using the verb forms from the box.

They weren't able to	~~You're allowed to~~
You're not allowed to	You have to
Do you mind if	Do you mind ... -ing
You didn't need to	You were supposed to
They're unable to	Do you want me to

1 You may bring one bag with you on the plane.
You're allowed to bring one bag with you on the plane.
2 You can't speak during the exam.
....
3 May I put my feet on this chair?
....
4 You should have practised harder.
....
5 You must wear a helmet.
....
6 You needn't have bought me a present.
....
7 They can't sing!
....
8 They couldn't find our house.
....
9 Can you speak more slowly, please?
....
10 Shall I cook tonight?
....

C Read the rules for a drama club, then complete the email, using the correct forms of *have to, need to, be supposed to* or *be allowed to*.

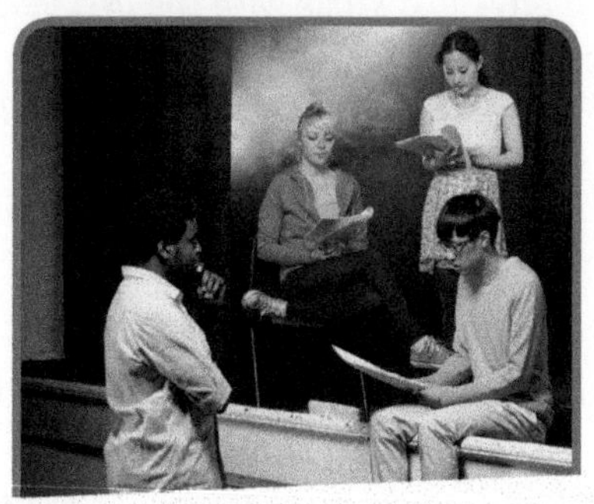

Rules
1 Members must attend all rehearsals.
2 Members may not leave rehearsals without permission.
3 Members must sell at least 10 tickets for each performance.
4 Members must not speak to any journalists about future performances without permission.
5 Members may request a meeting with the club directors only on Thursday mornings.
6 Members should not bring food or drink to rehearsals.

Dear Gary,

I'm thinking of leaving the drama club – the rules are horrible. We 1 ..have to attend.. all rehearsals, whether we're in those scenes or not. And we 2 .... without permission! Not even to go to the toilet! We 3 .... at least 10 tickets for every performance – last month we had 8 performances so I 4 .... 80 tickets! Can you believe it? To make matters worse, we 5 .... to any journalists about the shows. That's crazy! How 6 .... sell tickets if there's nothing in the newspapers? I wanted to speak to the directors about it, but we 7 .... ask for a meeting only on Thursday mornings! Who's free at that time? Anyway, I guess they'll make me leave the club soon. I was eating a kebab at our last rehearsal, even though we 8 .... or drink anything. The director was so angry, but I don't really mind if they throw me out. Anyway, I 9 .... stop writing now – I 10 .... learn my lines tonight.

Tim

D Complete each sentence, using a modal or non-modal form which is most similar to the underlined verb.

1 Last year we only <u>had to</u> practise four times a week, but next year we *will have to* practise at least six times a week.
2 I <u>can</u> usually eat a whole pizza, but last night I wasn't feeling good, so I .... eat only about half of it.
3 You really <u>must</u> go to bed earlier. When I was your age, I used to .... go to bed at 9 pm.
4 You <u>may not</u> leave the building during the lecture, but of course you will .... leave at the end.
5 I <u>didn't manage to</u> complete the race last week. When I was younger, I .... run much further every week.
6 You <u>should</u> always prepare for every performance, and you really .... prepared for last week's performance because they were filming it for TV.
7 You <u>needn't</u> worry about tomorrow's show, just like you .... worried about last night's show.
8 Your microphone is broken again. I <u>can't</u> hear you now and I .... hear you when you were singing.

E Write or complete a criticism for each situation, using the word in brackets.

1 Your friend invited you to a party but didn't tell you to bring a birthday present. (might)
You might have told me to bring a present!
2 Your friend arrives at your house completely wet because it's been raining. (should)
.... an umbrella.
3 Your friend offered to help you with some work, but then didn't reply to your emails. (supposed)
....
4 Your friend says something you don't understand or don't like. (supposed)
.... mean?
5 Your friend has heard some gossip about you. (shouldn't)
....
6 Your friend didn't ask you to help, and got a bad grade in a test. (ought to)
....
....
7 Your friend promised to bring you something back from his holiday, but forgot. (supposed)
....
....
8 Your friend sometimes treats you like a child. (I won 't)
....
....
9 You cooked a meal for your friend, but she didn't tell you she had already eaten. (could)
....
....
10 Your friend has painted a picture but you have no idea what it is. It looks horrible. (supposed)
.... be?

MY TURN!

Complete the sentences to make them true for you, using verb forms from this unit.

1 When I was a child, I used to have to .... but now ....
2 I wasn't able .... but I hope I'll be able ....
3 I think teenagers should be allowed .... but they shouldn't ....
4 I should have .... but I didn't because ....

MY TEST!

Circle the correct option.

1 I don't feel very well today, so do you mind .... at home? a that I stay b if I stay c I stay
2 Alexei wanted to film the sunrise yesterday, so he .... get up at 3.00. a has to b had to c must
3 You .... told us he was a famous director – we'd have asked for his autograph! a could have b would have c had
4 We were going to go by bus but in the end we .... because Simon gave us a lift. a needn't b didn't need to c needn't have
5 It took me three hours before I was finally .... fix my computer. a could b managed to c able to

My Test! answers: 1b 2b 3a 4b 5c

11 Other ways to express modality

There's no point doing nothing.

Check your fitness!

1 What **would** you **rather** do on Saturday morning?

- **a** Stay in bed – **it's not worth** getting up early.
- **b** Go for a run – **there's no point** doing nothing.
- **c** Go shopping – **it's about time** you bought something nice!

2 Your friend invites you to the gym. Which argument would persuade you?

- **a You're coming** with me whether you want to or not!
- **b** Come on – **it's time to** get fit!
- **c** If you come, **maybe** I'll buy you a burger later.

3 Would you **be capable of** running 10 km?

- **a** No problem!
- **b I'm not sure if** I'll manage more than 5.
- **c No way**!

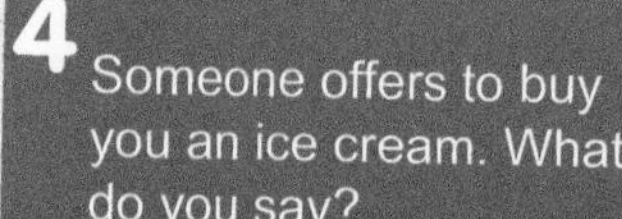

4 Someone offers to buy you an ice cream. What do you say?

- **a I'd just as soon** have an apple.
- **b There's no sense** saying no – I'll have two!
- **c** I shouldn't, but **I'd better** have one so I don't seem rude.

Check your score:

1 a 0 **b** 10 **c** 5 **2 a** 5 **b** 10 **c** 0
3 a 10 **b** 5 **c** 0 **4 a** 10 **b** 0 **c** 5

30–40: Congratulations! There's **no need for you to** change anything.

15–25: There's still a good **chance** you can get fit. **It's** not **likely to happen**, but it's not impossible.

0–10: Your only exercise **is sure to be** a walk to a burger bar. **You'd better** do something about it – now!

?
1 What was your score?
2 Do you agree with the advice?

Other ways to express modality

Probability

1 We use adjectives, adverbs, nouns and modal verbs to talk about how likely something is.

certainly	*She's **bound** to know.*
	*It's **almost certain** that she knows.*
	*There's a good **chance** that she knows.*
	*She's **very likely** to know.*
	*She **could** well know.*
	*She **probably** knows.*
maybe	*She **might** know. / **Perhaps** she knows.*
	*She **might** not know.*
	*It's **possible** that she knows.*
	*There's a slight **possibility** that she knows.*
	*I'm not **sure** if she knows.*
	*She's **unlikely** to know. / She **probably** doesn't know.*
certainly not	*I'm **sure** she doesn't know.*

▶ See Unit 9 for modal verbs of probability.

2 We can use adjectives to describe probability in three ways:

it **+** ***be*** **+ adjective + (*that*) + clause:**
It's ***unlikely*** *that he'll win.*

subject (person) + ***be*** **+ adjective + (*that*) + clause:**
I'm ***certain*** *she'll come.*

subject + ***be*** **+ adjective +** ***to*****-infinitive:**
Your only exercise ***is sure to be*** *a walk to a burger bar.*

There are different ways of talking about past probability.

He's ***likely*** *to have gone.* (= I think now it's likely that he went.)
He was ***likely*** *to go.* (= I thought then that it was likely that he would go.)

We can use *if* / *whether* after *not sure*.

I'm ***not sure if*** *I'll manage more than five.*

▶ See Unit 22 for more information on structures like *He was likely to go.*

3 **We can use *maybe* / *perhaps* at the beginning, in the middle, or at the end of a sentence.**

Maybe *I'll buy you a burger. / I'll* ***maybe*** *buy you a burger. / I'll buy you a burger,* ***maybe.***

We usually use *definitely, certainly, probably* and *possibly* in the middle of a sentence. In negative sentences, they come <u>before</u> the negative word.

*You'****ll definitely*** *meet her tonight.*
You ***probably won't*** *meet her tonight.*

▶ See Unit 24 for the position of adverbs.

4 **We can use *there is* + *a* / *the chance* / *possibility* / *likelihood* to talk about probability. After these nouns we can put a statement (with or without *that*) or *of* + -*ing*. We often put adjectives like *good, strong* or *slight* before these nouns, or quantifiers like *no* and *every*.**

There's *still* ***a good chance*** *you can get fit.*

We can also use *There's no way* + clause to express strong impossibility.

There's no way *she'll agree!*

We sometimes use *No way!* to refuse strongly.

A: Can I borrow your computer? *B:* ***No way!***

Suggestions

5 **We can use *had better* (*not*) + infinitive without *to* or *It's* (*high* / *about*) *time* + past simple or past continuous to make strong suggestions.**

I'd better *have one so I don't seem rude.*
It's about time *you bought something nice.*

It's time **+** ***to*****-infinitive just means that something needs to happen now.**

It's time to *get up!*

We also make suggestions with *Let's, could, Why don't* (*we* / *you*), *How about* + -*ing* and *How about* (*if*).

Let's *go out tonight.*
How about *having a salad?*

Commands and refusals

6 **We can give commands with the present continuous or with *be* + *to*-infinitive.**

*You'****re coming*** *with me, like it or not!*
*You'****re to phone*** *as soon as you arrive.*

We can also use the present continuous to refuse something strongly.

*I'****m*** *not* ***eating*** *this! It's disgusting!*

Lack of necessity

7 **We can use the following expressions to say something isn't necessary:**

There's no ...	*need* (*for* somebody) + *to*-infinitive / *point* / *sense* (*in*) (somebody) + -*ing*
It's not worth ...	*it* (*for* somebody) + *to*-infinitive / (somebody) + -*ing*

There's no need for you to change *anything.*
It's not worth getting up *early.*

▶ See Unit 15 for more information on *it* and *there*.

Preference

8 **We can use these expressions to talk about preference:**

would prefer + *to*-infinitive (*... than* + infinitive):
*We'****d prefer to go*** *swimming* ***than*** *go shopping.*
would prefer it + *if* + somebody + past simple:
I'd prefer it if you didn't stay *out late.*
would rather / *sooner* + infinitive (*... than* + infinitive):
*He'****d sooner drive*** *around for hours* ***than*** *ask the way.*
would rather + somebody + past simple:
I'd rather you didn't open *the window.*
would just as soon + infinitive (*... as* + infinitive):
I'd just as soon *have an apple.* (= I have no strong preference.)

Ability

9 **We can use *be capable of* + -*ing* to talk about abilities based on physical or mental qualities.**

Would you ***be capable of running*** *10 km?*

We use *manage* / *fail* + *to*-infinitive to talk about success or failure in specific situations.

I wanted to run 10 km, but I only ***managed to run*** *6.*

Practice

A Put the sentences in order, 1 to 3. 1 should be the strongest opinion or prediction.

1. a I'd rather you didn't eat that burger in here. 3
   b You are not eating that burger in here. 1
   c You shouldn't eat that burger in here. 2
2. a It's not impossible that we'll be late. ☐
   b It's possible that we'll be late. ☐
   c There's a strong possibility that we'll be late. ☐
3. a We could have a pizza but I'd sooner have a salad. ☐
   b We could have a pizza but I'd just as soon have a salad. ☐
   c We could have a pizza but I'd much rather have a salad. ☐
4. a You're to stop eating hamburgers immediately. ☐
   b It's about time you stopped eating hamburgers. ☐
   c You really had better stop eating hamburgers. ☐
5. a I'm not sure she'll be there. ☐
   b I'm fairly sure she won't be there. ☐
   c She's sure to be there. ☐
6. a There's every chance that he'll have finished by now. ☐
   b He's bound to have finished by now. ☐
   c He could have finished by now. ☐
7. a There's no way you'll beat me. ☐
   b Maybe you'll beat me. ☐
   c It's really unlikely that you'll beat me. ☐
8. a There's absolutely no point in you coming now. ☐
   b It's really not worth it for you to come now. ☐
   c Perhaps it might not be worth you coming now. ☐

C Complete the sentences, using the information in the table and *be capable of*, *manage to* and *fail to*.

Name	Sport	Personal best	Yesterday's result
Dan	high jump	2.10 m	2.05 m
Ruth	100 m running	15 sec	did not finish
Marion	marathon	3 hours 20 min	3 hours 39 min
Pete	long jump	5.40 m	5.40 m
Greg	diving	1st place	4th place

1. Dan is capable of jumping 2.10 ...
2. ... but yesterday he only managed to jump 2.05 .
3. Ruth ...
4. ... but yesterday .
5. Marion ...
6. ... but yesterday .
7. Pete ...
8. ... and yesterday .
9. Greg ...
10. ... but yesterday .

B <u>Underline</u> the correct option.

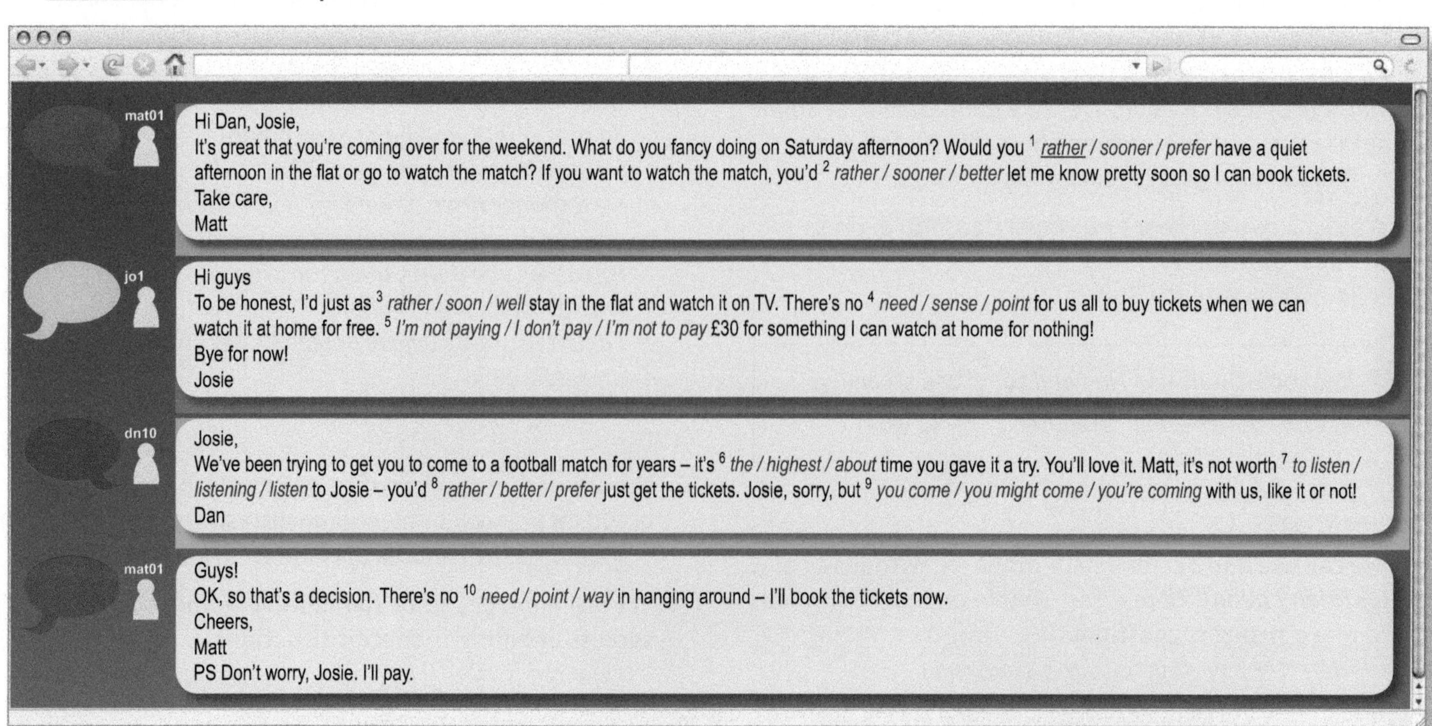

mat01

Hi Dan, Josie,
It's great that you're coming over for the weekend. What do you fancy doing on Saturday afternoon? Would you [1] *rather / sooner / prefer* have a quiet afternoon in the flat or go to watch the match? If you want to watch the match, you'd [2] *rather / sooner / better* let me know pretty soon so I can book tickets.
Take care,
Matt

jo1

Hi guys
To be honest, I'd just as [3] *rather / soon / well* stay in the flat and watch it on TV. There's no [4] *need / sense / point* for us all to buy tickets when we can watch it at home for free. [5] *I'm not paying / I don't pay / I'm not to pay* £30 for something I can watch at home for nothing!
Bye for now!
Josie

dn10

Josie,
We've been trying to get you to come to a football match for years – it's [6] *the / highest / about* time you gave it a try. You'll love it. Matt, it's not worth [7] *to listen / listening / listen* to Josie – you'd [8] *rather / better / prefer* just get the tickets. Josie, sorry, but [9] *you come / you might come / you're coming* with us, like it or not!
Dan

mat01

Guys!
OK, so that's a decision. There's no [10] *need / point / way* in hanging around – I'll book the tickets now.
Cheers,
Matt
PS Don't worry, Josie. I'll pay.

D Rewrite each sentence so that it has a similar meaning, using the words in brackets. Sometimes more than one answer is possible.

1 It's highly likely that she'll beat me at tennis. (every)
There's every chance that she'll beat me at tennis.

2 It's inevitable that he'll win the race. (bound)

3 I'm sure he'll play well. (He's)

4 It's fairly likely that the match will be cancelled. (good chance)

5 There's no chance of me being able to lift that weight. (way)

6 I'm sure they won't want to eat lettuce. (definitely)

7 I think your ideas might not work. (sure)

8 There's a slight chance she'll come with us for a run. (impossible)

9 There's no point her paying so much for a new bike. (worth)

10 We'd really rather you stayed at home tonight. (prefer it if)

E Rewrite these sentences to talk about probability in the past, present or future. Sometimes more than one answer is possible.

1 I'm convinced they went swimming in the morning. (future)
I'm convinced they'll go swimming in the morning.

2 There's likely to be plenty to eat. (past)

3 She's unlikely to have had a running machine at home. (present)

4 He's bound to spend the evening watching TV. (past)

5 It's possible that she's lost some weight. (future)

6 Perhaps she isn't at home. (future)

7 They're sure to be invited. (past)

8 There is no need for us to book a table. (past)

MY TURN!

Complete these sentences about your attitudes to health and fitness.

1 It's not worth *buying a running machine – I'd rather go running in the park*.

2 I'd rather ....

3 There's no way ....

4 I'm unlikely to ....

5 It's about time I ....

6 I'm capable of ....

7 I'd better ....

8 I'm not sure ....

MY TEST!

Circle the correct option.

1 Sam's not in – he's .... to be at the gym as usual. a probable b bound c possible
2 We're not .... if we can come to your birthday party. a likely b probable c sure
3 There's no .... we can all fit in only one car. a point b sense c way
4 It's about .... you started to look after yourself better. a time b better c rather
5 Gabrielle and Jo decided they'd .... not go camping again this year. a soon b prefer c rather

My Test! answers: 1b 2c 3c 4a 5c

R1 Review: present simple and continuous; past and perfect tenses; the future; the passive; modals

A Complete the sentences with the present simple or present continuous form of the verbs in the box.

apologise	arrest	have	not look forward
~~know~~	press	think	use

1 I ....know.... what you mean.
2 This party's great! I .... a great time.
3 In order to set the alarm you .... this button twice to change to the alarm mode.
4 I lost my phone so I .... my dad's until I can buy a new one for myself.
5 I was wrong to say those things. I .... for that.
6 The movie ended the usual way: the police eventually .... the criminals and at the end everyone's happy.
7 A: School starts again next week. I .... to it right now, though I'm sure I'll feel OK after a day or two.
8 I .... of going skiing if I can afford it.

B Match the pairs.

1 I've never played — b
2 I haven't been playing — a
a computer games recently.
b a computer game like that before.

3 While Amy was at the supermarket
4 By the time Jo reached the supermarket
a she lost her list of things to buy.
b she'd lost her list of things to buy.

5 Lee has been running a lot
6 Ryo had been doing a lot of exercise
a – that's why he's so fit.
b – that's why he was in good shape.

7 I lived
8 I've lived
a in Canada for about three years when I was a child.
b in four different countries in the last ten years.

9 I've been reading
10 I've read
a the third Ricky Parks book and I should finish it soon.
b every Ricky Parks book at least twice.

11 It's been raining a lot
12 It rained non-stop for days
a so the ground's very wet.
b the last time I was in Ireland.

13 I was hoping to get a new phone
14 I'd been looking for a new phone
a for about a month when I found one I liked.
b but I can't really afford one right now.

C Underline the correct option.

William Davies is an artist who makes incredibly small things. Recently, he [1]*<u>has been working</u> / had been working* on a sculpture of two polar bears which is about 0.005 millimetres high. 'I [2]*haven't been finishing / haven't finished* it yet,' the artist said, 'but it's for an exhibition about endangered animals.'
In his 40-year career, Davies [3]*made / has made* hundreds of tiny sculptures, most of them so small that they can only be seen under a microscope. How does he do it?
'[4]*I was developing / I've been developing* my techniques for over 40 years, ever since [5]*I've been / I was* 5 or 6 years old,' he says. 'As a child, I [6]*was having / had* learning difficulties and hardly any friends, so I [7]*had spent / used to spend* a lot of time on my own. In those days, [8]*I was always playing / I've always been playing* with insects in my mum's garden. In particular, I was fascinated by ants and [9]*I'd made / I would make* things for them like little houses, furniture and bicycles out of all sorts of materials. By the time I left school, my art [10]*took over / had taken over* my life.'
To create his tiny works of art, Davies [11]*was having to / has had to* learn to control his body in amazing ways because even the smallest wrong movement can destroy his work. 'I [12]*used to make / was making* lots of mistakes when I was younger. Once I [13]*painted / was painting* a sculpture of a scene from *Alice in Wonderland* when I accidentally [14]*breathed in / was breathing in*. The whole piece flew into my mouth and I swallowed it! It seems funny now but I was really upset at the time because [15]*I'd been working / I've been working* on it for two whole weeks.' Nowadays, Davies sells his work at very high prices so he's extremely careful how he breathes.

D Cross out ONE incorrect option.

1 A: I'm going to Moscow next week.
B: Really? How long ... there?
a will you be staying? b are you staying? c ~~will you have stayed?~~

2 A: Sorry. Have I come at an inconvenient time?
B: Well, actually we were ... to go out.
a bound b just about c going

3 A: Have you had your job for a long time?
B: No, not that long. In January ... for exactly three years.
a I'll have worked here b I'll be working here
c I'll have been working here

4 A: Did the election results surprise you?
B: Oh yes. I thought ... again.
a the government were bound to win
b it was obvious the government were going to win
c the government will be winning

5 A: Oh dear! Pete doesn't look very happy.
B: No, you're right. He looks like ... his temper.
a he's to lose b he's on the verge of losing c he's going to lose

6 A: Do you have any plans for the weekend?
B: Well, on Sunday afternoon ... on a plane to Malaysia.
a I'll be b I'm sitting c I'm going to be sitting

7 A: Have you watched series 3 of *Happy Families* yet?
B: No, but I have the programmes on DVD and when I see you next ... them all.
a I'll have watched b I'll watch c I'll have been watching

E Circle the correct option(s). Sometimes more than one option is possible.

1 I .... a very interesting email.
a was send (b) have been sent c have been being sent

2 I don't remember .... to Andrea's mum.
a to be introduced b being introduced c having been introduced

3 Simpson .... Footballer of the Year on two different occasions.
a was declared as b was voted c was named by

4 The work .... last week.
a was completed b had completed
c should have been completed

5 Is there anything else that needs .... around here?
a doing b done c to be done

6 Children in that school .... two hours homework every evening.
a have been made b are made do c were made to do

7 We .... a new sofa delivered.
a are having b were c had

8 Your bike might .... stolen if you leave it there unlocked.
a be b get c have

F Complete each sentence b so that it has a similar meaning to sentence a, using three to five words including the word in brackets.

1 a He definitely won't change his mind. (way)
b There's ...no way he'll... change his mind.

2 a Vanessa refused to fill in the form. (filling)
b Vanessa said: '.................... this form.'

3 a We probably won't be able to finish everything today. (unlikely)
b It .... be able to finish everything today.

4 a I think it's a good idea for them to stop now. (had)
b I think .... stop now.

5 a Helen thinks we really should go home. (high)
b Helen thinks it .... home.

6 a Sophie has the ability to become a really good writer. (capable)
b Sophie .... really good writer.

7 a My preference would be to go out today and not tomorrow. (rather)
b .... today and not tomorrow.

8 a If you could keep quiet about this I'd be happier. (sooner)
b .... nothing about this.

12 Determiners 1: articles and demonstratives

A hand came through the window.

Can ghosts drive cars? Do you believe in such things? Those of you who don't like ghost stories should stop reading now.

This guy was walking along **a mountain road** one stormy night. Suddenly he saw **a light** – there was **a car** coming along **the road**. He waved for **the car** to stop so he could have **a lift**. **The car** stopped, so he opened **the door** and got in. When he turned to thank **the driver**, he was shocked to see **the seat** was empty.

The frightened traveller sat and watched as **the car** started moving slowly and silently along **the road**. Suddenly, **the man** realised it was heading towards **the edge** of **a** cliff. Then, at **the last moment**, **a hand** came through **the window** and turned **the** steering wheel so that **the car** passed safely round **the corner**. **This** happened several times – every time **the car** was about to go over **a cliff**, **the hand** appeared and turned **the wheel**.

Eventually, **the man** managed to open **the door** and jump out of **the car**. He ran all **the way** to **the nearest town**, where he found **a café** and sat down. **The people** in **the café** noticed he was shaking, so he started explaining what had happened.

Just as he was finishing **this story**, two **men** came into **the café**. 'Look,' said one. 'There's **that crazy guy** who got into our car while we were pushing it.'

?

1 Why was the man scared?
2 Who did the car and the hand belong to?

Answers: 1 He thought a ghost was driving the car. 2 Two men who were pushing it.

Determiners 1

Articles

1 **We use *a* / *an* or no article to say something new. We use *a* / *an* for singular countable nouns and no article for plurals and for uncountable nouns. We use *the* to talk about something which is not new to the listener or reader.**

*There was **a** car coming. He waved his arms for **the** car to stop.*

TIP In jokes and stories, we sometimes use *this* to introduce a new character instead of *a / an.*

This guy was walking along a mountain path ...
OR *A guy ...*

We use *a / an* or no article for new information, even when you have used the same word before.

*The car was heading towards **a** cliff. Every time the car was about to go over **a** cliff* (= a different cliff)

We can use *another* with singular nouns to mean 'one more'.

*Would you like **another** glass of water?*

TIP Use *other*, not *another*, with plural and uncountable nouns, and after words like *the, this, my*, etc.

*I love reading about **other** countries.*
NOT ~~*... another countries.*~~
*Where's my **other** shoe?* NOT ~~*... my another shoe.*~~

We use *the* for known information even when you use a different word to describe it.

*This guy was walking ...; **The** traveller sat ...; **The** man realised ...*

We use *the* for information that is clear from the context. For example, after we introduce *a car*, we don't need to introduce all the things that cars usually have.

*The car stopped, so he opened **the** door and got in.*
*When he turned to thank **the** driver, he was shocked to see **the** seat was empty.*

TIP We use *the* in phrases like *the edge of a cliff* or *the middle of a field* because cliffs always have edges, and a field always has a middle.

*It was heading towards **the edge of a cliff**.*

2 We use *the* if the noun is defined by an adjective, clause or prepositional phrase before or after it.

*He ran to **the nearest** town.*
*Then, at **the last** moment, ...*
*We couldn't believe **the** story **that the man was telling**.*
***The** people **in the café** noticed ...*

3 We don't use an article with plurals or uncountable nouns to talk about things in general.

*Can **ghosts** drive **cars**?*

We can use *a / an* + singular noun to talk about things in general when we want to treat each thing separately.

*Everybody should have **a computer**.* (= one computer each)

We can use *the* + singular noun, or a plural noun, to make general statements about all members of a group.

***The computer** has made life much easier.*
OR ***Computers** have made life much easier.*

▶ See Unit 32 for *the* + adjective for general statements.

Demonstratives and determiners

4 We use *this, that, these* and *those*, with or without a noun, to refer to something 'here / now / with me' or 'there / then / with you'.

*Listen to **this** story and decide for yourself.*
*There's **that** crazy guy who got into our car.*

We can use *this / these* to emphasise that we're still talking about the same thing.

*He started explaining what had happened. Just as he was finishing **this** story ...* OR *... **the** story ...*
*The car made it safely round the corner. **This** happened ...* (= the same process)

We sometimes use *one of those* + plural noun to talk about typical things that everyone is familiar with.

*Have you ever had **one of those** days when everything goes wrong?*

TIP We can use *those* (*people / of us / of you*) with a relative clause to refer to types of people.

***Those of you** who don't like ghost stories should stop reading now.*

▶ See Unit 42 for more information on *this, that* and *it*.

5 We don't use *a / an* or *the* with *this, that, these* and *those* or with possessives (e.g. *my, your, his, her, Paul's*, etc.).

*It was **my** worst journey ever.*
NOT ~~*It was my the worst journey ever.*~~

6 We use *such* (*a / an*) + noun to mean 'the same kind as that'.

*I've never heard **such a scary story**!*
*Do you believe in **such things**?*

▶ See Unit 40 for *so / such* for emphasis and exclamations.

Practice

A Write S if each sentence b means the same as sentence a and D if it means something different.

1 a This man was walking down the street. Suddenly the guy started shouting.
  b This man was walking down the street. Suddenly a guy started shouting. ....D....
2 a Can you open a door, please?
  b Can you open the door, please? ....
3 a The car has changed a lot since it was invented over 100 years ago.
  b Cars have changed a lot since they were invented over 100 years ago. ....
4 a She was driving home when she thought she saw a ghost getting into the car.
  b She was driving home when she thought she saw a ghost getting into a car. ....
5 a I've got the books you wanted.
  b I've got those books you wanted. ....
6 a We have a ghost in a bedroom in my flat.
  b We have a ghost in the bedroom in my flat. ....
7 a I was lying in bed when I heard a strange noise.
  b I was lying in bed when I heard this strange noise. ....
8 a It was the most terrifying dream I'd ever had.
  b It was my most terrifying dream ever. ....
9 a Have you ever seen such beautiful paintings?
  b Have you ever seen these beautiful paintings? ....
10 a Anne was one of those people who always get the best grades.
  b Anne was the person who always got the best grades. ....

B Complete the sentences, using *this, that, these, those* or *such.*

1 A: Thanks for all your help. B: ....That....'s fine.
2 Would you like one of .... cakes? I made them myself.
3 He only talks about himself all the time. I can't stand .... people.
4 Please listen carefully. .... is really important.
5 Why are .... men waving their arms? Perhaps we should stop the car.
6 It's one of .... films about the end of the world. They're all the same.
7 What was .... noise? It sounded like a person outside.
8 I'll tell you a joke. .... man went to the doctor and said, 'Doctor, doctor, ...'.
9 I've never eaten .... a terrible meal.
10 I bought .... shoes here yesterday, but they're too small. Can I change them?

C Complete the story with *a, an, the* or – (= no article).

Many years ago, this [1] ....–.... train was approaching a bridge across [2] .... river. Suddenly [3] .... driver saw [4] .... strange figure ahead. [5] .... person seemed to be trying to make the train stop.

[6] .... noise of the brakes was terrible. When the train had stopped, the driver got out to ask the strange person what was wrong, but there was nobody around. He took his [7] .... lamp and walked a few steps along [8] .... track. Then he stopped suddenly – [9] .... bridge they had been about to cross had fallen into the river.

The man ran back to the train and found [10] .... large dead moth on the train's [11] .... lamp. When he lit the lamp, he saw that the moth's shadow looked exactly like the strange figure he had seen. The moth had saved the driver and all [12] .... other people on the train.

D Combine the pairs of sentences to complete one new sentence. Think carefully about articles and determiners.

1 I saw a man. You were talking about him earlier.
  I saw ....the man you were talking about earlier.... .
2 She had a mobile phone. It was a really thin one – I'm sure you know them.
  She had one ....
3 I heard a sound. It was a dog barking in the distance.
  I heard ....
4 Some of you have finished. If so, you can go home.
  Those of ....
5 She was driving down a road. It went to London.
  She was ....
6 It was a terrible meal. He's never cooked a worse one.
  It was ....
7 In his pocket I could see a handle. It was part of a gun.
  In his ....
8 I stayed in a hotel. You recommended it.
  I stayed ....

E **Change these headlines into normal sentences. You can use your imagination to add details.**

1 **Teenager prevents train crash by pulling emergency brake after dream**

A teenager prevented a train crash last night by pulling the emergency brake. She pulled the brake after a dream about a train crash.

2 **Man walking home from friend's house sees strange lights in sky**

....

....

3 Ghost whisper mystery solved after radio found under floor

....

....

4 **Woman finds keys under sofa – 40 years after losing them**

....

....

5 TV company apologises after Egyptian mummies terrorise city centre

....

....

6 Owner reveals secrets of 'flying car' film – 'I used model and fishing line'

....

....

7 **Man discovers woman sitting next to him in theatre is twin sister missing for 20 years**

....

....

8 Birthday card from grandfather delivered to woman's house 12 years late.

....

....

MY TURN!

Complete this ghost story, using your own ideas. The letters always refer to the same thing, e.g. (A) could be *old lady*.

One ....dark...., ...stormy.... night, this .... (A) was walking through the forest. It was .... and .... and the .... (A) felt .... Suddenly the .... (A) heard the sound of a / an .... (B).

The .... (B) was a long way away, but it was coming closer and closer. The .... (A) started running. He / She felt very .... Suddenly he / she saw a / an .... (C) standing among the shadows. The .... (C) was carrying a / an .... (D). The .... (A) screamed.

Then ....

....

....

....

....

Fortunately, ...

....

....

....

....

MY TEST!

Circle the correct option.

1 I've had .... terrible headache since I woke up this morning. **a** a **b** – **c** the

2 Joanna's feet are hurting her. She should have worn her .... shoes. **a** other **b** another **c** the other

3 As I was driving home, I thought I saw a ghost standing at .... side of the road. But it was just a reflection in the window. **a** – **b** a **c** the

4 I got really scared walking home in the dark last year, and since .... experience I always take the bus. **a** the **b** that **c** such

5 I can't believe he did that – I've never seen .... bad behaviour! **a** the **b** that **c** such

My Test! answers: 1a 2a 3c 4b 5c

13 Determiners 2: quantifiers

A good deal of progress has been made.

Alan Turing

For **several** decades, the idea of 'thinking machines' has been something **a lot of** people accept as part of modern life. Work on intelligent machines began in the 1950s when the mathematician Alan Turing suggested **all** computers could be programmed to think 'intelligently'. He developed the 'Turing Test', which said we can describe **any** machine as 'intelligent' if it can make a human believe it is a person. The term 'artificial intelligence' (AI) was first used by a group of American scientists, led by John McCarthy. **Each** of these scientists has played an important role in the development of AI since then.

Although **a good deal of** progress has been made, **much** work is needed before AI will equal human intelligence. **Some** scientists think **any** computer that can think like us would cost **too much** money to make. **Many** others think there is **no** reason why computers need to be more powerful than they are already. Instead, the problem is how to program them. The challenge for **every** AI scientist is that we don't have **enough** knowledge of how people learn. **Much of** a child's learning is through physical experience, but **no** computer programs exist which can learn effectively this way and there isn't **any** obvious possibility of this changing in the near future.

?

1 Who invented the term 'artificial intelligence'?
2 What is the difference between the way children and computers learn?

Answers: 1 A group of American scientists, led by John McCarthy 2 Children learn through physical experience but no computer programs can (currently) learn this way.

Determiners 2

Quantifiers

1 Quantifiers are words or phrases which usually go before a noun and give information about quantity. Examples include:

	countable	uncountable
zero	I don't have **any** books. / I have **no** books.	I don't have **any** time. / I have **no** time.
	I have **hardly** / **barely any** books.	I have **hardly** / **barely any** time.
	I have **(a) few books.** / I don't have **many** books.	I have **(a) little** time. / I don't have **much** time.
	I have **some** books. / Do you have **any** books?	I have **some** time. / Do you have **any** time?
	I have **quite a lot of** / **several** books.	I have **quite a lot of** time
	I have **a lot of** books. / Do you have **many** books?	I have **a lot of** time. / Do you have **much** time?
↓	I like **most** books.	I like **most** music.
100%	I like **all** books.	I like **all** music.

Use *no*, not *not ... any*, as the subject of the sentence or to add emphasis.

No computer programs exist which ...
NOT ~~*Not any computer programs ...*~~
*There is **no** reason why computers ...*
OR *There is**n't any** reason ...*

▶ See Unit 11 for some more common phrases with *no*.

We don't usually use *much* / *many* in affirmative sentences; we use *a lot of* instead.

*I have **a lot of** work to do.*
NOT ~~*I have much work to do.*~~

In more formal situations, we sometimes use *much* / *many* in affirmative sentences, especially as the subject.

***Many* / *A lot of* others think ...**

2 **We usually use *some* in affirmative sentences and *any* in negatives and questions with plural and uncountable nouns.**

__Some__ people think ...
There isn't __any__ obvious possibility ...
Is there __any__ possibility that ...?

Some exceptions:

– we usually use *some* in questions which make an offer:

Do you want __some__ ketchup?

– we use *any* in affirmative sentences to mean 'it doesn't matter which one' or 'if something exists':

We can describe __any__ machine as 'intelligent' if ...
__Any__ computer that can think like us ...

– we can use *some* with singular countable nouns, where it means 'I don't know which one'. In informal situations, we can add *... or other*.

There was __some__ man (__or other__) looking for you earlier.

3 **We use *both* / *either* / *neither* with two things: *both* = A + B; *either* = A or B; *neither* = not A or B.**

She can write with __both hands__ / __either hand__.
__Neither__ man wanted to accept responsibility.

▶ See Unit 41 for other uses of *both*, *either* (*or*) and *neither* (*nor*).

4 **We use *a few* / *a little* to talk about small quantities, and *few* / *little* to emphasise that the amount is less than you might expect, especially with *very*.**

I'll try to help you. I have __a little__ time.
I'm sorry – I can't help. I have __very little__ time.

We use *more* / *most*, *fewer* / *fewest* and *less* / *least* to compare quantities.

I made __fewer__ mistakes than last time.

TIP

In informal language, we often use *less* with plural nouns, instead of *fewer*.

There were __less__ people at the party than we expected. OR *There were __fewer__ people ...*

5 **We use *all* with a plural or uncountable noun, and *each* or *every* with a singular noun.**

She's good at __all__ sports.
I like to visit at least one new country __each__ / __every__ year.

We use *all* plus a singular noun without *the* to talk about complete periods of time.

I studied __all day__ / __night__ / __week__.

Use *each* with very small numbers and *every* with larger numbers.

The challenge for __every__ AI scientist ...
NOT ~~*The challenge for each AI scientist ...*~~

Use *every* with a singular time expression to talk about regular repeated events.

I go dancing __every week__ / __every__ Friday / __every now and then__ / __every once in a while__.

6 **In informal situations, we can use *a couple* / *bit of* and *plenty* / *lots of*. *Loads of* / *Tons of* are very informal.**

	countable	uncountable
small quantity	We've got a couple of friends.	We've got a bit of time.
large quantity	We've got plenty / lots / loads / tons of friends.	We've got plenty / lots / loads / tons of time.

In formal situations, we can use *a good deal of* with uncountable nouns and *a large* / *small number of* with plural countable nouns.

__A good deal of__ progress has been made.

7 **We can also use quantifiers as pronouns, without *of*.**

Have some biscuits – we've got __lots__.
NOT ~~*We've got lots of.*~~

We use *none* as a pronoun instead of *no*, and *each one* / *every one* instead of *each* / *every*.

I wanted to buy some milk but there was __none__ left.

8 **To combine quantifiers with other determiners or pronouns we usually use *of*. Use *none* instead of *no*.**

__Each of__ these scientists has played an important role ...
__Much of__ the learning a child does ...
__None of__ my friends live near me. NOT ~~*No of my friends ...*~~

TIP

We use *too* + *much* / *many* / *few* / *little* to talk about excessive quantities.

... would cost __too much__ money to make.

We don't necessarily include *of* when we use *all* / *both* with articles or determiners + nouns.

__All__ (__of__) __the computers__ in the world ...
__Both__ (__of__) __my parents__ are French.

TIP

Use *whole*, not *all*, with most singular nouns to emphasise completeness.

She read __a whole book__ in one night.
NOT ~~*She read all a book.*~~

Practice

A Match each sentence 1–8 to a sentence a–h which is closest in meaning.

1 I like some computer games.
2 I like any computer game.
3 I have few computer games.
4 I have some computer games.
5 I have hardly any computer games.
6 I have a lot of computer games.
7 I don't have enough computer games.
8 I like no computer games.

a I have plenty of computer games.
b I have almost no computer games.
c I like every computer game.
d I don't have many computer games.
e I don't like any computer games.
f I like several computer games.
g I have too few computer games.
h I have a few computer games.

B Match the pairs.

1 You should take plenty
2 You should take less
3 You should take fewer

a money next time you go on holiday.
b clothes next time you go on holiday.
c of books next time you go on holiday.

4 A: Do you want a pizza or a burger?
B: Neither,
5 A: Do you want a pizza or a burger?
B: Both,
6 A: Do you want a pizza or a burger?
B: Either,

a I don't mind.
b I'm not hungry.
c I'm really hungry.

7 I studied all day.
8 I studied every day.
9 I studied the whole day.

a I only had a few breaks.
b I didn't stop until midnight.
c It was a very hard week.

C If necessary, add *of*, *a* or *the* to the underlined quantifiers in this email, or tick (✓) the ones that are already correct.

Delete Reply Reply All Forward Print

Hi Will,

I've just got back from a week in the Italian Alps with Beth and Paula. We had a fantastic time, but it didn't really go as we'd expected. We'd planned to spend [1] the whole .... holiday skiing, but there wasn't [2] .... enough ✓ snow. There were [3] .... few .... snowy days, but not [4] .... enough .... We spent [5] .... most .... days walking in the mountains. It was wonderful. Unfortunately, I didn't take [6] .... much .... money with me – I was told there were [7] .... loads .... cash machines, but [8] .... all .... them were broken. Fortunately Beth had brought [9] .... lots .... money with her! I can speak [10] .... little .... Italian, which was really useful. I made [11] .... loads .... mistakes, but Beth and Paula didn't notice – [12] .... neither .... them can speak Italian!

Anyway, that's all I have time for! See you soon,

Emily

D Rewrite these sentences to make them less formal / more formal, using the words in brackets.

1 I have read many books on this subject. (lot)
Less formal: I've read a lot of books on this subject.
2 I spent a lot of time preparing this presentation. (deal)
More formal: ....
3 Some woman rang, but she didn't tell me her name. (or other)
Less formal: ....
4 There were a lot of mistakes in the report. (number)
More formal: ....
5 Don't worry. We still have a lot of time. (plenty)
Less formal: ....
6 I'm afraid you don't have enough correct answers to pass the test. (too)
More formal: ....

7 I've seen this film a lot of times. I know every word. (loads)
Less formal: ....

....

8 I'll be ready in two or three minutes. (couple)
Less formal: ....

....

9 We don't have much information about the delay. (very)
More formal: ....

....

10 There were fewer people than we expected. (many)
Less formal: ....

....

E Complete this report, using the information from the chart in the next column and the quantifiers from the box.

all both a couple of every a few fewer hardly any many many of most ~~most of~~ too much

I asked 100 teenagers how often they play computer games. 1 ......*Most of*...... them said they play computer games at least sometimes – 2 .... said they never play computer games. 14% said they play only 3 .... times per year. Slightly 4 .... people (13%) play computer games 5 .... times per month. 19% said they play 6 .... week. 7 .... people play at least twice per week, and 8 .... them (18%) play almost every day.

I asked these regular players how 9 .... hours they spend playing games. Two teenagers told me they are addicted to computer games. 10 .... of them said they spend around six hours playing every day, and often play 11 .... night. In my opinion, this is 12 ....

How often do you play computer games?

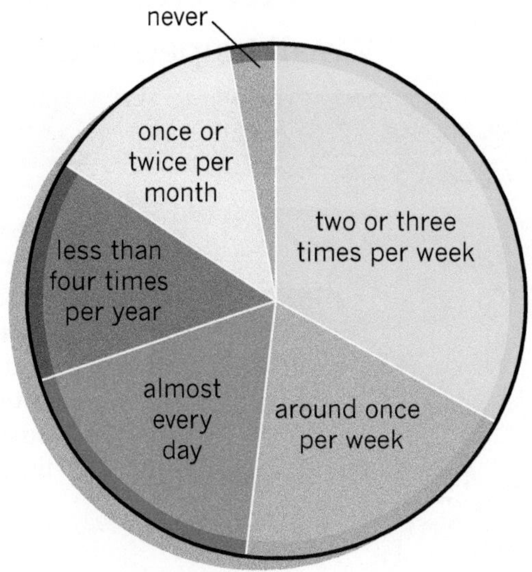

MY TURN!

Ask your friends how often they play computer games, watch television or go to the cinema. Write a short report, using plenty of quantifiers.

Example: *All my friends love going to the cinema. Most of them*

MY TEST!

Circle the correct option.

1 There is .... way of knowing if computers will ever think like humans. a none b no c any
2 Are there .... other people doing the same course as you? a many b much c a lot
3 .... change to the programme must be approved by the committee. a Any b Some c Several
4 It's nice to spend a day out of the city .... now and again. a every b each c any
5 I'm interested in .... kinds of science, especially information technology. a whole b either c all

My Test! answers: 1b 2a 3a 4a 5c

14 Pronouns and possessives

We all helped one another.

We arrived in 1849. The famine in Ireland had made **everything** difficult. **Our** kids had no food and **we** found **ourselves** in a desperate situation. **We** didn't know **what** to do. I **myself** had been out of work for years and **everyone** was talking about the opportunities in America, so my wife **and I** decided to go. **We** went to Pennsylvania, where **we** stayed in **my cousin and his wife's** house until **I** found work in a coal mine and **we** got **ourselves** a house. The work was hard but **it** was well-paid – **I** earned four times what **I'd** earned in Ireland. There were Irish people **everywhere**, and **we** all helped **one another**; for example, staying in **each other's** houses if we needed a place to stay. **Anyone** with a problem knew a friendly Irish neighbour would give them **whatever** help **they** needed.

After a few years **we** had enough money to move **somewhere** else. **It** was hard to leave **our** friends, but in the Midwest **you** could buy a farm for the price of a one-bedroom house in Dublin, and **we** decided to buy **one**. **Ours** was small for America, but compared with Irish farms **it** was enormous. Plenty of Irish people never adapted to America, but **I** guess **we** were among the lucky **ones**.

1 Why did the writer move to America?
2 Was his move to America a successful one?

Answers: 1 Because of the famine in Ireland 2 Yes. He found a well-paid job and was able to buy a farm.

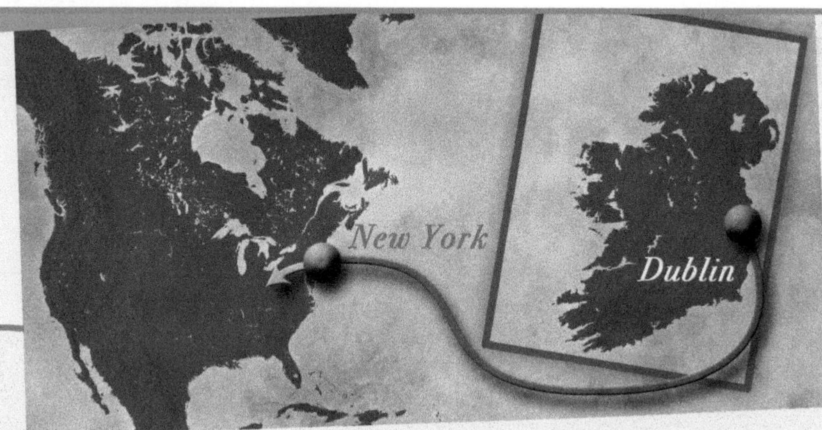

Pronouns and possessives

Pronouns

1 We use subject pronouns (*I, you, he, she, it, we, they*) for the subject of a sentence, and object pronouns (*me, you, him, her, it, us, them*) for all other functions. When there is no verb, we use object pronouns.

*She's taller than **me**.* OR *... than **I** am.*
*A: Who said that? B: **Me**.* OR ***I** did.*

When we use *and* to join pronouns with other words, we usually put *I* / *me* last.

*My sister **and I** decided to go.*

TIP

We sometimes use *you both, you all, you two,* etc., to make it clear we are talking about more than one person.

*Can **you two** please be a bit quieter?*

2 In direct and indirect questions, we use the pronouns *who, whose, what* and *which* for both the subject and other functions.

*We didn't know **what** to do.*
***Which** looks better?*
***Whose** are these clothes?* OR ***Whose** clothes are these?*

In very formal situations, we use *whom* as the object form of *who.* If there is a preposition, we put it before *whom.*

*To **whom** were you talking?* OR ***Who** were you talking to?*

▶ See Unit 36 for *who* / *whom* as relative pronouns.

3 **The most useful pronouns for talking about people in general are *you, we* and *they*.**

__You__ could buy a whole farm ...
__We__ need to do more to protect __our__ planet.

In more formal situations, we can use *one* to talk about people in general.

Does __one__ need a visa to go to Cyprus?
__One__ does __one's__ best.

4 **We use *it* to replace a noun with *the*, and *one* to replace a noun with *a / an*.**

__The work__ was hard but __it__ was well-paid.
You could buy __a farm__ ..., and we decided to buy __one__.

We can use *one* or *ones* as a pronoun with a determiner or adjective.

I've got two brothers, an older __one__ and a younger __one__.
I guess we were among the lucky __ones__. (= lucky people)

5 **We can use most determiners (e.g. *this, some, both, either, neither*) and numbers as pronouns.**

You'll love __this__ joke → You'll love __this__.
A: Do you want salad or soup?
B: Could I have __both__, please? / __Either__. I don't mind.

▶ See Unit 12 for *this, that, these, those* and Unit 42 for *the / it*.
▶ See Unit 13 for quantifiers as pronouns.

6 **We use possessive determiners (*my, your, his, her, its, one's, our, their*) before nouns. We use possessive pronouns (*mine, yours, his, hers, ours, theirs*) instead of nouns.**

It was hard to leave __our__ friends.
__Ours__ (= our farm) *was small for America.*

7 **We use reflexive pronouns (*myself, yourself, himself, herself, itself, oneself, ourselves, yourselves, themselves*) when the subject and object refer to the same person. We use reciprocal pronouns (*each other* and *one another*) when they refer to different people.**

We found __ourselves__ in a desperate situation.
We all helped __one another__ / __each other__.

We can use reflexive pronouns as indirect objects to emphasise 'for the same person'.

We got __ourselves__ a house.

We use reflexive pronouns after a noun or pronoun to emphasise a particular person or thing.

I __myself__ had been out of work for years.
We had lunch with the President __himself__.

We can use *myself* at the beginning of a sentence to emphasise that we are giving our personal opinion.

__Myself__, I'd prefer to stay at home.

8 **We form indefinite pronouns with *some / any / every / no + body / one / thing / where*. Indefinite pronouns are singular.**

__Everyone was__ talking about the opportunities ...
NOT ~~*Everyone were talking ...*~~

We can use adjectives or prepositions after indefinite pronouns.

We had enough money to think about moving __somewhere else__.
__Anyone with__ a problem knew a friendly Irish neighbour ...

▶ See Unit 13 for *some, any, no* and *every*.

9 **Use the pronouns *whatever* and *whoever* to mean 'it doesn't matter what / who' or 'I don't know what / who'.**

They would give them __whatever__ help they needed.
__Whoever__ told you that wasn't being completely honest.

▶ See Unit 37 for words like *whatever* and *whoever*.

Possessives

10 **To make a possessive from a noun, we add *'s*. We add an apostrophe (') to regular plurals, and we add *'s* to irregular plurals.**

What's the baby's name?
What are the babies' names?
What are the children's names?

To make a possessive from a long noun phrase, we add *'s* at the end.

We stayed in __my cousin and his wife's__ house.
NOT ~~*... in my cousin's and his wife's house.*~~

We don't use apostrophes in possessive pronouns.

Is this car __hers__? NOT ~~*Is this car her's?*~~

TIP

We don't use an apostrophe in possessive *its*. *It's* (with an apostrophe) means *it is* or *it has*.

What a beautiful baby! What's __its__ name?
NOT ~~*What's it's name?*~~

We add *'s* to make the possessive forms of indefinite and reciprocal pronouns.

Please don't use __anyone else's__ computer.
... staying in __each other's__ houses.
NOT ~~*... each others' houses.*~~

Practice

A Circle the correct option.

1 She lives in the same town as … .
(a) me   b I   c mine

2 A: Who tidied the apartment? B: … .
a I and Tom   b Tom and me   c Tom and I

3 I'd like to thank my father, … I could never have won.
a without whom   b without who   c who without

4 I'm going to have a cup of tea. Do you want … too?
a this   b it   c one

5 This book's really interesting. Do you want to read … when I finish?
a this   b it   c one

6 We're very proud – we built this house … .
a each other   b one another   c ourselves

7 Everything … really expensive.
a in the shop was   b were in the shop   c in the shop were

8 … gets the most points will be the winner.
a Anyone   b Which   c Whoever

9 We've got a new computer, but I think … was better.
a ours old   b our old   c our old one

10 … , I've never really been interested in computers.
a I   b Myself   c Mine

B Decide if the <u>underlined</u> nouns belong to one person / thing (1) or to more than one person / thing (1+).

1 This <u>football</u> isn't yours, it's mine. [1]

2 That's Julie's friends' <u>car</u>. [ ]

3 That's the phone number of the company, not its <u>fax number</u>. [ ]

4 Excuse me, I think this <u>table</u> is ours. [ ]

5 Everyone else's <u>room</u> had a beautiful view, but mine had a view of the car park! [ ]

6 Her <u>test results</u> are much better than we expected. [ ]

7 The <u>big house</u> on the corner is my cousins'. [ ]

8 These people's <u>houses</u> are really small. [ ]

9 The woman next door's <u>cats</u> are always playing in our garden. [ ]

10 These <u>paintings</u> are among the most valuable ones in his collection. [ ]

C Complete each sentence, using an indefinite pronoun (*something, everybody*, etc.) and a word or phrase from the box.

cool and dark   too crowded   else   good enough   hot   in Europe   in the shops   ~~nice~~   rich and famous   special

1 It's Rob's birthday, so we should buy him ......*something nice*...... .

2 I don't want to go .... – I want to spend some time alone.

3 A: What do you want to drink? B: .... Tea, coffee, I don't mind.

4 We wanted to find a new drummer for our band, but unfortunately, there was ....

5 I didn't buy anything. .... was really expensive.

6 You need to keep this plant .... for two months, like your fridge.

7 A: What are you doing at the weekend?
B: .... I'll probably just stay at home.

8 He's been almost .... , but he's never been to Africa.

9 I can't go to the concert, so if .... wants my tickets, please let me know.

10 I want to marry ....

D Complete the text with the correct pronouns.

Rachel and Mike lived next door to [1] ......*one*...... another, but they didn't get on at all. Rachel thought Mike was too self-centred – he never stopped talking about [2] ...., and wasn't interested in [3] .... else's problems. Then one day, Mike bought [4] .... a dog the same day that Rachel bought [5] .... one too. Mike's dog was a small grey [6] ...., and Rachel's was big and black. At first, the two dogs played by [7] .... in their own gardens, but then one day Rachel's dog got into Mike's garden and the dogs started playing together. Mike and Rachel watched the dogs playing happily in the garden and [8] .... of them realised there was no point in being enemies. So they started speaking to one [9] .... again. And a few weeks ago, they got married ... to [10] .... other!

E Rewrite the sentences, changing the underlined words, to make them sound more natural / informal.

1 If <u>any customer</u> would like to complain, <u>he / she</u> should write to the manager.
If you would like to complain, you should write to the manager.

2 When <u>one</u> meets new people, <u>one</u> should not talk about <u>oneself</u> too much.
....

3 My glasses are broken. I need to get some new <u>glasses</u>.
....

4 I don't know who it was, but <u>the person who</u> said English was easy was joking.
....

5 She swims much better than <u>I swim</u>.
....

6 Their house is more modern than <u>our house</u>.
....

7 A: Do you want to go dancing or watch a film?
B: <u>Go dancing or watch a film</u>. I don't mind.
....

8 <u>About whom</u> are you talking?
....

MY TURN!

Write at least four true sentences about your family history. Use some of the words and phrases from the box.

each other's	everything	her	mine	myself	nobody	one another	their	themselves	whatever

Example: *My grandmother brought up her brothers and sisters on her own.*

....
....
....
....
....
....
....
....

MY TEST!

Circle the correct option.

1 When we bought the farm, we couldn't believe it was actually .... a our's b our c ours
2 My room was freezing when I woke up because the heating had turned .... off during the night. a it b its c itself
3 Don't try and lift that box .... – I'll give you a hand. a you b yourself c yours
4 When we arrived in America, ... really friendly and helpful. a everyone was b anyone was c everyone were
5 At the end of our course we all signed .... other's course book. a every b each c one

My Test! answers: 1c 2c 3b 4a 5b

It and *there*

It's a good idea to make sure you're reasonably fit.

There are nearly 10 million people in Mexico City, 4 million cars, and hardly any cycle paths. **It**'s surprising, then, that the city's Ecobici bike-sharing scheme has been so successful! **It** costs $24 to buy an Ecobici card, which lets you use the bikes for a year; but you can only use a bike for 30 minutes per trip, then **it**'s necessary to wait ten minutes before borrowing another. **It**'s taken just two months for the number of people with Ecobici cards to reach 4,000, and **it**'s hoped that by next year **there** could be 24,000 users. Since Mexico City is very high (2,240 metres), **it**'s a good idea to make sure you're reasonably fit before you cycle there. But **there** are several things in cyclists' favour. Firstly, **there**'s no need for cyclists to worry about hills because Mexico City is relatively flat. **It**'s usually dry and sunny too. And **it** helps that the police are careful to protect cyclists' rights.

There are already similar systems in operation in other places. **There** are the ones operating in several cities in Canada, for example, and **it**'s said that more countries are planning similar projects – **it** was actually in France that the first such system was introduced. But **it**'s in Mexico that the idea of bike-sharing is reaching new levels of popularity.

?

1. What is the price of an Ecobici card?
2. What are the advantages of cycling in Mexico City?

Answers: 1 $24 2 It's flat; it's usually dry and sunny; the police protect cyclists' rights.

It and *there*

1 **We sometimes use *it* and *there* as 'dummy' subjects when there is no other suitable word / phrase to act as subject, to emphasise new information by putting it later in a sentence, to simplify the presentation of information, or to make a statement more impersonal.**

It's usually dry and sunny.
There are already similar systems in other places. (instead of *Similar systems are already ...*)
It helps that the police are careful ... (instead of *That the police are careful ... helps ...*)
It's sometimes hard to breathe. (more impersonal than *You have problems breathing.*)

▶ See Unit 11 for some idioms with dummy *it* and *there*.
▶ See Unit 14 for more information on *it* as a pronoun.

2 We use ***there*** + ***be*** to introduce new information with ***a*** / ***an***, no article, quantifiers / numbers or indefinite pronouns (e.g. ***nobody***).

__There__ are several things in cyclists' favour.

We don't usually use ***there*** for known information with ***the***, demonstratives (e.g. ***this***), possessives (e.g. ***my***), names (e.g. ***Paul***) or personal pronouns (e.g. ***him***).

John has been living here for five years.
NOT ~~*There has been John living here for five years.*~~

In informal English, we can sometimes use ***there*** for known information (with ***the***, etc.) to remind someone that something exists.

__There__ are the ones operating in several cities in Canada, for example.
If you can't afford a taxi, __there's__ always the bus.

Dummy ***there*** does <u>not</u> mean ***in that place***. Note the difference:

Is __there__ (dummy subject) *a hotel __there__* (in that place)*?*

3 We use a plural form of ***be*** (e.g. ***are, were, have been***) after ***there*** when the noun is plural.

__There__ are nearly 10 million people in Mexico City.

TIP

In informal spoken English, we often say ***there's*** + a plural noun, especially when we mention a number.

__There's__ about 40 chairs in this room. OR ***There are*** *about 40 chairs ...*

4 We use ***it*** to talk about times, dates and the weather.

__It__'s late / Thursday / half past two / dark / cold / snowing / windy.

We use ***it*** with an adjective to make general statements about a place.

__It__'s really nice in our new flat.

5 We use some common adjectives with ***it*** + ***that***-clause or ***to***-infinitive, such as adjectives of possibility (e.g. ***likely***), opinion (e.g. ***surprising***), frequency (e.g. ***usual***) and necessity (e.g. ***necessary***).

__It__'s __surprising that__ the city's Ecobici scheme has been so successful.

▶ See Unit 22 for adjectives followed by *to, -ing* and *that*.

Some nouns / noun phrases used with ***it*** + ***that***-clause or ***to***-infinitive are ***a good idea, a shame, a pity*** and ***good news***.

__It's a shame__ (that) you didn't tell me before.
__It's a good idea__ to make sure you're ...

Some verbs used with dummy ***it*** and a ***to***-clause are ***take, feel*** and ***cost***.

__It's taken__ two months for the number to reach 4,000 ...
__It costs__ $24 to buy an Ecobici card.

Some verbs used with a dummy ***it*** and a ***that***-clause are ***seem, appear*** and ***turn out***.

__It turns out__ that Gemma can't come with us after all.

Some verbs used with a dummy ***it*** and a question clause are ***depend*** and ***doesn't / didn't matter***.

__It depends__ what the weather's like.
__It doesn't matter__ where you sit.

Some passive verbs used with a dummy ***it*** and a ***that***-clause are ***thought, believed, said, rumoured, hoped, expected*** and ***argued***.

__It__'s __hoped that__ by next year ...

▶ See Unit 8 for more information on passive verbs with dummy *it*.

TIP

We use dummy ***it*** with ***worth*** + ***-ing***.

__It__'s __worth spending__ plenty of time on this.

We use dummy ***it*** twice in structures with ***worth*** + ***for***.

__It__'s not __worth it for__ you to come too.

6 We use dummy ***it*** + ***is*** / ***was*** / ***will be*** to emphasise a particular part of a sentence (this is called clefting).

__It__ was in France that the first scheme was introduced.
(instead of *The first scheme was introduced in France.*)

▶ See Unit 40 for more information on *it*-clefting for emphasis.

7 We can replace dummy ***it*** with the subject of a ***that***-clause and verbs and adjectives like ***seem*** / ***appear*** / ***turn out***; ***(un)likely*** / ***certain*** / ***sure***; ***said*** / ***thought*** / ***believed*** / ***expected***.

__It turned out__ that he was wrong. → ***He turned out*** *to be wrong.*
__It's unlikely__ that you'll know this. → ***You're unlikely*** *to know this.*
__It's said__ that more countries are planning ... → ***More countries are said*** *to be planning ...*

▶ See Unit 11 for more information on *likely / bound / sure / certain + to*.
▶ See Unit 27 for more information on *seem / appear / turn out*.
▶ See Unit 39 for more information on *said / thought / rumoured / believed / expected + to*.

We can do the same with dummy ***there***.

__It seems__ that __there__'s a problem. → ***There seems*** *to be a problem.*

Practice

A Match the sentence beginnings to the correct endings.

1	It's a	a	any problems?
2	There's no	b	that wanted to come here, not me!
3	Was there	c	in the city centre.
4	It's very noisy	d	anyone there?
5	It took	e	me a long time to get home.
6	Were there	f	pity we didn't win.
7	It's essential	g	it for you to study all night.
8	It doesn't matter	h	what you wear.
9	It's not worth	i	need to cry. Everything'll be fine.
10	It was you	j	to wear a safety helmet at all times.

B Complete the sentences with *it* or *there*.

1. It's very cold in our bathroom in the winter because ..there..'s no heating.
2. No one told me that ....'s going to be a party.
3. ....'s not worth going to the shop now – it closes in five minutes.
4. How many people are .... in your family?
5. I know she's very busy, but if we can't find anyone else ....'s always Tanya.
6. ....'s no point trying to have a picnic today – the weather forecast is terrible.
7. Maybe ....'ll be snow this weekend, but I don't think it's very likely.
8. ....'s nothing to do where I live – I get really bored sometimes.
9. However long .... takes, or whatever the cost, I really need to get my computer fixed.
10. ....'s said that this is the Queen's favourite restaurant.

C Rewrite the sentences, using *there* to make them more natural or less personal.

1. You don't need to have a ticket.
   Less personal: There's no need to have a ticket.
2. Lots of books are in my office.
   More natural: ....
3. Some useful information might be on the Internet.
   More natural: ....
4. We have three rooms in our flat.
   Less personal: ....
5. A castle used to be where this shopping centre is.
   More natural: ....
6. They're going to have a competition.
   Less personal: ....
7. We expected more people to be at the concert.
   More natural: We expected there ....
8. We were worried about an accident happening.
   More natural: We were worried ....

D Put the lines of the text in the correct order.

1. Trixis are taxis with a difference, because with a trixi there
2. a bicycle, but with space at the back for two passengers! There's
3. was a company in Barcelona which had the idea for trixis, and there
4. the driver himself who does all the work! That's because a trixi isn't a car – it's
5. is now a branch of the company in Madrid as well, and it is
6. expected that more branches will open around Spain before long. It
7. a beautiful sunny day outside, but with trixis there is now an alternative. It
8. is no noise, no pollution, and no engine – it's
9. are better ways to see a city than through the window of a hot car or smelly tour bus!
10. no point wasting time in the back of a taxi when it's
11. seems that both locals and tourists have realised there
12. has been such a high demand for this new form of city transport that there

1, 8, ..., ..., 10, ...,
....., 12, ..., ..., ..., ...

E Complete each sentence, using *It* or *There* and including an appropriate form of the word in brackets.

1 ......It seems to me...... that she likes English. (seem)
2 .... to be long delays on the roads this weekend. (likely)
3 .... to be a beautiful day, even though it was raining when I got up. (turn out)
4 .... that more of these schemes will be introduced soon. (expect)
5 .... being so depressed – you can't do anything about your exam results now. (no point)
6 .... that a new director has been appointed. (rumour)
7 .... that she was lying. (believe)
8 .... to be an official announcement about the future of the company soon. (certain)
9 .... if you don't have any money – I can lend you some. (matter)
10 .... to be an English-speaking receptionist in the hotel, and she helped us. (happen)

MY TURN!

Complete at least four of these sentences so that they are true for you (or for people you know).

1 It's ....
2 It's difficult ....
3 There's no chance ....
4 If it turns out ....
5 There are many things ....
6 It's not worth it for me ....
7 There's no need for me ....
8 It doesn't matter if ....

MY TEST!

Circle the correct option.

1 If you're really desperate for somewhere to eat, ... the takeaway in the High Street.
a they're always b there's always c it's always
2 There .... for you to hire a car – you can rent a bike instead. a isn't need b is no need c doesn't need
3 .... keep a copy of the application form somewhere safe.
a There's a good idea b It's a good idea c It's a good idea to
4 .... for you to buy a bike because you can easily borrow one when you need one.
a Is not worth b It's not worth c It's not worth it
5 .... sure to be lots of people trying to buy tickets, so make sure you get there early.
a It's b They're c There are

My Test! answers: 1b 2b 3c 4c 5c

16 Nouns and noun phrases 1

A spoonful of cheese ice cream

These **days**, cooking is more like a science than an art, as many world-famous **chefs** increasingly use scientific **methods** to create imaginative new **dishes**. **Ferran Adrià**'s El Bulli is in a small town to the north of Barcelona, away from the area's busy **beaches**. It is actually open only six **months** of the year. Adrià spends half the year working in his **laboratories** in **Barcelona**, inventing new cooking **techniques**, such as taking ordinary **ingredients** and mixing their basic **flavours** with a special gas. In this way he can make **foams** made from **peas**, **beans** or **coconuts**, or even **parmesan cheese ice cream**. Adrià also likes to separate traditional **dishes** into their individual **flavours** and put them together again in strange **ways**. His Spanish **omelettes**, for example, are served in **glasses** and have **onion** at the bottom and **egg** at the top, separated by **pieces** of **potato**.

Led by Adrià, El Bulli's **team** of **chefs is** changing the way we think about and enjoy food. You may not fancy **a plateful of beetroot jelly** or **a spoonful of cheese ice cream** for your dinner today, but the science which inspired such **creations** is definitely here to stay. And dinner at El Bulli is **an experience** you will never forget!

?
1 Who is Ferran Adrià?
2 What is unusual about his work?

Answers: 1 A chef and restaurant owner 2 He uses scientific methods to invent new cooking techniques.

Nouns and noun phrases 1

Countable nouns

1 **Countable nouns refer to people, places or things which we can count. We add *-s* to make the plural of many countable nouns, e.g. *days, chefs, pieces*.**

We usually add *-es* if the noun ends in *-ss, -ch, -sh* or *-x*.
glass → glasses, dish → dishes, beach → beaches, box → boxes

We usually replace *-y* with *-ies* if the word ends in a consonant + *-y*.
baby → babies, city → cities, story → stories, laboratory → laboratories

2 **Some countable nouns have unusual plurals.**
-f, -fe → -ves: half → halves, loaf → loaves
wife → wives, knife → knives, life → lives
-o → -oes: potato → potatoes, tomato → tomatoes, hero → heroes, echo → echoes
-is → -es: crisis → crises, analysis → analyses
-us → -i: cactus → cacti, nucleus → nuclei, stimulus → stimuli
-on → -a: phenomenon → phenomena
-um → -a: continuum → continua, bacterium → bacteria
-oo- → -ee-: foot → feet, tooth → teeth, goose → geese
woman → women, man → men, child → children, mouse → mice, person → people

TIP

The words *data* and *agenda* were originally plurals. Now *data* can be either singular (more common) or plural. *Agenda* is always singular.

*The **agenda** for the meeting **is** quite short.*
***This data is** very interesting.* OR ***These data are** very interesting.*

3 Some nouns ending in *-o* add *-s*, not *-es*, to make the plural.
piano ➜ *pianos, radio* ➜ *radios, studio* ➜ *studios*

4 Some countable nouns, e.g. ***sheep, species, means, series, fish, aircraft***, have the same singular and plural form.
*Scientists have discovered a new **species** of insect.*
*Many **species** of animal are in danger as a result of climate change.*

Collective nouns

5 We describe many collections of countable nouns with ***a*** + noun + ***of*** + plural noun.
a herd of cows, a flock of sheep, a bunch of flowers, a box of chocolates, a pack of cards, a crowd of people

6 Some nouns which refer to groups of people can use singular or plural verb forms, e.g. ***team, government, army, class, committee***.
*El Bulli's **team** of chefs **is** / **are** changing the way we think about food.*

▶ See Unit 46 for British and American English.

Uncountable nouns

7 Uncountable nouns refer to things which we can't count. They do not normally have a plural form.
*Your **advice was** very helpful.*
NOT ~~*Your advices were very helpful.*~~

Some uncountable nouns look like plurals, but are in fact singular, e.g. ***news, politics, mathematics, measles, economics, athletics***.
*The **news was** very exciting.* NOT ~~*The news were ...*~~

▶ See Units 12 and 13 for the use of determiners with countable and uncountable nouns.

Plural nouns

8 A few plural nouns normally have no singular form.
clothes, stairs, congratulations, thanks, outskirts, remains, belongings

Some plural nouns have two similar parts which are always together.
glasses, trousers, jeans, shorts, pyjamas, scissors

Unit nouns

9 We use unit nouns with uncountable nouns when we want to refer to countable units. The most common unit noun is ***piece***. We use specific unit nouns with specific uncountable nouns. Some unit nouns are containers.
a piece of cake / wood / advice
a gust of wind, a sheet of paper, a loaf of bread
a cup of tea, a glass of milk, a packet of crisps

We can add ***-ful*** to some nouns when we refer to them as containers.
a plateful of jelly, a spoonful of ice cream, a handful of coins

Nouns which can be countable or uncountable

10 Many nouns can be countable (if they refer to specific examples of something) or uncountable (if they refer to a material, something abstract or a process as a whole).
*Dinner at El Bulli is **an experience** you will never forget!*
*Amy has lots of **experience** in this business.*

Some countable nouns for animals (e.g. ***chicken, turkey, lamb, duck***) can also be uncountable when they refer to the meat.
*My uncle keeps **chickens** and **turkeys**.*
*Would you like **chicken** or **turkey** in your sandwich?*

Proper nouns

11 Proper nouns give names to specific people, places, organisations, etc. They start with capital letters.
***Ferran Adrià** spends half the year in his laboratories in **Barcelona**.*

Names of rivers, seas and some countries take ***the*** before them.

the (River) Thames, the Mississippi (River)
the Atlantic (Ocean), the Mediterranean (Sea)
the United Kingdom NOT ~~*the Great Britain*~~

12 Some proper nouns are well-known brand names (e.g. ***Coca-Cola, Pepsi, Rolex, Porsche***). We can use these as singular countable nouns. Some brand names (e.g. ***hoover, sellotape***) are so familiar that they can be used as common nouns starting with lower-case letters.
*Where's the **hoover**? I've dropped some cake on the carpet.*

Practice

A Complete the table with the singular or plural forms of the nouns.

singular	plural	singular	plural
dish	dishes	knife	knives
species	....	....	taxes
person	....	....	potatoes
city	....	....	phenomena
crisis	....	....	mice
tomato	....	....	stimuli
fish	....	....	families
switch	....	....	teeth
box	....	....	crises
studio	....	....	means

B Underline the correct option. Sometimes both options may be possible.

1. I've just heard the news, and unfortunately *it's* / *they're* not good.
2. The government *has* / *have* many difficult decisions to take in the next few weeks.
3. The stairs *is* / *are* a bit wet, so be careful when you leave.
4. The only trousers I ever wear *is* / *are* jeans – and sometimes shorts in summer.
5. What *was* / *were* the best advice you received when you were growing up?
6. When I was at school I thought mathematics *was* / *were* really difficult.
7. Measles *is* / *are* very common among schoolchildren.
8. The latest data *show* / *shows* that the situation is improving gradually.
9. The remains of a Roman villa *was* / *were* discovered on this site.
10. Can you pass me the scissors which *is* / *are* on the kitchen table?

C Complete each sentence, using one word from box A and one from box B.

A

box crowd glass gust herd loaf ~~piece~~ plateful sheet spoonful

B

~~advice~~ bread chocolates cows honey paper pasta people water wind

1. Let me give you a ....piece.... of ....advice.... – never listen to what other people tell you!
2. If you pass the bakery, can you buy a .... of ...., please?
3. Would you like a .... of .... to drink with your meal?
4. A .... of .... had gathered in the square to listen to the President's speech.
5. Sorry I'm late – I got stuck behind a .... of .... on their way back to the farm.
6. Fiorelli's is the best value Italian restaurant I know – a big .... of .... for only €6!
7. My grandfather was walking with his dog yesterday when a .... of .... blew his hat into the canal!
8. The best remedy for a sore throat is a cup of hot water with lemon juice and a .... of .... in it.
9. On her birthday Sara got a big .... of .... with a note saying 'With love from Mum and Dad'.
10. Before answering any questions, please write your name at the top of the first .... of ....

D Write the plurals of the nouns in the box, if possible (not all of the nouns have plurals – put ✗ if not). Then add each singular noun to the correct group of nouns below.

bacterium	basis	belief ....
church	echo	information ....
~~kilo~~ kilos	means	pyjamas ....
shelf	stimulus	thermos ....

1 video, studio, piano .... kilo
2 potato, hero, tomato ....
3 leaf, wife, thief ....
4 species, aircraft, deer ....
5 crisis, oasis, thesis ....
6 chief, house, doctor ....
7 fungus, cactus, nucleus ....
8 furniture, advice, news ....
9 shorts, binoculars, jeans ....
10 hoover, tippex, sellotape ....
11 medium, memorandum, continuum ....
12 catch, beach, stitch ....

MY TURN!

Write down ...

1 ... two things you eat now but didn't eat when you were a child.
mangoes and turkey
2 ... your favourite and least favourite subjects at school.
....
3 ... three people from history that you would love to have dinner with.
....
4 ... two countries you would like to visit in the future.
....
5 ... three well-known brand names in your country.
....
6 ... five things that you own at least two of.
....

E Cross out all the incorrect nouns in this text.

It sometimes seems that hardly a week passes without a new cookery [1]~~*serie*~~ */ series* appearing on our televisions or [2]*radios / radioes*. Food has always been popular in the media, but the popularity of so-called 'celebrity chefs' is a relatively new [3]*phenomenon / phenomena*. Jamie Oliver's love of fresh, healthy [4]*ingredients / ingredientes* began during his childhood as he was growing up in his parents' pub. After leaving [5]*school / School*, he decided he wanted to become a chef, and his first jobs included working at Antonio Carluccio's Neal [6]*street / Street* Restaurant, and at the River Café. Inspired by these [7]*experience / experiences*, Oliver made his first TV show, *The Naked Chef*, which showed him preparing [8]*partys / parties* for his friends, and his lively presenting style made him popular with young and old [9]*persons / people*. Later programmes included *Jamie's Great Escape*, focusing on Italian [10]*food / Food*, and *Jamie's Fowl Dinners*, in which he showed how badly some farms treated their [11]*chicken / chickens*. Finally, in 2008, he opened his own chain of Italian restaurants, with [12]*branches / branchs* around the UK.

MY TEST!

Circle the correct option.

1 I heard .... very interesting news this morning. **a** a **b** some **c** these
2 When I passed my exams, my mother bought me a beautiful .... of flowers. **a** box **b** bunch **c** packet
3 I'm sorry your food is burnt. Our new chef hasn't got .... experience. **a** an **b** much **c** many
4 I bought .... trousers this afternoon. **a** these **b** a **c** this
5 My brother is going to spend next year training to be a chef in ....
a United States **b** the united states **c** the United States

My Test! answers: 1b 2b 3b 4a 5c

Nouns and noun phrases 2: gerunds

Bowing your head is the normal way to greet others.

Traveller and Tourist info!

One problem with **travelling** is **not knowing** about local customs, and many people have stories about **having said or done** the wrong thing. So, if you don't want to risk **offending** the locals, I've collected some tips on greetings from around the world:

***Kissing** is very popular here, between men as well as between women, and often when you say goodbye as well as hello.* (Alessandro, Italy)

*To greet someone, I suggest **nodding your head**, although **shaking** hands is common these days too.* (Ming, China)

***Bowing** your head is the normal way to greet others.* (Michiko, Japan)

*We usually kiss the right cheek, but the **kissing** can be complicated near the Dutch border – **kissing** three times is common there!* (Elise, Belgium)

***Hugging** is common between men. But if you don't feel like **being hugged**, **shaking** hands is fine!* (Luis, Brazil)

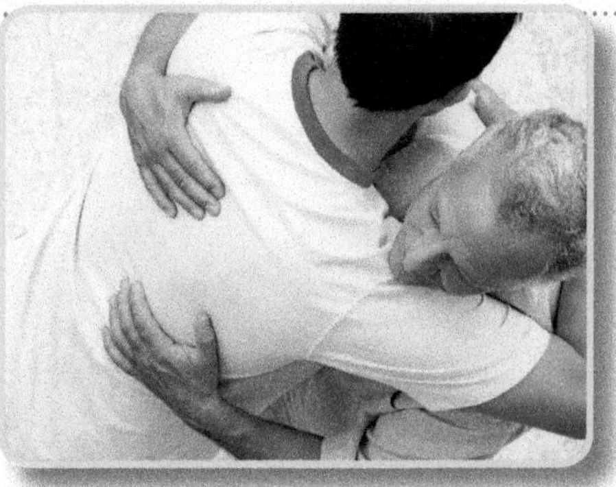

***Shaking** hands is very important and we don't mind **spending** ages on greetings. In fact, **not greeting** everyone in the room personally is rude.* (Kinoro, Kenya)

*Avoid **kissing** and **hugging**. The normal greeting is **saying** Namaste, 'I bow to you', after **touching** hands with the other person.* (Krishnan, India)

So, **greeting** people around the world is more complicated than I thought! But I'm looking forward to **trying** some of these greetings myself when I go somewhere new!

?

1 How many different greetings are mentioned?
2 Which of these greetings do you use in your country?

Answers: 1 Seven: kissing, bowing, hugging, shaking hands, saying Namaste, touching hands, nodding your head

Nouns and noun phrases 2

Gerunds as subjects and objects

1 A gerund is the *-ing* form of a verb when we use it as a noun. We can use a gerund as the subject or object of a verb.

__Kissing__ is very popular here.
Most teachers don't allow __eating__ in class.

2 The negative form of a gerund is *not + -ing.*

__Not greeting__ everyone in the room personally is rude.

3 The past form of a gerund is *having* + past participle of the verb.

Many people have stories about __having said__ the wrong thing.

Gerunds as complements

4 We often use gerunds to define words referring to processes, situations or activities.

One problem with travelling is __not knowing about local customs__.

We can also use gerunds after the object of some verbs, e.g. *consider, call, declare, have, take* and *spend.*

You wouldn't really __call his work painting__ – a child could paint better than him!
My sister __spends hours chatting__ with friends on her mobile.

5 We can sometimes use determiners and possessive forms with gerunds.

__The kissing__ can be complicated.
__Their leaving__ early was a surprise.

In informal conversation, we usually use object forms, not possessives, before a gerund.

Do you mind __me sitting__ here? (instead of *Do you mind __my sitting__ here?*)

We don't usually use possessive determiners before gerunds if it is already clear who we are referring to.

The first job I had was __selling__ ice cream.
NOT ~~*... was my selling ice cream.*~~

TIP

We often use *No* with a gerund in public notices to say that something is not permitted or not possible.

***NO SMOKING** INSIDE THIS BUILDING*

Gerunds before nouns

6 Many compound nouns are formed with a gerund + a noun. The gerund works like an adjective and usually describes the purpose or function of the noun.

Please take a seat in the __waiting room__. (= a room where you can wait)

We can use *-ing* forms before nouns to describe what a person or thing is doing.

The sound of a __crying baby__ kept me awake all night.

▶ See Unit 21 for participle adjectives.
▶ See Unit 31 for compound nouns.

Gerunds after some verbs

7 Many verbs are normally followed by a gerund instead of a *to*-infinitive, e.g. ***admit, avoid, consider, deny, enjoy, imagine, involve, like / love / hate, mind, prefer, risk,*** (***can't***) ***stand, start / stop*** and ***suggest***.

__Avoid kissing__ and __hugging__.
We __don't mind spending__ ages on greetings.

TIP

If you *feel like* doing something, you are in the mood to do it.

I __feel like going__ dancing. Do you want to come?

We can also use some of these verbs, e.g. ***admit, consider, deny, mention, suggest***, with a *that*-clause.

I __suggest nodding__ your head. OR *I __suggest that you nod__ your head.*

TIP

We sometimes use ***hate, like, love*** and ***prefer*** with a *to*-infinitive instead of a gerund.

I __like getting up__ early. OR *I __like to get up__ early.*

▶ See Unit 26 for other verbs which can be followed by a gerund or an infinitive.

Gerunds after prepositions

8 If we put a verb after a preposition, we always use a gerund, not an infinitive.

One problem __with travelling__ is ...
NOT ~~*One problem with to travel is ...*~~

TIP

We use *for* + gerund after a noun or *thing / something / anything* to talk about the general purpose of an object or substance.

Have you got anything __for cleaning__ carpets?

Practice

A Match the sentence beginnings to the correct endings.

1 Please take your shoes off before entering — c
2 I'm really looking forward to seeing
3 You can download the programme by clicking
4 The main argument against allowing
5 I've got some new software for protecting
6 I changed my mind after thinking
7 There's no harm in asking
8 The main difference between travelling
9 The trouble with driving
10 What are your reasons for applying

a in a city is finding somewhere to park.
b carefully about what you told me.
c the house.
d you again at the party next week.
e free music downloads is the cost to musicians.
f for this job?
g on the icon.
h but I know Mum won't let me go to the concert.
i my computer from viruses.
j by plane or train is the price.

B Write instructions with 'NO ....' or '............ ALLOWED' to match the signs. Use gerunds formed from the verbs in the box.

camp cycle dive eat or drink fish overtake park run ~~swim~~ talk

1

NO SWIMMING

2

....

3

....

4

....

5

....

6

....

7

....

8

....

9

....

10

....

C Complete the sentences, using compound nouns made with one word from box A and one word from box B.

A

boarding chewing ~~dining~~ driving parking running swimming waiting walking washing

B

card gum licence list machine pool shoes stick ~~table~~ ticket

1 At 7 o'clock the family sat round the ....dining table.......... to have dinner.
2 I had to take my clothes to the launderette because our .... is broken.
3 My grandfather is 93, but he can still walk without a ....
4 I only left the car for ten minutes, but when I got back there was a .... stuck to the windscreen.
5 I bought myself some new .... this morning – I've decided to start doing more exercise!
6 My cousins live in a big house with its own open-air .... in the garden.
7 The gym isn't accepting more new members, but I've put my name down on the ....
8 To open a bank account, you need a passport, ..., or other form of identification.
9 Don't talk when you've got .... in your mouth – it's very rude.
10 Your flight leaves from Gate 7. Here's your passport and .... Enjoy your flight.

D **Use any of the words from Exercise C (or other words you choose yourself) to make compound nouns with gerunds.**

swimming lesson ....

....

....

....

E **Rewrite the underlined words in each sentence so that they have a similar meaning, using a form of the verb in brackets and a gerund.**

1 Don't drive through the city between 6 and 7 – that's the rush hour. (avoid)
Avoid driving
2 She said she hadn't done anything wrong. (deny)
....
3 Do you want to go out for a drink after work? (feel)
....
4 My dad thought he might buy a new car soon. (consider)
....
5 Why has Joe gone already? He didn't say he had to leave early. (mention)
....
6 Bill's idea was that we could go for a walk along the river. (suggest)
....
7 When you've written all the reports, let me see them to make sure they're OK. (finish)
....
8 After the police questioned her for an hour, the woman finally said that she'd stolen the books. (admit)
....
9 I really hate it when I have to walk to work in the rain. (can't stand)
....
10 Can you open the window for me? (mind)
....

MY TURN!

Complete six or more of these sentences so that they are true for you. Include at least one gerund in each sentence.

1 Typical ways of greeting people in my culture are ....
2 I'm really looking forward to ....
3 One thing I really like doing is ....
4 Something I can't stand other people doing is ....
5 Two things I've always really enjoyed doing are ....
6 The household job I always try to avoid doing is the ....
7 Two things I get nervous about are ....
8 Something I am more fond of now than in the past is ....
9 An unusual habit I have is ....
10 Two things I spend a lot of time doing are ....

MY TEST!

Circle the correct option.

1 .... is not recommended unless you know each other very well. a Hug b Hugging c To hug
2 .... the best way to greet someone can make communication difficult. a No knowing b Not know c Not knowing
3 Can you recommend something .... stopping birds from eating my seeds? a to b by c for
4 Would you mind .... me that magazine? a passing b pass c to pass
5 She denied .... who had stolen the money. a that she knew b her knowing c to know

My Test! answers: 1b 2c 3c 4a 5a

R2 Review: determiners; pronouns and possessives; *it* and *there*; nouns and noun phrases

A Underline the correct option. (– means no word.)

I was really worried [1]*the / a* first time that [2]*a / –* virus got into my computer. It was quite new, so I took it back to [3]*a / the* shop where I'd bought it. They managed to get rid of [4]*– / the* virus and installed new security software.
[5]*These / This* worked really well for six months. Then my computer got [6]*other / another* virus. [7]*A / The* friend of mine who's really into computers tells me it's just one of [8]*these / those* things that happen all the time.

Nowadays, we can give much more help to [9]*an / the* unemployed than we ever did in [10]*that / the* past. Here in [11]*this / the* part of town, for example, we provide [12]*a / –* practical advice about how to look for [13]*a / the* job, training in [14]*the / –* interview techniques and various [15]*other / another* services.

B Write D next to the sentence which has a different meaning.

1 a We have plenty of things to do before we go.
b We need to do several things before we go. D
c There are loads of things to do before we go.

2 a We spent every summer at my grandparents' house.
b We stayed at my grandparents' house the whole summer.
c We were at my grandparents' house all summer.

3 a There were fewer traffic problems than before.
b All the traffic problems had been solved.
c There were no problems with traffic any more.

4 a Neither of the rooms is any good for a party.
b We can't use either of the rooms for a party.
c Both of the rooms can be used for a party.

5 a He spoke a good deal of sense.
b He said a few sensible things.
c Much of what he said made sense.

6 a I'd been looking forward to some of that cake but there was none left.
b Each person had had a bit of the cake I'd been looking forward to.
c I'd been looking forward to the cake but the whole thing had gone.

7 a Would you be able to answer a couple of questions?
b I'd like to ask you about two or three points if that's all right with you.
c Do you mind if I ask you a number of questions?

8 a There's very little space in the kitchen for anything else.
b The kitchen has a little room for something else.
c We've got barely any more room for other things in the kitchen.

9 a A large number of these pens don't work.
b All these pens are useless.
c None of these pens are any good.

10 a Excellent! This time there are hardly any mistakes in your homework.
b Well done! This homework has very few mistakes in it.
c Great! You haven't made any mistakes in your homework this time.

C Complete each sentence, using TWO of the words in brackets.

1 ....These.... are the salty biscuits and those are the sweet ....ones.... . (them / ~~ones~~ / ~~these~~)

2 Tell me .... of the two singers you prefer and .... you like about them. (what / which / who)

3 I don't know .... he is or .... friend he is. (whose / who / which)

4 To .... should I address this letter and .... would you like me to write in it? (what / whose / whom)

5 The pizza was delicious and .... was cheaper than the .... I'd had in Rome. (that / it / one)

6 My parents say I can invite .... I like to the party but .... is allowed to go upstairs in the house. (whatever / whoever / no one)

7 From time to time, my mum likes to be by .... and not have to worry about .... else. (each other / anyone / herself)

8 A: Have they got a bath or a shower in their bathroom?
B: They have .... Their bathroom's much bigger than .... (ours / us / both)

9 My sisters really enjoyed .... at the festival last year and they've been trying to persuade .... they meet to go there with them this year. (either / everybody / themselves)

10 When I was a child, I had some friends who lived in the same street – Ewa, Anna, Mariana and a few .... We were always going in and out of each .... houses. (other / others / other's)

D Complete the text with *it* and *there*.

The London Eye

About 8 million people live in London and, on top of that, [1] ...there... are over 25 million visitors to the capital of the UK each year. 3.5 million of these people visit the London Eye, making [2] .... one of the most popular attractions in the city.

[3] .... was in 1999 that the great wheel first opened to the public. A few years earlier, [4] .... had been a competition for ideas to celebrate the year 2000, and [5] .... is hardly surprising that the beautiful steel and glass structure, looking like a giant bicycle wheel, turned out to be the competition winner. [6] .... are taller wheels in other parts of the world but none has quite the same appeal. Because of its popularity, [7] .... is often a long queue for visitors to get on the wheel, so [8] .... is a good idea to buy tickets in advance and get there early.

[9] .... is best to go on a clear day, but even when visibility is limited, the flight, as they call [10] ...., is still worth [11] .... The wheel never stops but moves slowly enough for passengers to walk on and off and [12] .... takes about 30 minutes to do a full rotation. As you go up into the sky, the great city of London spreads out below you. [13] .... is a wonderful sight and [14] .... is great fun to try to identify the buildings and landmarks that you see on all sides.

E Circle the correct option. Sometimes two options, or all three, may be possible.

1 The news about South Africa ... quite positive.
(a) was (b) is c were

2 Stevie Wonder is one of my all-time ... .
a heros b hero c heroes

3 Do you think Edina would like a ... of flowers?
a pack b bunch c crowd

4 They're looking for someone who has ... of working with disabled people.
a experiences b an experience c experience

5 Would you like a ... of this lovely home-made bread?
a sheet b piece c slice

6 The government ... to spend more on education.
a want b wants c wanted

7 You can't take ... scissors onto the plane.
a a b that c those

8 The agenda for the end-of-term meeting ... too long.
a are b is c were

9 I had a sandwich with ... in it and it was delicious.
a organic chicken b an organic chicken
c some organic chicken

10 I wonder if you could give me ... , please.
a some informations b an information
c some information

11 After a number of major ... , the team recovered and are now doing well.
a crisis b crisises c crises

F Complete each sentence b so that it has a similar meaning to sentence a, using three words including the word in brackets.

1 a When we were younger, we used to play in the park for hours. (spend)
b When we were younger, we used to ...spend hours... ...playing... in the park.

2 a In his job, Daniele has to travel a lot around Europe. (involves)
b Daniele's .... a lot around Europe.

3 a I said goodbye to Kurt and I don't remember anything after that. (was)
b The last thing I remember .... to Kurt.

4 a Why do you want to become a vegetarian? (reasons)
b What are your .... a vegetarian?

5 a No one can ever talk in my Maths teacher's classes. (allows)
b My Maths teacher .... in his classes.

6 a Andrea says it's great that she doesn't have to get up early every day. (not)
b Andrea says .... get up early every day is great.

7 a I don't think it's a good idea for us to drive in these dangerous conditions. (risk)
b I don't think we .... in these dangerous conditions.

8 a The smile I saw on Nick's face told me he'd passed the test. (smiling)
b I knew Nick had passed the test when I .... face.

9 a Is it OK with you if I leave my bike here? (mind)
b Do you .... my bike here?

10 a These beans take a long time to get soft – that's what's difficult when you cook them. (trouble)
b The .... these beans is that they take a long time to get soft.

18 Prepositions

Hodja climbed up the ladder with the man behind him.

Hodja and the beggar

One day, Hodja climbed **up** his ladder **to** repair a hole **in** his roof. Just then he heard a knock **on** the door. Looking down, he saw a man **below** him **in front of** the door.
'What do you want?'
'Come down,' replied the man.
Hodja climbed **down** the ladder. 'Well? What do you want?'
'Money,' said the man.
Hodja thought **for** a second, then said: 'Ah, you want money, do you?' And he told the man to come **onto** the roof **with** him. Hodja climbed **up** the ladder **with** the man **behind** him. At the top, he turned **to** the man, who was **out of** breath **after** his climb, and said 'I'm sorry, but I'm afraid I have no money for you.'

Hodja and the chicken

One day, Hodja was walking **around** the market when he saw a man **with** a parrot. **Above** the bird was a sign: '**For** sale: 12 gold pieces'.
'Why so expensive?' Hodja asked.
'It can talk **like** a human!' the man replied.
Hodja had an idea. He went **to** the butcher's stall and bought a chicken **for** two gold pieces. He put the chicken **in** a box, returned **to** the man **with** the parrot, and stood **next to** him.
'Chicken **for** sale, ten gold pieces!' he shouted.
The man laughed **at** him, 'How can a chicken be worth so much?'
'Your parrot can talk **like** a human,' Hodja replied, 'but this chicken can *think* **like** a human.'

?
1 Why did Hodja tell the man to come up to the roof?
2 Why was the chicken so expensive?

Answers: 1 Because the man had told him to come down from the roof just to ask him for some money. 2 Because it could think like a human.

Prepositions

Prepositions of place, movement and time

1 The usual prepositions of place are *at*, *on* and *in*. Use *at* with a specific place or event, *in* to talk about somewhere inside a larger space, and *on* to talk about somewhere on a line or surface.

__at__ home, __at__ John's house, __at__ a party
__in__ France, __in__ a market, __in__ a box
__on__ the door, __on__ the roof, __on__ the ground

Other prepositions of place include:

above	*beneath*	*in front of*	*over*
against	*beside*	*inside*	*past*
among	*between*	*near*	*round*
behind	*beyond*	*opposite*	*under*
below	*by*	*outside*	*upon*

2 Prepositions of movement include *to, in / into, off, on / onto, out of, up, down, over, under, through, around* and *across.*

He told the man to come __on__ / __onto__ the roof

3 The usual prepositions of time are *at*, *on* and *in*. Use *at* with a specific point in time, *in* when you are talking about a longer period of time, and *on* with days and dates.

__at__ 4.00, __at__ the same time, __at__ the weekend
__in__ summer, __in__ April, __in__ 1974
__on__ Tuesday, __on__ my birthday, __on__ 24 May

We usually use *in* with parts of a day. However, we use *at night* to refer to nights in general, and *in the night* to refer to one particular night.

I sometimes find it hard to sleep __at night__.
I woke up __in the night__ with a headache.

We can use *in* to say how long something takes.

The album was recorded __in only two days__.

We can use *in / in ...'s time* to say when something will happen.

I'll call you __in a week__ / __in a week's time__.

Other prepositions of time include *after, before, between, by, during, for, from, to, until* and *within.*

In American English, *through* is used in time expressions to mean 'up to and including'. In British English, *to ... inclusive* and *to the end of* are used.

*The park is closed **from** November **through** February.*
OR ... ***from*** *November* ***to*** *February* ***inclusive.***
OR ... *from November* ***to the end of*** *February.*

4 We can use *after, as, before, since* and *until* as prepositions of time or conjunctions.

*They left **after** the meal.* (preposition + object)
*They left **after** we arrived.* (conjunction + clause)

Other prepositions

5 Other prepositions can indicate different kinds of relationship, e.g:

about	*concerning*	*of*	*versus*
against	*despite*	*regarding*	*via*
among	*except*	*than*	*with*
as	*for*	*unlike*	*without*
by	*like*	*upon*	

6 We use some groups of two or three words as prepositions.

according to	*as a result of*	*in front of*
ahead of	*as well as*	*in terms of*
along with	*away from*	*next to*
apart from	*due to*	*out of*

Commonly-confused prepositions

7 Some prepositions have meanings that are very similar and can be confused.

Use *over*, not *across*, to mean 'on / to the other side of something high'.

*The thief escaped by climbing **over** the wall.*

Use *above / below* when one thing is not directly over / under another. Use *over / under* when one thing covers / is covered by another.

*He saw a man **below** him.* NOT ~~*... under him.*~~
*The cat was hiding **under** the bed.* NOT ~~*... below the bed.*~~

Use *below* with measurements of temperature and height. Use *over / under* with speeds, ages, prices, etc.

*Temperatures can drop to 15° **below** zero.*
NOT ~~*... under zero.*~~
*You have to be **over** 16 to join this club.*
NOT ~~*... above 16 ...*~~

TIP

In books or documents, *see above / below* refers to something that came before / after in the text, and *see over* means 'Look on the next page'.

Use *between* with two separate things and *among* with a group of things.

*The café is **between** the flower shop and the shoe shop.*
*The house stood **among** the trees.*

Use *as* to say what someone or something is or does and *like* to make a comparison or to give examples.

*My uncle works **as** a lawyer.*
*This chicken can think **like** a human!*

In more formal English, use *such as* to give examples instead of *like*.

*We offer a wide range of activities, **such as** skiing and surfing.*

Use *during* to mean 'some time within a bigger period of time' and *throughout* or *all through* to emphasise a continuous state lasting the whole of a period. Use *over* to emphasise a change in state between the beginning and end of a period.

*We moved house **during** the summer.*
*I worked **throughout** / **all through** the summer.*
*I want to improve my English **over** the summer.*

Use *until* to talk about activities or states that continue up to a particular time and *by* to talk about activities that happen before or at a particular time.

*My sister lived with our parents **until** the day she got married.*
*I'll definitely be home **by** 9.*

We sometimes use *till* (British English) or *'til* (American English) instead of *until* in informal situations.

*I won't be back **till** / **'til** 10.* OR ... ***until*** *10.*

Use *except* (*for*) to mean 'not including'. Use *besides* to mean 'in addition to'. We can use *apart from* with both these meanings.

*She was alone in the building. Everyone **except** (**for**) / **apart from** her had left.*
*Bill was driving, and there were three other people in the car **besides** / **apart from** him.*

Use *beside* to mean 'next to'. Use *near* (*to*) or *close to* to mean 'not far from'.

*The hotel is **beside** / **next to** the casino and **near** (**to**) / **close to** the main shopping area.*

Use *towards* to mean 'in the direction of'. The opposite of *towards* is *away from.*

*I saw a dog running **towards** / **away from** me.*

Practice

A Circle the correct option.

1 My sister was born at ... .
a the afternoon b 20th November (c) home
2 It will be difficult for me to do both things in ... .
a only three days b the same time c Tuesday
3 Jan and Carla live in a beautiful house on ... .
a the end of a valley b the Alps c the road to Zurich
4 My cousin's getting married in ... .
a the end of the month b a month's time
c 29th April
5 Maggie's going to the dentist this morning because she had really bad toothache in ... .
a last night b the night c night
6 The winner is the person who has the most money at ... .
a the end of the game b 30 minutes' time
c their bank account
7 The museum is closed on Wednesday afternoons and on ... .
a Mondays b December c lunchtime
8 The First World War ended on ... .
a 1918 b November 1918
c Monday 11th November 1918
9 Matt's due to arrive at ... .
a about 4.00 b the morning c Thursday night
10 I hate having to get up early in ... .
a Sundays b winter c my day off

B Match the sentence beginnings to the correct endings.

1 It's already 11.30. The last bus will have left
2 Most of the time our cat stays
3 A lot of animals hibernate
4 Colin's test result was
5 In order to finish my assignment I had to work all
6 All their lives, Judith and Diana have lived
7 Can you pass me my keys? I think they're on the table,
8 It was a perfect holiday,
9 The party didn't finish
10 The gate was locked, so to get in we had to climb

a until after midnight.
b near each other.
c by now.
d over the garden fence.
e among the best in the country.
f inside the house.
g under my jacket.
h throughout the winter.
i apart from the wet weather.
j through the night.

1 ...c... 2 ...... 3 ...... 4 ...... 5 ......
6 ...... 7 ...... 8 ...... 9 ...... 10 ......

C Complete the story with the correct prepositions. Sometimes more than one preposition is possible, but you should use a different preposition in each space.

One day, a young boy was working [1] ...in... a field [2] ...... his village. He worked [3] ...... a shepherd boy, protecting the sheep, but [4] ...... only the sheep as company he soon became bored. To entertain himself, the boy suddenly shouted, 'Help! Help! A wolf is killing all the sheep!' The people from the village ran [5] ...... the field to help the boy, but he just laughed and said, 'Hahaha! There is no wolf! I was only joking!' The next day, and the day [6] ...... that, the boy repeated his joke. Each time, the villagers ran to help, and each time they found the boy sitting [7] ...... the sheep and saying, 'Hahaha! I was joking again. Of course there is no wolf!' [8] ...... now the villagers were very angry. Then the next day, a wolf really did start killing the sheep, so the boy again shouted, 'Help! Help! A wolf is killing all the sheep!' This time, [9] ...... the boy's cries, the villagers thought he was joking again, and [10] ...... the other days, they didn't run to help him. So the wolf killed all the sheep.

MORAL: If you tell lies, no one will believe you when you tell the truth!

D Rewrite each sentence so that it has a similar meaning, using the preposition in brackets.

1 We had a long journey to make, so we set off early. (ahead of)
We had a long journey ahead of us, so we set off early.

2 Maya is really good at volleyball and is an excellent tennis player too. (as well as)

3 I know I've got a good salary, but it's a terrible job if we think about job satisfaction. (in terms of)

4 Not checking your answers carefully caused most of your mistakes in the test. (due to)

5 Because she worked hard during the year, Julia was offered a promotion. (as a result of)

6 The weather forecast said it might snow later today. (according to)

7 The police put up a sign warning people not to go near the edge of the cliff. (away from)

8 We were the only people in the park, if you don't include an old man and his dog. (apart from)

9 Jim had to brake suddenly when a cat ran across the road as he was driving. (in front of)

10 Pasta is definitely one of my favourite meals, and pizza is too, of course! (along with)

E Complete each sentence in an appropriate way.

1 We decided to go out, despite the cold weather.

2 After …………, they needed a long holiday!

3 As a result of …………, Andy was in a really bad mood.

4 Janet stayed at home all weekend, apart from ………….

5 Besides …………, you should also visit the castle.

6 Sally never goes anywhere without ………….

7 Dan had six months of Spanish lessons before ………….

8 To get to …………, you have to go through …………, under …………, past …………, and across ………….

MY TURN!

Write at least six true sentences about yourself, using a different preposition from the box in each sentence.

about as as a result of at before between by during except for in next to throughout until without

Example: I have to wait until July for my exam results.

MY TEST!

Circle the correct option.

1 My cousins live ………… a big house in the country. a in b into c at
2 He didn't sleep very well – the rain was dripping through his roof all ………… the night. a over b along c through
3 The new shopping centre is in the city centre, ………… the train station. a close b near c next
4 ………… the cold weather, we decided to go for a walk. a Despite b Against c In terms of
5 ………… from Hodja and his chicken, the market was completely empty. a Apart b Besides c Except

My Test! answers: 1a 2c 3b 4a 5a

19 Prepositions after adjectives and nouns

Without doubt the perfect solution to your problems

Have you ever wondered how adverts work? We explain the three secrets of advertising:

1 Describe a problem. A good **way of doing** this is by asking questions which get people **interested in** the product.

shine

Do you have no control over your hair? Are you disappointed with your usual shampoo?

Faced with life's daily demands, it's hard to find time to take **pride in** your appearance, especially when you're always **in a hurry**. That's why we've created ... shine.

Free from anything unnatural, shine is for anyone who is **tired of** not looking good **in public**. And it's **kind to** your skin!

shine – it brings your hair under control!

2 Be personal. Develop a **relationship with** your customers, by using language which shows you are **aware of** their problems.

Are you worried about how much you eat? Were you under the impression that healthy food is boring?

We have **sympathy for** you. So we've created ...

the Mega Bar!

Packed with vitamins, the Mega Bar is **without doubt** the perfect **solution to** your problems. The Mega Bar is **good for** you – in **fact** it provides 10% of your recommended daily vitamins! And it tastes great!

The Mega Bar – on sale now!

3 You have more **chance of selling** your product if people have **a reason for buying** it. **In other words**, tell them what's so **good about** it.

?

1 What is the name of each product?
2 What kind of product is each one?

Answers: 1 *Mega Bar* and *Shine* 2 A *Mega Bar* is a vitamin bar; *Shine* is a shampoo.

Prepositions after adjectives and nouns

Prepositions after adjectives

1 **We use a specific preposition after many adjectives.**

- ***about:*** *anxious / worried* ***about****, confused* ***about****, curious* ***about****, sad* ***about****, (un)sure* ***about***
- ***at:*** *clever* ***at****, skilled* ***at****, adept* ***at***
- ***for:*** *desperate* ***for****, ready* ***for****, impatient* ***for****, famous / known* ***for****, responsible* ***for***
- ***from:*** *absent* ***from****, different* ***from****, free* ***from****, safe* ***from***
- ***in:*** *interested* ***in****, absorbed* ***in***
- ***of:*** *afraid / scared / frightened* ***of****, ashamed* ***of****, fond* ***of****, (un)aware* ***of****, ignorant* ***of****, (in)capable* ***of****, tired* ***of****, full* ***of****, proud* ***of****, typical* ***of***
- ***on:*** *dependent* ***on****, reliant* ***on***
- ***to:*** *used* ***to****, addicted* ***to****, resigned* ***to****, similar* ***to****, engaged / married* ***to****, kind* ***to***
- ***with:*** *satisfied* ***with****, faced / confronted* ***with****, acquainted* ***with****, packed* ***with****, crowded* ***with****, bored* ***with****, familiar* ***with****, obsessed* ***with***

2 **We can use more than one preposition after some common adjectives, with a change in meaning.**

angry / annoyed / upset / furious
Julie was ***annoyed about*** *her poor exam result.*
Julie's parents were ***annoyed with*** *her.*

disappointed
Are you ***disappointed with*** *the results?*
Fiona was ***disappointed at / about*** *failing the test.*
I'm very ***disappointed in*** *you. You should have done better.*

fair
We can't leave without Kim. It's not ***fair on*** *her.*
I don't think it would be ***fair of*** *us to leave without Kim.*

good / bad
Harry's very ***bad at*** *swimming, but* ***good at*** *running.*
Eating too much chocolate is ***bad for*** *you.*
Thanks for offering to help – it was very ***good of*** *you.*
He's ***good with*** *children.*
Tell them what's so ***good / bad about*** *it.*

happy / pleased / delighted / thrilled
*Are you **happy about / with** your new house?*
*Congratulations! I'm really **pleased for** you.*

right / wrong
*I don't think Gary's new job is **right for** him.*
*You were **right about** Gary's job; he hates it.*
*It was **wrong of** you to steal the money.*
*You were **wrong about** Hans – he's Dutch, not German.*
*There's something **wrong with** my computer.*

sorry
*I'm **sorry about** all the noise last night – we had a party.*
*I feel **sorry for** Scott – no one ever listens to him.*

Prepositions after nouns

3 **Many nouns are followed by the same preposition as their related verb or adjective.**
*to agree **with** → agreement **with***
*to believe **in** → belief **in***
*to complain **about** → complaint **about***
*to invest **in** → investment **in***
*to participate **in** → participation **in***
*to respond **to** → response **to***

A few nouns are followed by a different preposition from the related verb or adjective.
*fond **of** / fondness **for***
*proud **of** / pride **in***
*to sympathise **with** / sympathy **for***

Nouns are usually followed by a preposition even if the related verb is not.
*to ban → a ban **on***
*to control → control **of** / **over***
*to decrease → a decrease **in** / **of***
*to discuss → a discussion **about***
*to fear → a fear **of***
*to increase → an increase **in** / **of***
*to solve → a solution **to***
*to support → support **for***
*to threaten → a threat **to***

> **TIP**
> **We use *increase / decrease in* to talk about what is increasing / decreasing. We can use *increase / decrease of* to talk about the size of the increase / decrease.**
> *There has been an increase **of** 5% **in** the price of petrol.*

4 **Some nouns can be followed by *to*-infinitive or *of* + gerund with the same meaning, e.g. *idea, aim, opportunity, way.***
*A good **way of doing** this is by asking a question.*
OR *A good **way to do** this is ...*

Some nouns can be followed by *of* + gerund but not *to*-infinitive, e.g. *cost, effect, fear, possibility, probability, problem, risk.*
*There's no **risk of damaging** your health.*
NOT ~~*There's no risk to damage your health*~~.

> **TIP**
> **The word *chance* can be followed by *of* + gerund or *to*-infinitive with a different meaning.**
> *You have more **chance of selling** your product.* (= a higher probability)
> *A long weekend gives you a **chance to relax** for a few days.* (= an opportunity)

5 **Other common noun + preposition combinations are *effect on, exception to, relationship with* and *reason / room for.***
*Develop a **relationship with** your customers.*

6 **There are many common preposition + noun phrase combinations.**

at:	***at** home, **at** fault, **at** least, **at** once, **at** present / the moment, **at** any rate, **at** risk, **at** stake, **at** a time*
by:	***by** accident, **by** chance, **by** definition, **by** far, **by** mistake, **by** myself / yourself / himself,* etc., ***by** the way*
for:	***for** good, **for** now, **for** real, **for** that matter, **for** the time being*
in:	***in** addition to, **in** advance, **in** charge, **in** common, **in** control, **in** danger, **in** fact, **in** general, **in** a hurry, **in** a mess, **in** order to, **in** other words, **in** particular, **in** public, **in** touch, **in** trouble, **in** a way*
on:	***on** average, **on** business, **on** holiday, **on** my / your / his,* etc. *own, **on** purpose, **on** sale, **on** strike, **on** the phone, **on** time, **on** the / my / your / his,* etc. *way (to)*
out of:	***out of** control, **out of** date, **out of** order, **out of** place, **out of** sight, **out of** work*
under:	***under** the circumstances, **under** control, **under** the impression, **under** pressure*
with:	***with** the aim of, **with** the exception of, **with** the help of, **with** regard to, **with** respect to*
without:	***without** doubt, **without** warning*

> **TIP**
> **We use *out of order* to say that something is not working at the moment. We use *out of work* to say that someone is unemployed.**

Practice

A Put each adjective from the box under the preposition which is usually used after it. Try to do this first without looking at page 82, then check your answers.

capable clever dependent engaged ~~famous~~ free full interested obsessed proud ready reliant responsible safe satisfied similar skilled used

at	for	from	in
....	famous	....	....
....	....	....	
	....		

of	on	to	with
....	....	....	....
....	....	....	....
....		....	

B Match the sentence beginnings to the correct endings.

1 There's no way [c]
2 A new ban [ ]
3 Estevez is playing some very good tennis, but there is still some room [ ]
4 One of the most common phobias nowadays is a fear [ ]
5 I don't have any sympathy [ ]
6 People have a lot more respect [ ]
7 After he gave an excellent speech to the nation last week, support [ ]
8 If James continues to work hard he will have a good chance [ ]
9 It's only a general rule, and like all rules there must be an exception [ ]
10 New statistics show a decrease [ ]

a for improvement.
b to it.
c of knowing if your idea will work until you try it.
d in the number of unemployed, from 1.8 million to 1.6 million.
e for Luis. This situation is all his own fault.
f of flying.
g for the environment than they did 20 years ago.
h for the President increased.
i on the use of mobile phones in hospitals will take effect today.
j of passing his exam.

C Complete each sentence, using a preposition and a word or phrase from the box.

the circumstances least my way particular purpose regard ~~stake~~ touch

1 We need someone with experience to lead this project because there is a lot of money ...at stake... .
2 It was great to see you again, and we must make sure we keep .... more regularly in future.
3 We don't normally let people come in without a ticket but .... we can make an exception – I can see it's not your fault.
4 Sorry, I can't stop now. I'm .... to an important meeting.
5 Do you think Kevin kicked you ...., or was it an accident?
6 There are lots of things wrong with that idea, ... the fact that it would be really expensive.
7 I am writing .... to the advertisement for an Accounts Clerk on JobSearch.com.
8 I don't feel like going to Frank's party, but .... Jess is going, so I'll have someone to talk to.

D Complete the questions by adding the missing letters to the expressions from this unit.

1 Where did you go on h_o_lid_a_y last year?
2 How much time do you spend o_ t_e p_o_e each day?
3 Can you suggest one good w_y o_ improving your English?
4 Are you still i_ t_u_h w_t_ any of your childhood friends?
5 What habits do you have which are b_d f_r you?
6 Do you know anyone who is always i_ a h_r_y?
7 What has there been an i_c_e_s_ i_ where you live in the last few years?
8 Are you happy spending long periods of time o_ y_u_ o_n?
9 Is your bedroom usually tidy or do you leave it i_ a m_s_?
10 Have you ever done something embarrassing i_ p_b_i_?

Now answer the questions for yourself.

E Complete the advert with the correct prepositions.

Are you confused [1] ....about.......... all the different health advice you find in the media these days? Most of us are resigned [2] .... having a life which is full [3] .... stress, but if we don't look after ourselves, we are putting ourselves [4] .... risk of developing health problems in the future. Although we are all [5] .... pressure to look and feel good, finding a fitness programme which is right [6] .... us can be difficult – and expensive. But now there is a solution [7] .... all your health and fitness problems! Here at FEEL GOOD FITNESS we have a firm belief [8] .... the importance of regular exercise, and with the help of your own personal fitness trainer you will soon discover the benefits [9] .... following a training programme which you actually enjoy – so there's no chance [10] .... you getting bored and giving up after a week! FEEL GOOD FITNESS helps you to FEEL GOOD NOW!

MY TURN!

Complete at least six of the sentences, starting with an appropriate preposition in each case.

1 At the moment I'm a bit worried ..about my next English test.. .
2 I very quickly get bored ....
3 I've never really got used ....
4 My home town is famous ....
5 When I was younger I was scared ....
6 As a child I was obsessed ....
7 I would love to be skilled ....
8 I was disappointed ....
9 I get furious ....
10 Something surprising about me is that I'm good ....

MY TEST!

Circle the correct option.

1 Good advertisements are important for attracting customers who are unsure .... which product to buy. a with b about c of
2 You shouldn't eat so much fast food because it's really bad .... you a for b at c about
3 She's a terrible teacher. She has no control .... her students. a for b to c over
4 Your idea .... offering customers a special deal was a really good one. a of b to c for
5 I can't talk now – I'm .... my way to meet my sister and I'm a bit late! a in b on c by

My Test! answers: 1b 2a 3c 4a 5b

20 Verbs + prepositions; prepositional verbs

If the moon loves you, why worry about the stars?

Proverbs can tell us a lot about life. Have a look at these examples from around the world:

1 If you ***climb up*** a tree, you must ***climb down*** the same tree. (Sierra Leone)

2 If the moon loves you, why **worry about** the stars? (Tunisia)

3 *If you **run after** two rabbits, you won't catch either of them.* (Japan)

4 **Ask for** advice, then use your head. (Norway)

5 **No one is more afraid of ghosts than those who don't believe in them.** (China)

6 The tiger **depends on** the forest; the forest **depends on** the tiger. (Cambodia)

7 Don't **blame** the sun **for** the darkness of the night. (Georgia)

8 You cannot **prevent** the birds of sadness **from** flying over your head, but you can **stop** them **from** building nests in your hair. (China)

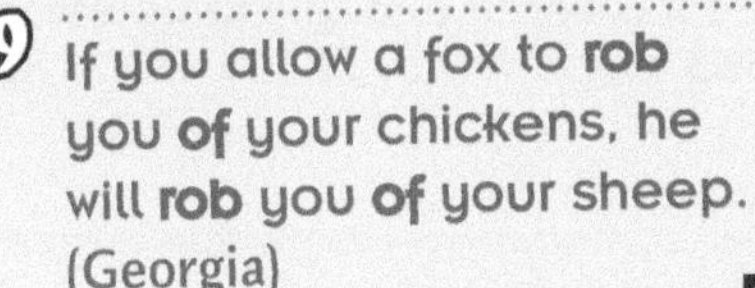

9 If you allow a fox to **rob** you **of** your chickens, he will **rob** you **of** your sheep. (Georgia)

10 *One camel does not **make fun of** another camel's hump.* (Ghana)

11 *If you can't catch a fish, don't **put the blame on** the sea.* (Greece)

12 *To **set fire to** the wood, you need the help of the wind.* (Tibet)

13 Let every fox **take care of** his own tail. (Italy)

? 1 Which proverbs are connected with animals?
2 Which ones also exist in your language?

Answers: 1 3, 6, 8, 9, 10, 11, 13

Verbs + prepositions; prepositional verbs

Verbs + prepositions

1 We can use many different prepositions after most verbs of movement, e.g. *go in, go to, go up, go along, go under.*

*If you **climb up** a tree, you must **climb down** the same tree.*

2 We can separate the preposition from its following noun phrase in some kinds of sentences:

– *wh*-questions
on what **→** ***What*** *were you working* ***on****?*

– relative clauses
up that mountain **→** ***That mountain*** *is the one we're going to climb* ***up****.*

– passive sentences
across the bridge **→** ***The bridge*** *is driven* ***across*** *thousands of times every day.*

– infinitive structures
to classical music **→** *I think most* ***classical music*** *is very relaxing to listen* ***to****.*

We can omit *to* in questions with verbs of movement (e.g. *go, fly, take, drive*), particularly in informal contexts.

*Where are you **going**?* OR *Where are you **going to**?*

Prepositional verbs

3 Many verb + preposition combinations are fixed. These fixed combinations are called prepositional verbs, and their meaning is sometimes different from the meaning of the verb on its own.

*I **came across some old photographs** when I was cleaning my room.* (= I found them by accident.)

4 Some common prepositional verbs are:

about:	*be **about**, complain **about**, dream **about**, hear **about**, protest **about**, talk **about**, worry **about***
after:	*look **after**, run **after***
against:	*advise **against**, argue **against**, decide **against**, vote **against***
at:	*laugh **at**, look **at**, glance **at**, smile **at***
between:	*choose **between***
for:	*account **for**, allow **for**, apply **for**, apologise **for**, ask **for**, care **for**, charge **for**, go **for**, hope **for**, look **for**, pay **for**, prepare **for**, stand **for**, wait **for***
from:	*benefit **from**, differ **from**, result **from**, suffer **from***
in:	*believe **in**, specialise **in**, succeed **in**, trust **in***
into:	*break **into**, get **into**, run **into***
like:	*feel **like**, look **like**, smell **like**, sound **like***
of:	*approve **of**, consist **of**, hear **of**, know **of**, smell **of***
on:	*call **on**, comment **on**, concentrate **on**, decide **on**, depend **on**, insist **on***
to:	*apply **to**, attend **to**, belong **to**, confess **to**, lead **to**, listen **to**, object **to**, refer **to**, see **to***
with:	*(dis)agree **with**, cope **with**, deal **with**, interfere **with**, play **with***

▶ See Unit 25 for phrasal verbs.

Some verbs form two common prepositional verbs with slightly different meanings.

*This cake **tastes of** coffee.* (= I think it contains coffee.)
*This coffee **tastes like** water.* (= It has a similar flavour to water.)
*I don't want to go to the party but I can't **think of** a good excuse.* (= I can't imagine a good excuse.)
*I'm **thinking about** / **of** going away for a few days.* (= I'm considering this possibility.)

5 There are some fixed expressions that consist of verb + prepositional phrase, e.g. ***bear in mind, fall in love, get into trouble, go into detail, take into account, take into consideration, put into practice, come as a shock / surprise.***

*Salaries are higher now, but **bear in mind** that prices are higher too.*

6 Some verbs need an object before the preposition.

about:	*tell ... **about**, warn ... **about***
against:	*advise ... **against***
for:	*blame ... **for**, buy ... **for**, do ... **for**, make ... **for**, thank ... **for***
from:	*ban ... **from**, discourage ... **from**, prevent ... **from**, protect ... **from**, stop ... **from***
of:	*accuse ... **of**, deprive ... **of**, remind ... **of**, rob ... **of***
on:	*base ... **on**, blame ... **on**, congratulate ... **on***
to:	*confine ... **to**, explain ... **to**, give ... **to**, introduce ... **to**, say ... **to**, send ... **to**, tell ... **to***

We can use *stop* + object with or without *from*. The meaning is the same.

*... but you can **stop** them (**from**) building nests in your hair.*

7 Some verb + object + preposition combinations are fixed expressions. These expressions are usually with very common verbs, e.g. *have, make, put*.

have:	***have a go / look at, have a word with***
help:	***help oneself to***
make:	***make a difference to, make a point of, make an impression on, make contact with, make friends with, make fun of, make room for, make the most of, make way for***
put:	***put a stop to, put pressure on, put the blame on, put your mind to***
set:	***set fire to, set foot in***
take:	***take advantage of, take an interest in, take care of, take exception to, take note of, take part in, take pity on, take responsibility for***

*One camel does not **make fun of** another camel's hump.*
*We **took advantage of** the good weather to have a barbecue in the garden.*

Practice

A Match the questions to the correct replies.

1 What are you looking for?
2 Where are you from?
3 Who are they waving at?
4 What are you listening to?
5 Who do you live with?
6 What kind of house do you live in?
7 How long will the hill take to walk up?
8 What's your necklace made of?

a Some jazz music. It helps me to relax.
b Us, I think!
c My wallet. Have you seen it?
d About two hours.
e Silver. Do you like it?
f A small one, with only two bedrooms.
g My parents and my younger brother.
h Warsaw. The capital of Poland.

1 ...c... 2 .... 3 .... 4 .... 5 .... 6 .... 7 .... 8 ....

B Circle the correct option.

1 She fell in ... with the dress as soon as she saw it in the shop, and begged her dad to buy it.
a happiness b attraction ⓒ love d like
2 It's a good idea in theory, but it's going to be hard to put it into ... .
a practice b trial c test d examination
3 Stefania's decision to give up her job came as a ... to all her colleagues.
a concern b delight c pleasure d surprise
4 It sounds like a great job, but bear in ... that you'll need to work very long hours.
a consideration b thought c account d mind
5 My little brother is really naughty, and he's always getting into ... at school.
a problem b trouble c punishment d disturbance
6 Without going into ... , the trip was a complete disaster.
a fact b detail c information d list
7 If you take into ... stopping for lunch on the way, the journey should take about four hours.
a thought b allowance c reminder d account
8 It came as a ... to my parents when I told them I wanted to leave school.
a nightmare b shock c horror d right

C Complete the sentences with the correct prepositions.

1 I nearly bought a new car the other day but in the end I decided ...against... it.
2 The secret to dealing .... stress is to recognise the symptoms as quickly as possible.
3 I offered to give Louise a lift to work but she insisted .... walking.
4 Do you know .... any good places to eat near here?
5 Our company makes lots of different things but we specialise .... electrical instruments.
6 The service in the hotel was so bad that I wrote to the manager to complain .... it.
7 Do you know who this umbrella belongs ....? I found it in one of the classrooms.
8 I ran .... David in town this afternoon. I hadn't seen him for ages.

D Complete each sentence b so that it means the same as sentence a, using a form of the verb in brackets and the correct preposition.

1 a What can I do so that the birds don't steal all the berries off the tree? (stop)
b How can I ...stop the birds from stealing all the berries off the tree?...
2 a Giorgia told Cristina that Alex had a really bad temper. (warn)
b Giorgia .... really bad temper.
3 a Michelle told Jackie that she thought she had stolen her purse. (accuse)
b Michelle .... her purse.
4 a The police have said that people can't park in front of the building. (ban)
b The police .... in front of the building.
5 a The author used real-life events as the basis of her book. (base)
b The author .... real-life events.
6 a We'd like to say thanks to our families and friends. We appreciated all their support. (thank)
b We'd like to .... all their support.
7 a As a result of several injuries, Williams didn't have a long career as a professional tennis player. (rob)
b Several injuries .... a long career as a professional tennis player.
8 a The teacher said 'Well done' to Tom when he won first prize in the school competition. (congratulate)
b The teacher .... first prize in the school competition.

E Write the verbs from Box A next to the correct numbers 1–6 in the table.

A

have help make put ~~take~~ set

1 ......take......	2	3 ....
part in	a word with	pressure on
pity on	....	a stop to
the trouble to		....
....		
4	**5 ....**	**6 ....**
friends with	yourself to	foot in
a point of		....
the most of		
....		

Now write the expressions from Box B in the correct sections of the table.

B

your mind to contact with fire to care of a go at

MY TURN!

Complete these proverbs with your own ideas, using prepositional verbs.

1 A cat likes to eat fish, but it will not ....*go into the water.*....
....

2 Look after your own house before you ....
....
....
....

3 An empty stomach will not ....
....
....
....

4 Before the water drains away, ...
....
....
....

5 When a blind man leads, ...
....
....
....

MY TEST!

Circle the correct option.

1 If you want your children to look .... you when you're old, take good care of them when they're young. a to b after c over
2 If we take the cost of the train tickets .... consideration, it could be an expensive weekend. a for b to c into
3 The museum has a modern alarm system to prevent anyone .... stealing the exhibits. a from b of c for
4 Take care not to .... fire to yourself when you're putting out a fire. a put b start c set
5 Lorraine's friends all .... fun of her new hairstyle. a made b took c did

My Test! answers: 1b 2c 3a 4c 5a

21 Adjectives 1

There's an amazing golden statue.

Day 4

Well, I'm in Beijing, and it's a really **interesting** city. The Chinese are very **friendly** and they're really **interested** in me just because I'm **different**! Beijing is extremely **noisy** and **overcrowded**, with cyclists everywhere – crossing the road can be **utterly terrifying**. It was boiling **hot** today, so I got out of the **city** centre and cycled to the **Summer** Palace. Because of the **sheer** size of Beijing it felt like I never really left the city until I got to the Palace itself, but I'm really **glad** I went because it was very **peaceful**. It's an **enormous royal** park with lots of palaces and towers, as well as **incredible ornamental** gardens and a **large blue boating** lake. It was built so that the **old Chinese** emperors had somewhere **quieter** to relax – they used to spend their **summer** holidays there. It's now a **popular tourist** attraction, and it's **easy** to see why – there are beautifully **decorated** palaces everywhere, showing you how the **rich** used to live! And there's a hill with a **40-metre-high stone** tower, the Tower of **Buddhist** Incense. Inside there's an **amazing golden** statue, and although climbing up the tower was quite **hard** work, there are absolutely **stunning** views from the top. Anyway, it's been an **exhausting** day, so …

1 Where is the Summer Palace?
2 Name two of its attractions.

Answers: 1 Beijing, China 2 A park, ornamental gardens, a boating lake, decorated palaces, the Tower of Buddhist Incense, a golden statue

Adjectives 1

Gradable and ungradable adjectives

1 **Gradable adjectives describe characteristics that can be more / less intense, e.g. *big, noisy*. They can be used after adverbs like *very, too, a bit* and *extremely*, before the adverb *enough*, and in comparative / superlative forms.**

*Beijing is **extremely noisy**.*
*... somewhere **quieter** to relax.*

▶ See Unit 23 for comparative and superlative forms of gradable adjectives.

2 **Ungradable adjectives usually describe extreme (e.g. *freezing*) or absolute characteristics (e.g. *dead*). They are not normally used with adverbs like *very, too*, etc., or in comparative / superlative forms.**

*Today is **freezing** / **the coldest** day of the year.*
NOT ~~*... the most freezing day ...*~~

We can use *quite* with both gradable and ungradable adjectives, but with a different meaning.

*Climbing up it was **quite hard** work.* (= not very hard, but not easy)
*The food in our hotel was **quite superb**.* (= extremely good [very formal])

Ungradable adjectives can often be emphasised with *absolutely, completely, totally* and *utterly*.

*Crossing the road can be **utterly terrifying**.*

> **TIP**
> We sometimes use ***boiling, freezing*** and ***soaking*** as adverbs to emphasise ***hot, cold*** and ***wet***.
> *It was **boiling hot** today.*

Ungradable adjectives can be modified using ***nearly, virtually***.

*This crossword puzzle is **nearly impossible**!*

> **TIP**
> We can use ***really*** with both gradable and ungradable adjectives.
> *The views are **really beautiful** / **stunning**.*

Some ungradable adjectives define the subject or area of activity which the noun refers to, e.g. ***chemical, digital, mental, environmental, historical, economic.***

*My sister is a nurse specialising in **mental** health.*

3 Some adjectives can be gradable and ungradable, with different meanings, e.g. ***common, critical, odd, original, clean, old.***

*An **old** couple live in the flat next to mine.* (gradable = elderly)

*... the **old** Chinese emperors ...* (ungradable = the ones in the past)

Participle adjectives

4 We can use the ***-ing*** form and the past participle (***-ed*** form) of a verb as adjectives.

*It's been an **exhausting** day.*

*There are beautifully **decorated** palaces.*

> **TIP**
> Don't confuse the ***-ed*** and ***-ing*** forms of the same verb. The ***-ing*** form has an active meaning and usually describes things. The ***-ed*** form has a passive meaning and usually describes people.
> *It was a very **exciting** film.*
> *I was **excited** about going to the cinema.*

5 Some nouns which refer to places, seasons and materials can be used as adjectives.

*I decided to get out of the **city** centre.*

*There's a hill with a 40-metre-high **stone** tower.*

Some materials have two or more adjective forms, e.g. ***wood / wooden, gold / golden***. In general, the ***-en*** form is more common, particularly when the meaning is metaphorical.

*There's an amazing **golden** statue.* OR *... an amazing **gold** statue.*

*The actor gave a very **wooden** performance.*

NOT ~~*... a wood performance.*~~

▶ See Unit 31 for compound nouns.
▶ See Unit 32 for adjectives used as nouns.

Adjective position

6 Most adjectives can be used before a noun or after a verb like ***be, look, seem, feel, become*** or ***appear***.

*These are very **comfortable shoes**.* OR *These **shoes are** very **comfortable**.*

▶ See Unit 27 for more information on verbs followed by adjectives.

7 Some adjectives are normally only used before nouns, e.g. ***main, only*** and ***whole***.

*This is the **main entrance**.* NOT ~~*This entrance is main.*~~

We can use ***sheer, mere*** and ***very*** before nouns to add emphasis: ***sheer*** to emphasise something big or powerful, ***mere*** to emphasise something small or simple, and ***very*** to emphasise 'exactly this one'.

*Because of the **sheer size** of Beijing ...*

*The **mere thought** of food makes me hungry.*

*You're the **very person** I need.*

8 Some adjectives are normally only used after verbs like those in 6 above, e.g. ***well, ill*** (= not healthy), ***alive, asleep***.

*The student **looked ill**, so I called a doctor.*

NOT ~~*The ill student ...*~~

> **TIP**
> We can use adjectives after words like ***something / anything, somewhere / anywhere, nothing***, etc.
> *... their families could have **somewhere quiet** to relax.*

9 Some adjectives have a different meaning depending on their position in a sentence, e.g. ***present, opposite, concerned*** and ***late***.

*Mrs Jones and her **late** husband lived here for 50 years.* (= her husband died)

*Juan was **late** for class again this morning.* (= not on time)

Adjective order

10 If several adjectives are used together, they usually appear in this order:

size – age – shape – colour – origin – material – type / purpose

*a **small round wooden dining** table*

*an **enormous royal** park*

Adjectives describing opinions or attitudes usually come before all others.

*a **beautiful long blue silk** dress*

*an **amazing golden** statue*

Practice

A Match the gradable adjectives to the ungradable adjectives with extreme meanings.

1	funny (→ c)	a	fascinating
2	big	b	superb
3	stupid	c	hilarious
4	surprising	d	terrified
5	good	e	furious
6	angry	f	starving
7	attractive	g	gorgeous
8	hungry	h	idiotic
9	interesting	i	enormous
10	scared	j	astonishing

B Circle TWO correct options.

1 The book I'm reading at the moment is absolutely … .
a interesting (b) terrifying (c) hilarious

2 This drink has a very … flavour.
a unusual b delicious c sweet

3 The views from the top of the mountain were utterly … .
a spectacular b great c stunning

4 My brother has a very … job in a bank.
a responsible b hard c bored

5 The child got a lot of attention because she was … .
a young b only c ill

6 The project was very successful and we would like to thank everyone … .
a particular b concerned c involved

7 Her last book was interesting because the story was extremely … .
a original b unique c odd

8 There was a / an … cat on the sofa.
a huge b asleep c beautiful

9 The Indian restaurant was … expensive, so we got a takeaway instead.
a too b enough c extremely

10 The company's … owner, Eduardo Sanchez, inherited it from his father.
a alive b late c present

C Complete the sentences by putting the words and phrases in the correct order.

1 thought / up / the / getting / mere / of / early
The mere thought of getting up early puts me in a bad mood.

2 ate / pizzas / she / whole / on her own / two
Marion was so hungry ....
....

3 by the time / soaking / were / we / wet
It was raining so hard that ....
.... we got home.

4 you / reliable / know / do / anyone
....
who can babysit for us on Friday night?

5 couldn't / to watch / interesting / I / anything / find
I sat down and turned on the TV but
....

6 reason / is / don't like / main / Jake / the / I
....
that he's always so rude to me when I see him!

7 alive / didn't / the / seem / lizard
....
so I was surprised when it suddenly moved.

8 always / equipment / should / you / proper / take
If you go walking in the mountains,
....

D Complete the blog with adjectives made from the words in brackets.

Wow – I've just got back from Jin Shan Ling, a really [1] *beautiful* (beauty) part of the Great Wall of China. It was absolutely [2] .... (stun). I got up really early this morning and took the bus from Beijing to Si Ma Tai. It's not as touristy as some other parts of the Wall, so it felt much more [3] .... (peace) than the Badaling Great Wall. As I wrote last week, I was a bit [4] .... (disappoint) when I visited it – it was almost too perfect. Then I walked the 10 km along the wall to Jin Shan Ling, which was absolutely [5] .... (exhaust). It was a [6] .... (boil) hot day and there wasn't much shade from the sun.

While I was walking, I had a good chat with some American tourists – it was a [7] .... (gold) opportunity to practise my English. One guy I spoke to had read the history of the Wall – absolutely [8] .... (fascinate). I guess I need to read more books and blog about it soon! Looking back, it was probably too [9] .... (tire) for a single day – next time I'll take a sleeping bag and take more time to enjoy the experience. Also, I'd take more food and drink – mine ran out after a few hours, which was really [10] .... (annoy). And don't forget to take some toilet paper!

E **Write descriptions of these things using at least two adjectives. You can use the adjectives from the box or your own ideas.**

1 
2 
3 
4 

5 
6 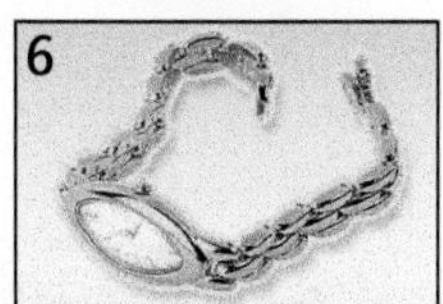
7 
8 
9 
10 

beautiful black Chinese city comfortable dark deserted exciting expensive gold horror leather little long modern new old overcrowded popular running square terrifying tropical wooden young

1 *an extremely comfortable black leather* sofa
2 .... table
3 .... singer
4 .... film
5 .... shoes
6 .... watch
7 .... hair
8 .... restaurant
9 .... beach
10 .... centre

MY TURN!

Write sentences describing at least five of the following, using adjective structures from the unit.

1 Your best friend

2 The weather yesterday

3 The last film you saw

4 An activity which you don't like

5 A good meal you had recently

6 A present you got for your last birthday

7 A famous person from your country

8 The English language

Example: 2 *Yesterday was a beautiful sunny day, with a clear blue sky and boiling hot temperatures.*

MY TEST!

Circle the correct option.

1 I'm reading a / an .... interesting book about China at the moment. **a** absolutely **b** really **c** completely
2 There has been a small increase in .... growth in this country this year. **a** economic **b** economics **c** economy
3 I find the .... idea of running a marathon exhausting. **a** quite **b** sheer **c** mere
4 During the .... months, the emperors and their families used to move away from the city. **a** winters **b** winter's **c** winter
5 Everyone .... voted to go on strike. **a** current **b** present **c** actual

My Test! answers: 1b 2a 3c 4c 5b

22 Adjectives 2

My daughter said it would be pointless complaining.

To: Alfredo's Pizzeria
From: Melissa Watson
Subject: Dinner last night

Dear Sir or Madam,

My daughter celebrated her 18th birthday in your restaurant last night and I am **afraid that** I must complain about the way she and her friends were treated.

I thought it would be **nice to arrange** a surprise birthday meal for my daughter, so I reserved a table for twelve. However, when the guests arrived they were **disappointed to be** told that it was **impossible to have** everyone on the same table. They were **surprised to find** that in fact the group had to sit at three separate tables, and my daughter was particularly **upset that** two friends had to eat in a different room.

I am sure that I asked for everyone to sit together when I reserved the table, although I think it is **obvious that** friends **should want** to sit together. My daughter felt it was **not worth complaining** at the time because the waiters were **busy serving** other customers. She thought it would be **wrong of her to cause** any problems, but she felt **terrible having to tell** her friends to sit at different tables.

My daughter said it would be **pointless complaining**, but I am not **prepared to accept** this because I am **unhappy to have been treated** with so little respect. However, I am **confident that** you will apologise, in which case we may be **willing to** use your restaurant again in the future.

Sincerely,

Melissa Watson

?
1 Why did Melissa Watson write the email?
2 What does she want the manager to do?

Answers: 1 She wanted to complain about her daughter's birthday meal in a restaurant. 2 Apologise

Adjectives 2

Patterns after adjectives

1 **Adjectives can be followed by a *to*-infinitive, a gerund or a *that*-clause.**

*I am not **prepared to do** this.*
*She felt it was **not worth complaining** at the time.*
*I am **confident that** you will apologise.*

We can sometimes use *easy, good, hard, impossible* or adjectives describing feelings + *to*-infinitive in these two ways, with a similar meaning:

*It's always **interesting to talk** to Jon.* OR *Jon's always **interesting to talk** to.*
*It's very **easy to use** this printer.* OR *This printer is very **easy to use.***

We can use some adjectives with *of* + a person + *to*-infinitive, e.g. ***good, great, interesting, lovely, nice, right*** and ***wrong.***

*It would be **wrong of me to cause** any problems.*

In formal situations, we sometimes use *should* in a *that*-clause after adjectives.

*It is **obvious that** friends **should want** to sit together.*

We can leave out *that* in a *that*-clause after adjectives.

*I am **confident** you will apologise.* OR *I am **confident that** you will apologise.*

Adjectives that follow only one pattern

2 The following adjectives can take a *to*-infinitive only: ***(un)able, due, free, prepared, ready, welcome*** and ***willing.***

*I may be **willing to eat** in your restaurant again.*

3 The following adjectives can take a gerund only: ***busy, no good*** or (***not***) ***worth.***

*All the waiters were **busy serving** other customers.*

4 The following adjectives can take a *that*-clause only: ***aware, clear, confident, hopeful, obvious*** and ***positive.***

*It is **clear that** we need to find a better solution.*

Adjectives that follow more than one pattern

5 Some adjectives can take a gerund or a *to*-infinitive after *It*, e.g. ***dangerous, easy, hard, hopeless, pointless*** and ***useless.***

*It would be **pointless complaining**.* OR *It would be **pointless to complain**.*

6 The following adjectives can take a *to*-infinitive and a *that*-clause: ***afraid, angry, annoyed, ashamed, disappointed, glad, pleased, (im)possible, shocked, sorry, sure, surprised*** and ***upset.***

*I was **disappointed to be** told ...* OR *I was **disappointed that** we couldn't ...*

TIP

We say *I'm sure* (*that*), not ~~*It's sure (that)*~~.

***I am sure that** I asked for everyone to sit together.* NOT ~~*It's sure that I asked ...*~~

TIP

When we say *sure* + *to*-infinitive, it is the speaker who is sure, not the subject of the sentence.

***She** is sure to be disappointed.* (= I am sure that she will be disappointed.)

The subject of a *that*-clause can be different from the subject of the main clause.

*She was particularly **upset that** two friends had to eat in a different room.*

TIP

The meaning of *afraid* (*that*) is different from the meaning of *afraid to.*

*I am **afraid** (**that**) I would like to complain.* (= I am sorry.)

*I am **afraid to** walk home on my own.* (= I am scared.)

7 The following adjectives can take a gerund or a *that*-clause after *feel*: ***awful, awkward, bad, (un)comfortable, good, guilty*** and ***terrible.***

*She **felt terrible having** to tell ...* OR *She **felt terrible that** she had to tell ...*

If the adjective is followed by a new subject, we use a *that*-clause instead of a gerund.

*I felt **guilty that you** got in trouble.*

NOT ~~*I felt guilty you getting in trouble*~~.

8 Some adjectives can take all three forms, e.g. ***(un)happy.***

*I am **unhappy to have** been treated with so little respect.* OR *... **unhappy having** been treated ... / ... **unhappy that** I was treated ...*

The following adjectives can often take all three forms after *It*: ***awful, bad, funny, good, great, helpful, interesting, lovely, nice, strange, terrible*** and ***useful.***

*It was **strange having** to move to different tables.* OR *... **strange to have** to move ...* OR *... **strange that** we had to move ...*

TIP

The adjective *funny* can have two different meanings.

*It was very **funny to watch** the cat playing.* (= It made me laugh.)

*It's **funny to think** I've only known you a few days.* (= It's strange.)

Practice

A Complete each group of sentences / sentence with one word from the box.

awful free guilty obvious surprised ~~useless~~ worth

1 It's ......useless...... to talk about it.
It's ......useless...... talking about it.

2 It was .... that we had to say goodbye.
It was .... having to say goodbye.
It was .... to have to say goodbye.

3 I'm .... that you're here.
I'm .... to see you're here.

4 She felt .... doing it.
She felt .... that she did it.

5 You're .... to leave.

6 It's .... going to find out.

7 It's .... that he's not at home.

B Circle the correct option. Sometimes both options are possible.

1 ⓐ It was nice being able
ⓑ It was nice that we were able
... to spend time together.

2 **a** I'm pleased that you can come
b I'm pleased you coming
... to my party.

3 **a** Is it safe leaving **b** Is it safe to leave
... the door open, or shall I lock it?

4 **a** Did you feel guilty to tell
b Did you feel guilty that you told
... me Susan's secret?

5 **a** It's not worth to go **b** It's not worth going
... shopping today. Most of the shops are closed.

6 The words to this song ... .
a are impossible to me to understand
b are impossible for me to understand.

7 I felt awkward ... .
a not knowing anyone at the party
b that I didn't know anyone at the party

8 **a** Tina was sure she had seen
b It was sure Tina had seen
... the man somewhere before.

9 The players are confident ... .
a to be able to win the match
b that they can win the match

C Complete the sentences with the adjectives from the box.

afraid awkward good ~~helpful~~ strange stupid sure upset willing wrong

1 It was ......helpful...... having the instructions when I built the table.

2 We were .... that you didn't invite us to your party.

3 Jack felt .... not remembering the woman's name.

4 Are you .... this is the right way?

5 Fiona is .... to think that nobody likes her – she's got lots of friends.

6 It's .... that nobody answered the door, because we could hear voices inside.

7 It was very .... of you to help me with my assignment.

8 I am .... that we have decided not to offer you the job.

9 You're .... riding a bike without a helmet – you could get hurt if you fall off.

10 Do you think Ruth would be .... to give us a lift to the train station?

D Complete each sentence b so that it means the same as sentence a. Use three to six words, including the word(s) in brackets.

1 a According to the schedule, Martin's train should arrive at 3.20. (due)
  b Martin's train ...is due to arrive... at 3.20.
2 a This year was hard, but we hope there will be an improvement in our situation next year. (hopeful)
  b This was a hard year but we're .... improve next year
3 a Don't apologise now. The damage has been done. (no good)
  b The damage has been done, so it's ....
4 a Dad was in the middle of cooking dinner when we got home. (busy)
  b When we got home, Dad ....
5 a I'm confident that my daughter will be angry. (sure)
  b My daughter ....
6 a We'll be happy if you don't want to walk and decide to come in our car. (welcome)
  b If you don't want to walk, you're .... in our car.
7 a There were two witnesses to the robbery, but they couldn't describe the thief. (unable)
  b Two people saw the robbery, but they .... the thief.
8 a Do you think it's a good idea to buy some tickets? They're €25. (worth)
  b The tickets are €25. Do you think it's .... ?
9 a Did you know it's Connie's birthday today? (aware)
  b .... Connie's birthday today?
10 a It was lovely that you sent me a card. (send)
  b It was lovely .... me a card.

E Complete each sentence in an appropriate way.

1 When he woke up, Karl was surprised ...to find it had snowed during the night... .
2 It was obvious to Chris's parents ....
3 Henry felt Judy had been rude ....
4 Cristina and her friends were glad ....
5 Michaela can't come out because she's busy ....
6 The girls felt guilty ....
7 Veronika's friends thought she was mad ....
8 It was nearly 8 o'clock before Alessandra was ready ....
9 Tonya's neighbours were annoyed ....
10 Ellie finally decided it wasn't worth ....

MY TURN!

Think of something you bought or a service you received, which you were not happy with. In your notebook, write a short email complaining about it, including at least six adjectives from the unit.

MY TEST!

Circle the correct option.

1 It was lovely .... you to invite me to your birthday meal. a for b of c to
2 I'm really pleased you .... your money back. a got b to get c to have got
3 It's no good .... to the restaurant now – it'll be closed. a go b to go c going
4 .... sure I told you to meet me at 5, not 5.30. a It's b I'm c That's
5 We felt awful .... about our party. a that Karen didn't know b Karen not knowing c not having known

My Test! answers: 1b 2a 3c 4b 5a

23 Adjectives 3

One of the most modern campuses in the world

Science City is a campus of ETH Zurich, a university in Switzerland. It is **one of the most modern** campuses in the world, a place which has been moving **closer and closer** towards achieving sustainability since it opened in 2003. Its energy-generating system is **so effective** that Science City does not use any fossil fuels, so it gives out **much smaller** quantities of CO_2 than similar, but **less advanced**, institutions.

Science City was constructed **in such a way** that it operates with **the greatest possible** energy efficiency and **the lowest possible** use of resources. The Information Science building, for example, has a low proportion of outside walls so heat energy is **less likely** to be wasted.

And Science City is trying to be **even kinder** to the environment. The university recognises that **the higher** the number of overseas trips made by its staff, **the greater** its 'carbon footprint', so it is investing in **the latest** communication technology, making it **easier** to do business with other countries without travelling and contributing to air pollution. And **just as important** an advantage of investing in communication technology is the need to use less paper. By using recycled paper and encouraging staff not to print documents, Science City is **as far** along the road to becoming a 'paperless institution' **as** anywhere in the world.

1 What, and where, is Science City?
2 Find one way that Science City tries to avoid damaging the environment.

Answers: 1 One of the most modern university campuses in the world, in Zurich, Switzerland.
2 Uses no fossil fuels; has low proportion of outside walls; invests in latest communication technology; less travel abroad; uses recycled / less paper.

Adjectives 3

Comparative and superlative adjectives

1 We usually make the comparatives / superlatives of one-syllable adjectives with *-er* / (*the*) *-est*.

great → *greater* → *the greatest*
high → *higher* → *the highest*

We use *more* / (*the*) *most* before a few one-syllable adjectives, e.g. *right, wrong, real,* and one-syllable participle adjectives like *bored* or *loved.*

Yes – you couldn't be ***more right.***
She is ***the most loved*** *singer in the world.*

TIP

We can add *-er* / *-est* to the first adjective in compound adjectives.

hard*-working* → ***harder****-working* → ***hardest****-working*

2 We usually make the comparative / superlative of two-syllable adjectives with *more* / (*the*) *most*.
afraid → ***more afraid* / *the most afraid***

We make the comparative / superlative of some two-syllable adjectives with *-er* / (*the*) *-est*, e.g. ***happy, funny, narrow***.

We can either add *-er* / (*the*) *-est* or put *more* / (*the*) *most* before some two-syllable adjectives, e.g. ***likely, clever, friendly, simple, stupid*** and ***quiet***.

3 We make the comparative / superlative of adjectives of three syllables or more with *more* / (*the*) *most*.
incredible → ***more incredible* / *the most incredible***

4 The comparatives / superlatives of ***good, bad, far, ill*** and ***well*** are irregular.
good / well → ***better* / *the best***
bad / ill → ***worse* / *the worst***
far → ***further* / *the furthest***

When we use *far* to refer to distance, we can also use *farther / the farthest*, although *further / the furthest* is more common.

5 We can use *less* / (*the*) *least* with all gradable adjectives.
It's ***less cold*** *today than it was yesterday.*
Heat energy is ***less likely*** *to be wasted.*

6 After verbs like ***be, seem, feel, become*** or ***appear***, we can use a *to*-infinitive after a comparative / superlative adjective, sometimes as part of a noun phrase.
This machine seems ***more difficult to use***.
This is ***the best place to have breakfast***.

7 We usually use *the* + superlative adjective + *of* before plural nouns and *the* + superlative adjective + *in* / *on* before singular nouns.
This is ***the most dangerous of*** *sharks.*
Chelly's is ***the cheapest restaurant in*** *town.*

8 We don't use *the* with superlative adjectives after possessive forms.
This is ***McEwan's most interesting*** *book.*
NOT ~~*... McEwan's the most interesting ...*~~

TIP

We can leave out *the* in informal situations when the adjective doesn't have a noun next to it.
You can get there in various ways, but going by train is ***easiest***. OR *... is* ***the easiest***.

9 We use two comparatives with *the*, if one change causes another.
The higher *the number of trips made by its staff,* ***the greater*** *its 'carbon footprint'.*

We can use the same structure with *more* on its own, or with nouns and adverbs.
The more *you spend,* ***the less money*** *you will save.*

10 With verbs of change we can add emphasis using two comparatives joined by *and*.
Science City has been moving ***closer and closer*** *towards its aim.*

Modifying comparative and superlative adjectives

11 We use ***much, even, far, a lot, rather*** and (informal) ***miles / loads*** before comparatives.
It emits ***much smaller*** *quantities of carbon dioxide.*

12 We use ***probably, one of, easily, far and away*** and ***by far*** before superlatives.
Science City is ***one of the most modern*** *campuses.*

13 We use *as* + adjective + *as* to show equal levels of something.
... ***as far*** *along the road* ***as*** *anywhere else.*

If there is a noun, we insert *a* / *an* after the adjective.
... as important an advantage ...

We can use ***about, almost, just*** and ***nearly*** before *as*.
Travelling by bus in my country is ***almost as expensive as*** *travelling by train.*

We can use *not as* / *so ...* + adjective + *as* to mean *less* + adjective + *than*.
This painting's ***not as valuable as*** *the others.*

We can often use *not such a* / *an* + adjective + noun, instead of *not as* + adjective + *a* / *an* + noun, with a similar meaning.
*It was****n't such a bad idea*** *as it seemed at first.* OR *It was****n't as bad an idea as ...***

14 We can also express comparison by using (*not*) *too* + adjective (+ *to*-infinitive) and (*not*) adjective + *enough* (+ *to*-infinitive).
The letters are ***too small to read***. OR *... are****n't big enough to read***.

If there is a new subject after *too* / *enough*, we use *for* + subject between the adjective and the *to*-infinitive.
His English is ***good enough for him to pass*** *the exam.*

Practice

A Write the adjectives under the correct headings. Try to do this without looking at pages 98 and 99, then check your answers.

afraid bad bored clever funny ~~great~~ ill low right simple stupid well

-er / (the) -est	more / (the) most	-er / (the) -est *or* more / (the) most	irregular
great			

B Complete the sentences, using the comparative or superlative forms of the words in brackets.

1 China and India have ......the highest...... populations in the world by far. (high)
2 Paris and Barcelona are among .... European cities. (visited)
3 The USA is a little .... in area than China. (big)
4 Russia is far .... than any other country in the world. (large)
5 Mexico City is one of .... cities in the world. (busy)
6 Asia contains far and away .... cities on Earth. (fast-growing)
7 The Pitcairn Islands have by far .... capital in the world. (small)

The capital of the Pitcairn Islands

8 Mongolia has quite a lot .... people per km² than any other country. (few)
9 Monaco is easily .... country. (crowded)
10 Tokyo is .... city in the world to live in. (expensive)

C Complete each sentence b so that it means the same as sentence a, using no more than five words including the word in brackets.

1 a Penny's cat is much younger than ours. (not)
  b Our cat is ......not as young as...... Penny's.
2 a Despite the weather forecast, it wasn't such a bad day. (as)
  b It wasn't .... the weather forecast had predicted.
3 a These onions are sufficiently soft now, so you can add the rice. (enough)
  b These onions are now .... to add the rice.
4 a Often, if you try to do something more quickly, you end up taking more time to do it. (longer)
  b Often, the more quickly you try to do something, ... to do it.
5 a The least expensive time to visit the city is in winter, which is the quiet season. (cheapest)
  b Visiting the city .... , which is the quiet season.
6 a Cristoph is no more likely to get the job than Marina. (as)
  b Marina .... Cristoph is to get the job.
7 a This box weighs so much that it's just impossible to pick it up. (too)
  b This box is just ....
8 a Some people say university courses are less difficult now than they were in the past. (so)
  b Some people say university courses .... they used to be.
9 a *Guernica* is probably the Picasso painting which people have heard of most. (famous)
  b Picasso's .... *Guernica*.
10 a Many snakes are poisonous, but sea snakes are more poisonous than any others. (most)
  b Sea snakes .... all snakes.

D Complete the sentences, using comparative expressions made from the words in brackets.

1 *The more money* people have, *the less satisfied* they often are. (money / satisfied)
2 .... I get, ... the years seem to pass by. (old / fast)
3 .... you have to do something, ... it takes you to do it. (time / long)
4 .... you go to bed, ... you will feel in the morning. (late / refreshed)
5 .... he eats, ... he will be. (fast food / healthy)
6 .... you do before an exam, ... the chance of passing it. (preparation / great)
7 .... people do, ... they tend to become. (travelling / open-minded)
8 Some people think that .... children are when they start to learn a second language, ... they will find it. (young / easy)
9 .... you have to travel to work, ... you should set off in the morning. (far / early)
10 .... you eat now, ... you'll be at dinner time. (biscuits / hungry)

E Complete the sentences, using appropriate comparative or superlative forms.

1 Computers were by far *the most useful invention of the last century*.
2 The moon is not as ....
3 This year we didn't have such ....
4 Maths and Science are far and away ....
5 Tomorrow will be one of ....
6 This soup is much too ....
7 Doing exercise is as ....
8 In 20 years' time, the world will be far .... than ....
9 Travelling by public transport is ....
10 The more work you do now, ...

MY TURN!

Write three or four sentences to answer each question, using different comparative or superlative forms from the unit.

How is your life now different from five years ago?

....

How would you like your life to be different five years from now?

....

MY TEST!

Circle the correct option.

1 By the time I finally went to bed I think I was .... tired I have ever been. a the more b most c the most
2 Science City is one of Europe's .... campuses. a the most famous b the more famous c most famous
3 The more you read in English, ... your vocabulary will become. a better b the better c the best
4 The amount of electricity used by Science City is .... high as in many other universities. a nothing like b nothing as c nothing like as
5 It was too far .... all the way in one day, so we stayed in a hotel overnight. a to drive b to driving c for driving

My Test! answers: 1c 2c 3b 4c 5a

24 Adverbs

Fortunately, however, it keeps missing.

Why doesn't the moon **just** fall and crash into the Earth? **Actually**, it may come as a surprise to you that it is falling **constantly**. **Fortunately** for everyone on Earth, **however**, it keeps missing.

Imagine standing right at the top of an **extremely** high mountain and shooting an arrow as **far** as you **possibly** can. **Initially** the arrow will fly **horizontally** away from you, but it will **soon** start to curve **downwards** due to the effects of gravity. But because you're on a mountain, it won't hit the ground **immediately** because the land is **also** curving **downwards**. **Eventually**, **however**, the arrow will be falling more **steeply** than the side of the mountain and, **finally**, it will hit the ground.

Now, remember that the Earth itself is curved. **Theoretically**, an incredibly strong person could shoot the arrow **so far** that the downward curve of the arrow would be **exactly** the same as the curve of the Earth and, **amazingly**, the arrow would then keep falling **forever** and **never actually** hit the ground. **Unfortunately**, of course, this experiment would **obviously never really** work because the air would **very quickly** slow the arrow **down**. **However**, in space, there is **absolutely** no air to slow the moon **down**, so it **just** keeps moving **forwards** **indefinitely**.

And **basically**, that is why the moon doesn't fall and crash into the Earth.

1 Why does an arrow start to curve downwards soon after you shoot it?
2 Why does the moon never slow down?

Answers: 1 Because of the effects of gravity. 2 Because there is no air.

Adverbs

Form of adverbs

1 **We form many adverbs by adding *-ly* to an adjective.**
gradual → gradually, absolute → absolutely

Adjectives ending in *-ic* become adverbs ending in *-ically*.
basic → basically, scientific → scientifically

Adjectives ending in *-le* become adverbs ending in *-ly*.
incredible → incredibly, simple → simply

Some adverbs are irregular.
good → well, whole → wholly

Some adjectives don't change when they become adverbs.
far, hard, fast, late, early

Adjectives ending in *-ly* can't become adverbs. Use *in a ... way* instead, e.g. *in a friendly way, in a silly way*.

TIP

***Hardly* and *lately* aren't the same as *hard* and *late*. *Hardly* means 'almost not'. *Lately* means 'recently'.**

*I've **hardly** seen you **lately**. Where have you been?*

2 Many common adverbs are not formed from adjectives, e.g. ***just, soon.*** We can also use many prepositions as adverbs, e.g. ***up, down*** and ***around.***

*Why doesn't the moon **just** fall **down**?*

Adverbs ending in *-ward(s)* describe directions, e.g. ***downward(s), forward(s), onward(s), upward(s), backward(s), outward(s), inward(s).***

*It keeps moving **forwards / forward**.*

We can make adjectives ending in *-ward.*

*The **downward** curve of the arrow*

Position of adverbs

3 An adverb can come at the beginning, middle or end of the sentence. If it comes at the beginning, there is usually a comma after it.

***Apparently**, the Earth looks beautiful from the moon.*

TIP

Don't put adverbs between verbs and objects.

*It won't hit the ground **immediately**.*

NOT ~~*It won't hit immediately the ground.*~~

If an adverb comes in the middle, we put it before the main verb, or after *be* or the first auxiliary verb. Adverbs in the middle or at the end of the sentence may or may not take commas.

*That is **basically** how the moon stays up.*

OR *That is, **basically,** how the moon stays up.*

*It will soon start to curve **downwards**.*

*This is the reason, **apparently**.*

In negative sentences, middle-position adverbs usually come before negative auxiliaries like ***don't.***

*I **probably won't** understand anything.*

Sometimes both positions are possible, but with a change of meaning.

*I **really** don't like astronomy.* (= I strongly dislike it.)

*I don't **really** like astronomy.* (= I don't like it very much.)

Use of adverbs

4 Adverbs of manner describe the way something happens. They usually come at the end.

*The arrow will fall **horizontally**.*

5 Most adverbs of frequency can come at the beginning, middle or end.

*I take the bus to work **occasionally**.*

OR ***Occasionally**, I take the bus ...* OR *I **occasionally** take the bus ...*

6 Adverbs of place and movement usually come at the end. Most adverbs of time can come at the beginning or end.

*How does the moon stay **up**?* (place)

*It keeps moving **forwards**.* (movement)

*I'm going to try the experiment **tomorrow**.*

OR ***Tomorrow**, I'm going to ...* (time)

7 Most adverbs of degree, e.g. ***very, quite, absolutely, extremely, roughly, approximately, so*** and ***too,*** come before the adjectives, quantifiers and other adverbs that they describe.

*... could shoot the arrow **so** far that ...*

*... there is **absolutely** no air.*

The adverb *enough* comes after adjectives or adverbs.

*You couldn't shoot the arrow far **enough**.*

NOT ~~*... enough far*~~.

We can use the adverb *right* before a preposition. It means *absolutely.*

*Imagine standing **right** at the top of a mountain.*

8 Some adverbs describe a whole sentence. Whole-sentence adverbs include:

actually	*generally*	*meanwhile*
apparently	*honestly*	*obviously*
basically	*hopefully*	*therefore*
eventually	*however*	*(un)fortunately*

Whole-sentence adverbs normally come at the beginning of the sentence, usually followed by a comma. Other positions are also possible.

***Apparently**, there's going to be a full moon tonight.*

OR *There's going to be a full moon tonight, **apparently**.*

OR *There's **apparently** going to be a full moon tonight.*

Maybe and ***perhaps*** usually come at the beginning without a comma. ***Probably, certainly, definitely*** and ***possibly*** usually come in the middle without commas.

***Maybe** we could go to the cinema tonight.*

NOT ~~*Maybe, we could go ...*~~

*John will **definitely** be coming with us.*

NOT ~~*John will, definitely, be coming with us.*~~

Don't use *though* at the beginning of a sentence.

*I'm afraid I can't come. Thanks for inviting me, **though**.* NOT ~~*Though, thanks for inviting me.*~~

9 We use adverbs such as ***well, now*** and ***anyway*** to start a new point or finish a topic or conversation. They usually come at the beginning of a sentence.

***Now**, remember that the Earth itself is curved.*

Practice

A Match the pairs.

1 I've been working late a lot. — a I'm trying to save some money.
2 I've been working a lot lately. — b That's why I usually don't get up early.

3 I asked him to leave quietly. — a But he was really noisy.
4 I asked him quietly to leave. — b I didn't shout.

5 I don't really want to go out tonight. — a Please can we stay at home?
6 I really don't want to go out tonight. — b But we can go if you want to.

7 I thought hard about my decision. — a I wanted to make sure it was the right one.
8 I hardly thought about my decision. — b I was too busy thinking about other things.

9 She didn't just sing well. — a So the concert wasn't very good.
10 She just didn't sing well. — b She also played the piano beautifully.

B Rewrite the sentences, changing the <u>underlined</u> nouns and adjectives into verbs and adverbs.

1 She's a <u>wonderful singer</u>.
She sings wonderfully.

2 His <u>driving</u> is very <u>dangerous</u>.

3 His <u>entrance</u> into the room was <u>dramatic</u>.

4 She always does a <u>silly dance</u>.

5 Her <u>performance</u> of the song was very <u>good</u>.

6 She's a very <u>fast swimmer</u>.

7 Please be <u>careful</u> with your <u>writing</u>.

8 Her <u>offer</u> to let us stay was <u>kind</u>.

9 He gave the door a <u>gentle push</u>.

10 I had a <u>deep sleep</u>.

C Put the adverbs from the brackets in the correct places, using the order given. Sometimes more than one place is possible.

1 Please speak *slowly* and *clearly* so they can hear you *properly*. (slowly, clearly, properly)

2 I'll sleep tonight because I've been training. (probably, well, very, hard)

3 It's important to prepare before doing yoga. (apparently, incredibly, carefully)

4 The arrow flies, and then curves until it is falling. (horizontally, gradually, downwards, vertically)

5 She threw the ball. (accidentally, too, far)

6 How can you say the alphabet? (fast, backwards)

7 She treats her children but she doesn't buy them presents. (kindly, often)

8 He fired the arrow that it flew over the target

and landed in a field.
(so, hard, right, eventually)

D **Complete the text with the adverbs from the box.**

Alternatively enough eventually Finally ~~Firstly~~ gradually However Moreover Similarly well

There are four main theories to explain where the moon came from. 1 Firstly, there is a theory that it was part of our Earth which was thrown into space because the Earth was spinning so fast. 2 ...., scientists believe the Earth has never spun fast 3 .... for this to happen. 4 ...., this theory does not properly explain the moon's current patterns of movement.

5 ...., perhaps the moon started life somewhere else in the universe and 6 .... came closer to our Earth before 7 .... becoming part of a two-body system. Scientists have calculated, however, that this almost certainly didn't happen.

8 ...., the theory that the Earth and moon were formed simultaneously is also not widely believed.

9 ...., there is the theory that the Earth was hit violently by a body as large as Mars. This seems to fit scientists' calculations 10 ...., although many questions remain.

E **Make this story more interesting by adding at least ten adverbs.**

The other evening, I was sitting at home, quietly reading my book. I heard a strange noise outside. It sounded like someone was screaming in the back garden. I opened the door and looked outside. The person was screaming, but I couldn't see who it was because it was dark. I walked out into the garden towards the trees at the back. The noise was becoming quieter and quieter. It stopped. All I could hear was a person whispering. I saw a movement on the ground by my feet and looked. There was a cat running towards my house. I felt relieved – it was only a couple of cats fighting. But I turned round and saw a bear ... it was looking at me.

MY TURN!

Write at least three possible adverbs to complete each sentence. Don't write the same adverb more than once. You can use a dictionary.

1 She laughed .... when I told her my joke.
politely, nervously, in a silly way, quietly, sarcastically

2 I hated astronomy at first, but I'm .... starting to like it.

3 A: Where's Karen? B: ...., she's gone home.

4 I don't know what presents I'm going to get for my birthday. .... I'll get a new bike!

5 The helicopter can fly ....

MY TEST!

Circle the correct option.

1 She always arrives .... – she's never on time. a lately b late c finally
2 He .... a played his guitar quietly b played quietly his guitar c played his quietly guitar
3 It'll be a long time before people live on the moon, but I'm sure it'll happen ....
a occasionally b apparently c eventually
4 In rugby, ...
a forwards you can't throw the ball b you can't throw forwards the ball c you can't throw the ball forwards
5 We don't know how our planet caught its moon. We do, ..., know how it kept hold of it.
a however b similarly c moreover

My Test! answers: 1b 2a 3c 4c 5a

R3 Review: prepositions; adjectives; adverbs

A **Underline the correct option.**

The Bronte sisters, Charlotte, Emily and Anne, wrote some of the best-loved novels [1]*for / by / in* the English language. Charlotte, who wrote *Jane Eyre,* and Emily, the author of *Wuthering Heights,* in particular, are regarded as [2]*between / among / in* the world's greatest novelists. [3]*As well as / In terms of / In front of* novels, they also wrote some outstanding poetry. Although the Brontes lived [4]*above / beyond / over* 150 years ago, their writing still seems fresh and exciting today. *Jane Eyre,* for example, is a powerful, romantic story with the main character being an independent, intelligent young woman. [5]*In terms of / According to / Out of* the themes it deals with, the novel is considered to be [6]*apart from / against / ahead of* its time. *Wuthering Heights,* Emily Bronte's only novel, is dark and tragic, and is [7]*despite / unlike / except* anything else that was written at the time. [8]*Like / With / As* most authors, the Bronte sisters used their own experiences, the landscapes and people [9]*among / around / upon* them as materials for their books. They lived together in their father's house in a remote village in the north of England [10]*until / to / by* their deaths. [11]*As / Like / From* children, they were only able to attend school [12]*throughout / over / for* a few years but they read many books at home, and [13]*over / during / among* their childhood wrote stories for each other about an imaginary world. When they first published their novels, the three sisters used men's names. This was [14]*due to / next to / according to* the fact that in those days writing books was not seen as a suitable thing for women to do. Things are very different today, of course.

B **Complete the sentences with the correct prepositions.**

1 Barry's teacher is satisfied ......*with*...... his progress in English, but he has plenty of room ......*for*...... improvement in Maths.
2 I was .... the impression that the beach would be packed .... holidaymakers, but I was wrong.
3 The government is faced .... a large increase .... the number of people wanting to go to university.
4 The kitchen was .... a terrible mess – it wasn't fair .... you to expect Jill to sort it all out.
5 I'm not aware .... any problems with taking food onto the plane, but perhaps we should check this .... advance with the airline.
6 People in this region are known .... their hospitality and their fondness .... good food.
7 Anisha takes great pride .... her work, which is why she got so upset .... the mistake she made.
8 This website should be safe .... any security threats, ... the time being at least.

C **Complete the questions by putting the words in the correct order. Then match the questions to the correct replies.**

1 for / charging / they / are / this / much
How *much are they charging for this?*
2 you / of / remind / she / does
Who ....?
3 being / of / accused / is / she
What ....?
4 taste / that / like / does / sauce
What ....?
5 as / did / you / surprise / to / a / it / come
Why ....
....?
6 of / choice / approve / my / you / don't / of / film
Why ....
....?
7 we / this / put / can / to / stop / a
How ....
....?
8 you / book / to / were / referring
Which ....
....?

a It's quite salty, actually.
b I just hadn't expected it.
c I've seen it before and it's awful.
d *Wuthering Heights.*
e Oh, it's quite cheap.
f By introducing stricter rules.
g Stealing from her employers.
h A company in Turkey.
i Your sister.
j Several weeks, I think.

1 ...*e*... 2 .... 3 .... 4 ....
5 .... 6 .... 7 .... 8 ....

D Circle the correct option.

I'm writing from the Iguazu Waterfalls, one of the most [1]… places I've ever been to. The waterfalls, which are right on the border between Argentina and Brazil, are [2]… beautiful and absolutely [3]… . Apparently, they are [4]… similar in size to the Victoria Falls in Africa but what's great about Iguazu is how close you can get to the water at the top of the falls and also at the [5]… bottom. Yesterday, I joined a boat trip to the foot of the falls and we actually went behind the falling water. It was quite [6]… and we got [7]… wet, of course, but I loved it. The day before, I was at the top of the falls, the place they call the Devil's Throat, and I was utterly [8]… by the noise and the [9]… volume of water that pours down. I've enjoyed myself the [10]… time I've been here actually. My hotel is [11]… fantastic. It's cheap and has a restaurant which serves very [12]… local dishes. To get to the falls, I've been taking the [13]… modern bus which has a [14]… young guide on board who can answer any questions you might have. Unfortunately, I have to fly home tomorrow but it's been a very enjoyable holiday.

1 a fascinated (b) amazing c incredibly
2 a too b sheer c extremely
3 a enormous b big c large
4 a utterly b very c completely
5 a very b really c quite
6 a afraid b scary c frightened
7 a freezing b boiling c soaking
8 a stunned b interested c excited
9 a mere b sheer c dead
10 a main b all c whole
11 a absolutely b fairly c virtually
12 a unique b tasty c delicious
13 a hotel b comfortable c tourist
14 a friendly b Brazilian c blond

E Match the pairs.

1 We're positive
2 We're prepared to work hard
a to find a solution.
b that we can solve this problem.

3 It's worth
4 It was nice of you
a waiting a bit longer.
b to wait for us.

5 It would be great
6 I'm hopeful
a that I'll see her again soon.
b to see you again soon.

7 I'm ashamed
8 I feel awful
a to say I can't remember her name.
b having to say that I don't know.

9 They're sure
10 They're busy
a looking for work.
b to find jobs.

11 It's obvious
12 It's hard
a we need more help.
b to find anyone who'll help.

13 I'm free
14 I felt uncomfortable
a to go and see him at the weekend.
b going at that time of the day.

15 Ali is willing
16 It's no good
a just doing what Monica says all the time.
b to do what Charmaine has suggested.

17 I'm confident
18 We would be mad
a that we'll reach an agreement.
b to agree to their proposal.

19 It was wrong of me
20 I was aware
a that there was a problem.
b to blame Lily for what happened.

F Complete each sentence by adding TWO of the adverbs in brackets in the correct places.

1 *Apparently* that book is *extremely* difficult to find. (though / ~~extremely~~ / ~~apparently~~ / tomorrow)
2 We .... saw the lake and it was .... wonderful. (however / eventually / hopefully / absolutely)
3 We were .... tired that we fell asleep almost .... (so / quite / therefore / immediately)
4 It's .... not good .... (enough / well / just / far)
5 I can't hear you ...., ... (never / unfortunately / properly / just)
6 .... we should go out more .... (often / absolutely / far / perhaps)
7 The best thing to do, ..., is to keep going .... (hardly / enough / forward / basically)
8 I don't .... think it's possible, ... (very / really / possibly / though)
9 He wasn't .... standing .... in front of you but I'm sure he wasn't far away. (too / right / necessarily / probably)

25 Phrasal verbs

We picked up our things and started walking off.

Mum: What'**s up**, Anna?

Anna: Oh, nothing really. It's just everyone seems to be getting at me these days. For example, I got **told off** today and it wasn't my fault.

Mum: What **were** you **up to**?

Anna: We were just **messing around** outside the shop, **kicking** a football **around**. And then the fire alarm **went off**. We **carried on** playing for a few minutes, then we **picked up** our things and started **walking off**.

Mum: **Go on** ...

Anna: Well, the shopkeeper **came up to** us and started shouting. I couldn't **make out** what she **was going on about**, then I **figured out** she thought we'd **set off** the alarm. The thing is, her son had been watching us.

Mum: And didn't he **back** you **up**?

Anna: No, he just **ran off**. And I **ended up** having to promise to go back on Friday night and tidy her shop for her. I'm a bit fed up about it, to be honest.

Mum: OK, **calm down**. I'll **go round** and speak to her. Maybe I can **talk** her **round**. But if it **turns out** that you've been lying to me, I won't be happy!

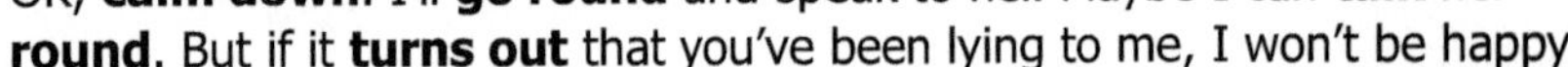

? 1 Why was the shopkeeper angry?
2 What is Anna's mum going to do?

Answers: 1 She thought Anna and her friends had set off the fire alarm.
2 Go round and speak to the shopkeeper.

Phrasal verbs

1 We form phrasal verbs from a verb and a short adverb like *in, up* or *around.*

*We were just **messing around.*** (= playing and having fun)

Some phrasal verbs can have an object.

*Didn't he **back** you **up**?* (= support you)

When the object is a pronoun, put it before the adverb.

*Maybe I'll be able to **talk** her **round**.*

NOT ~~... *talk round her.*~~

When the object is a noun or noun phrase, put it before or after the adverb.

*We **picked up** our things.* OR *We **picked** our things **up**.*

TIP

When the object is a long noun phrase, we usually put it after the adverb.

*We **picked up** our football, our bags and the coats we had with us in case it started raining.*
NOT ~~*We picked our football, our bags and the coats … started raining up*~~.

There is a difference between phrasal verbs and prepositional verbs. Unlike phrasal verbs, prepositional verbs are *always* followed by a noun or pronoun, which always comes *after* the preposition.

*The plane **took off**.*
*The shopkeeper **shouted at** them / the children.* (prepositional verb)
NOT ~~*The shopkeeper shouted the children at*~~ / ~~*… shouted them at*~~.
*The shopkeeper **told off** the children.* (phrasal verb)
OR *The shopkeeper **told** the children **off**. / … **told** them **off**.*

TIP

When you learn a new phrasal verb or prepositional verb, always learn the position of the pronoun object, e.g. *tell him off, shout at me.*

▶ See Unit 20 for more on prepositional verbs.

2 **We form many phrasal verbs simply by adding adverbs like *away, down* or *around* to verbs of action or movement, e.g. *go away, sit down* and *walk around.* Their meaning is clear from the meanings of the verb and adverb.**

*We were **kicking** the ball **around**.* (= from person to person)

3 **The meaning of many other phrasal verbs is not clear from the meanings of the verb and adverb, so we have to learn the phrasal verb separately.**

Common examples which normally have an object are:

back up	*let down*	*set up*
carry out	*make up*	*sort out*
give up	*pick up*	*take over*
give back	*put off*	*tell off*

Common examples which normally don't have an object are:

break down	*go ahead*	*shut up*
calm down	*go off*	*sit down*
come on	*hurry up*	*slow down*
get up	*mess around*	*wake up*

We can sometimes use objects with phrasal verbs that normally don't have an object.

*Please **wake up**! / The alarm **woke** me **up**.*

4 **Some phrasal verbs also have a preposition (and an object at the end).**

back out of	*get on with*	*look forward to*
blend in with	*go along with*	*look up to*
break up with	*go on about*	*put up with*
come up with	*live up to*	*run out of*
get away with	*look down on*	

*The film didn't **live up to** my expectations.* (= It wasn't as good as I expected.)

5 **Some phrasal verbs are followed by a *that*-clause or question clause (the clause always comes after the adverb), e.g. *find out, make out, work out, figure out, point out* and *turn out.***

*I couldn't **make out** <u>what she was going on about</u>.*

The phrasal verbs *end up, keep on* and *carry on* are usually followed by an *-ing* clause.

*We **carried on** playing for a few minutes.*
(= We continued playing for a few minutes.)

▶ See Unit 26 for *go on* + *-ing* and *go on* + *to*-infinitive.
▶ See page 203 for lists of verb patterns.

6 **Some common phrasal verbs with the verb *be* include:**

be in / out	*I thought she'd **be in** when I phoned, but she **was out**.*
be up	*What's **up**?* (= What's the matter?)
be off	***I'm off**.* (= I'm leaving.) OR *This milk's **off**.* (= It's not fresh.)
be on about	*… what she **was on about*** (= what she was talking about)
be up to	*What **are** you **up to**?* (= What are you doing?) OR *It's **up to** you what you wear.* (= It's your decision.)
be down to	*I've had a lovely day and it's all **down to** you.* (= You were the cause.)

7 **Many phrasal verbs have several different meanings. Note the difference:**

*The bomb **went off**.* (= exploded)
*The fire alarm **went off**.* (= started ringing)

*Can you **pick up** your bag?* (= lift it from the floor)
*I **picked up** English by watching TV.* (= learnt without studying)
*I'll **pick** you **up** from the airport.* (= collect you in my car)

Many phrasal verbs are informal. There is often a single word that you can use instead in more formal English, e.g. *let down* (= *disappoint*), *back up* (= *support*).

▶ See Units 44 and 45 for formal and informal English.

Practice

A Match the underlined phrasal verbs in sentences 1–10 to the more formal words a–j.

1 I'll try to talk her round.
2 Can you sort out this problem?
3 Don't put off making a decision.
4 I love to make up short stories.
5 Could you set up a meeting?
6 I really look up to my Uncle George.
7 How do you put up with that terrible noise all the time?
8 I need to work out how much money I'll need.
9 Please don't let me down again.
10 Please carry on writing until I tell you to stop.

a respect, admire
b postpone, delay
c organise
d solve, tidy
e tolerate
f calculate
g disappoint
h persuade
i continue
j invent, create

1 ...h... 2 ...... 3 ...... 4 ...... 5 ......

6 ...... 7 ...... 8 ...... 9 ...... 10 ......

B Decide on the best place to put the adverb, A or B. If both are possible, write A/B.

1 We were going to go out, but we ended [A] staying at home and watching a film [B]. (up)
...A...

2 You shouldn't let her get away [A] being so rude to you [B]. (with)
......

3 I want to find [A] who took my bike [B]. (out)
......

4 My files are in a terrible mess. Could you help me sort [A] them [B]? (out)
......

5 Do you think he'll carry [A] his promise to buy her a new car [B]? (out)
......

6 I'm really sorry for letting [A] you all [B]. (down)
......

7 Paul really looks down [A] me [B]. He thinks he's something special! (on)
......

8 I'm very busy so I had to put [A] the meeting I had arranged with our American suppliers [B]. (off)
......

9 We're having a barbecue tonight – can you help me to set [A] it [B]? (up)
......

10 You shouldn't believe her. She's always making [A] stories [B]. (up)
......

C Match the sentence beginnings to the correct endings.

1 We should stop talking and get [h]
2 If you like, I'll pick [ ]
3 She promised to help, but then she backed [ ]
4 When I told the truth, I came [ ]
5 I don't mind where we go. I'll go [ ]
6 I need to come [ ]
7 We thought it'd be a great match, but it didn't really live [ ]
8 He spent all his money on a new car and ended [ ]
9 When you go bird-watching, try to blend [ ]
10 I thought my story was terrible, but it turned [ ]

a out of it when she saw how much work there was.
b along with whatever everyone else wants.
c up to our expectations.
d up with nothing left to buy clothes.
e you up from the party.
f out that everyone else liked it.
g up with a great title for my story. Any suggestions?
h on with some work.
i in with the trees by wearing brown or green clothes.
j in for a lot of criticism from my friends, but I'm glad I did it.

D Replace the <u>underlined</u> words with the correct forms of the phrasal verbs in the box.

be down to	be off	be off	be on about	~~be out~~	be up	be up to	be up to

1 I'm afraid she ~~isn't at home~~ 's out at the moment. Can I take a message?
2 Some people think she's been lucky, but I know her success <u>is because of</u> her hard work.
3 I had to throw away those yoghurts because they <u>weren't fresh</u>.
4 She<u>'s always talking about</u> her holidays ... it's so boring!
5 Where <u>are you going</u> to? You need to stay and help us.
6 What<u>'s the matter</u> with Lucy? She looks really sad.
7 I don't mind what you bring. It<u>'s your decision</u>.
8 Here come the boys now – they look as if they've <u>been doing</u> no good.

E Complete the phrasal verb in each sentence, using one or two words.

1 You need to hurry ......up...... if you don't want to be late.
2 My cousin picked .... English while he was working in a hotel in London.
3 My auntie found a valuable old painting when she was sorting .... her cupboards.
4 She didn't get .... her parents very well, so she moved into her own flat instead.
5 I didn't plan on staying at the party for long, but I ended .... staying until midnight.
6 I really don't understand what you're going .... Start again, from the beginning.
7 She was very angry but she calmed .... when I said I was sorry.
8 I feel much healthier since I gave .... eating chocolate.
9 I'm really looking .... my holiday.
10 I ran .... money, so I had to borrow some from Jake.

MY TURN!

Check that you know the meanings of the eight verbs in the table. Then tick (✓) the boxes to show possible phrasal verbs (e.g. *run up*, *run down*, etc.). Use your imagination – they won't all be in a dictionary.

	up	down	in	out	around	off
run	✓	✓	✓	✓	✓	✓
climb						
swim						
wander						
push something						
chase someone						
kick something						
throw something						

Now choose six phrasal verbs ending with different adverbs and write sentences in your notebook.

Example: 

MY TEST!

Circle the correct option.

1 There weren't enough people for us to hold the meeting, so we had to .... **a** put off **b** put off it **c** put it off
2 We need to .... **a** come up with a plan **b** come up a plan with **c** come a plan up with
3 She kept on .... at us until we decided to go and play somewhere else. **a** to shout **b** shouting **c** shout
4 A: What time do you want us to be there? B: It's .... you. **a** on about **b** down to **c** up to
5 I thought Anna had been causing trouble, but it .... that she hadn't done anything. **a** turned out **b** pointed out **c** ended up

My Test! answers: 1c 2a 3b 4c 5a

26 Infinitives and *-ing* forms

I can't imagine being bored here!

*Artist Kate Brown has **spent** 12 months **painting**, and **thinking**, in Antarctica. Here she talks to Tim Scott about her experience.*

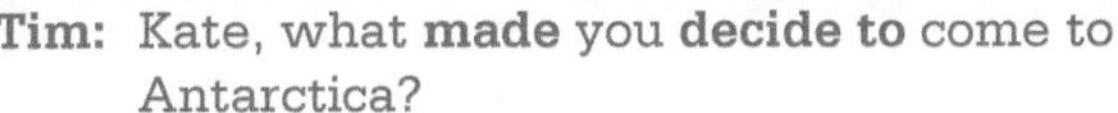

Tim: Kate, what **made** you **decide to** come to Antarctica?

Kate: I **happened to** see a photograph of Antarctica at an exhibition. I **stood staring** at it for ages, it was so beautiful. That's when I **decided to** come here to paint. I **remember** everyone **thinking** I was crazy, but that just **made** me **want to** prove I could do it.

Tim: Do you miss anything?

Kate: I certainly don't **miss working** in an office! But sometimes I **long to** go shopping. When the weather's bad, there isn't **much to** do.

Tim: Do you ever **regret coming** here?

Kate: Not now. At first, it was difficult **to get used to being** so cold. When I arrived, I **remember thinking**, how am I going to **face spending** a year like this? But I survived!

Tim: How do you **stop** yourself **getting** bored?

Kate: I can't **imagine being** bored here! I **like to** get up early and **watch** the sun **rise** – the colours are fantastic. And I **love hearing** the waves **crashing** against the cliffs.

Tim: What would you say to someone **considering visiting** Antarctica?

Kate: I'd **recommend doing** lots of research first – **try to** get an idea of what **to** expect. Also, **try spending** a week in a really cold place **to** see how you get on!

?
1 Why did Kate decide to spend a year in Antarctica?
2 What does Kate enjoy doing?

Answers: 1 She wanted to paint there. 2 Getting up early and watching the sun rise, hearing the waves crashing against the cliffs.

Infinitives and *-ing* forms

Infinitives and *-ing* forms after verbs

1 **Many verbs are followed by other verbs in the *to*-infinitive or *-ing* form.**

agree, expect, long + *to*-infinitive
allow, encourage + object + *to*-infinitive
admit, deny, imagine, keep, miss, spend time + *-ing*

Groups of verbs with similar meanings often have the same patterns. Most verbs looking forward to later events take the *to*-infinitive. Exceptions are the verbs *suggest* and *recommend*, which take *-ing*.

*That's when I **decided to come** here.*
*I **recommend doing** lots of research.*
NOT ~~*I recommend to do ...*~~

Many verbs referring to feelings, earlier events and events with no specific time take the *-ing* form. Exceptions are the verbs *fail, manage, tend* and *happen*, which take a *to*-infinitive.

*I don't **mind** not **being** able to go shopping.*
*Do you **regret coming** to Antarctica?*
*I **fail to see** what the problem is.* NOT ~~*I fail seeing ...*~~

▶ See page 203 for lists of verbs with each pattern.

2 **We also use verbs like *stand, sit* and *lie* with an *-ing* form to describe two actions happening at the same time.**

*I **stood staring** at it for ages.* (= I stood and stared at the same time.)

3 **Some verbs have two patterns with different meanings, usually a forward-looking meaning and a backward-looking meaning. These include *forget, go on, regret, remember* and *stop*.**

*I **remembered to pack** warm clothes.* (= I remembered that I should pack.)
*I **remembered packing** warm clothes.* (= I remembered that I'd packed.)

TIP

***Try** + **to**-infinitive means 'attempt'. **Try** + **-ing** means 'do as an experiment'.*

***Try to get** an idea of what to expect.*
***Try spending** a week in a really cold place.*

4 **Some verbs have two patterns but the meaning is the same, e.g. *begin, start, like* and *love*.**

*I **like to get up** early and **watch** the sun rise.* OR *I **like getting up** early and **watching** ...*

TIP

With *begin* and *start*, we usually use a *to*-infinitive after *starting* or *beginning*, and an *-ing form* after *to start* or *to finish*.

*I'm **starting to get** used to the cold.*
NOT ~~*I'm starting getting used ...*~~

5 **A few verbs can be followed by an infinitive without *to*, e.g. *make, let, have* and *help*.**

*What **made** you **decide** to come?*
*The scientists **let** me **stay** with them.*
*I'll **have** my assistant **send** you a form.* (= I'll arrange this.)

The verb *make* in the passive takes *to*.

*I **was made to fill in** lots of forms.*
NOT ~~*I was made fill in ...*~~

The verb *help* is possible with or without *to*.

*I'll **help** you **pack**.* OR *I'll **help** you **to pack**.*

6 **Verbs describing senses, e.g. *see, hear, watch, listen to* and *notice*, can be followed by an infinitive without *to* when they describe complete events and by an *-ing* form when they describe an unfinished process.**

*I **watch the sun rise**.* (from start to finish)
*As I was driving along the road, I **saw Mike washing** his car.* (a process with no finish)

Infinitives and *-ing* forms after nouns

7 **Many nouns can be followed by *to*-infinitives, especially nouns which have a forward-looking meaning.**

*Your **idea to go** to the museum was really good.*
*I don't regret my **decision to go**.*

▶ See Unit 36 for more information on *-ing* forms after nouns (shortened relative clauses).

-ing forms after prepositions

8 **We use the *-ing* form of verbs after prepositions.**

*Aren't you worried **about getting** ill?*

In the structures *be / get used to* and *look forward to*, *to* is a preposition.

*It was difficult to **get used to being** so cold.*
NOT ~~*... to get used to be ...*~~
*I'm not **looking forward to going** home again.*
NOT ~~*... looking forward to go ...*~~

Infinitives and *-ing* forms as subject of a sentence

9 **We do not normally use *to*-infinitives as the subject of a sentence; we usually use an *-ing* form or dummy *it* instead.**

***Coming** to Antarctica was always my dream.* OR ***It** was always my dream to come to ...*

▶ See Unit 15 for more information on dummy *it*.
▶ See Unit 17 for more information on *-ing* forms (gerunds).

Infinitives and *-ing* forms as a separate part of a sentence

10 **We use a *to*-infinitive to explain the purpose of something.**

*I came to Antarctica **to paint**.*

We can use a *to*-infinitive after pronouns such as *something* and *nothing*, quantifiers like *little* and *much*, and some nouns, to show that something must / can / can't be done.

*There isn't **much** (**work**) **to do**.*
*I don't have (**enough**) **time to watch** TV.*

11 **The following useful phrases use infinitives and *-ing* forms of the verb:**

not to mention
to be honest
to cut a long story short
to tell the truth
frankly speaking
considering

▶ See Unit 22 for verb patterns after adjectives.

Practice

A Complete the sentences, using the correct form of the verbs in brackets.

1 They allowed me ....*to stay}.......... . (stay)
2 I wanted .... (go) to the concert but I couldn't get a ticket.
3 These days I seem to spend hours .... (write) emails.
4 My parents always encouraged me .... (follow) my dreams.
5 I don't mind .... (be) outside in the cold, as long as it's not raining.
6 Sometimes I long .... (go) back to my old life.
7 I can't imagine not .... (be) able to use a mobile phone.
8 She keeps .... (talk) about resigning, but she never does.
9 I'm worried about .... (go) to the dentist this afternoon.
10 This film always makes me .... (laugh).

B Match the pairs.

1 I tried talking to Ruth — a but it didn't help.
2 I tried to talk to Ruth — b but she didn't answer the phone.

3 Oh no! I forgot
4 I'll never forget
a to go to that exhibition.
b going to that exhibition.

5 I regret telling you
6 I regret to tell you
a that we have lost your passport.
b my secret. I wish I hadn't.

7 After a year in Antarctica, she went on living
8 After a year in Antarctica, she went on to live
a in the Sahara for a year.
b there for another six months.

9 I stopped to have a coffee
10 I stopped having coffee for breakfast
a because I needed a break.
b about six months ago. Now I only have orange juice.

C Complete the rest of the interview with Kate Brown, using the correct form of the words in brackets.

Tim: Where do you live? I guess there aren't many flats to rent in Antarctica!
Kate: No, I live with a group of scientists. I wrote to them [1] ....*to ask*.......... (ask) if I could stay with them. Well, [2] .... (cut) a long story short, they wrote back and said they don't normally let other people [3] .... (stay) with them. But they suggested [4] .... (apply) for a job as an administrative assistant. So that's what I did.
Tim: And do they make you [5] .... (work) very hard?
Kate: Not really! I spend a lot of time [6] .... (help) them [7] .... (input) data after their experiments. I can't complain, [8] .... (consider) how much free time I have [9] .... (paint) my pictures.
Tim: That's good. One last question: are you looking forward to [10] .... (go) back home?
Kate: Not at all, [11] .... (tell) the truth. But I suppose I'll get used to [12] .... (live) there again after a few weeks.

D Make these sentences shorter and simpler, using a *to*-infinitive or an *-ing* form.

1 He told me ~~that I have to get~~ *to get* a visa.
2 She hopes that she'll go to the Antarctic one day.
3 She admitted that she had lied on her application form.
4 I agreed that I would help her.
5 We expect that we'll be away for at least a year.
6 Do you remember that you promised to fix my computer?
7 I forgot that I had to buy a ticket.
8 I don't recall that I told you about my trip.
9 I suggested that we come back the next day.
10 He denied that he had cheated in the exam.

E Complete each sentence b so that it means the same as sentence a.

1 a I didn't manage to take any photos.
  b I failed ......to take any photos...... .
2 a If by any chance you see Rob, please let me know.
  b If you happen ....
  ....
3 a They made me sign a form before I could come in.
  b I was ....
  ....
4 a We weren't allowed to take any photographs without permission.
  b They didn't let ....
  ....
5 a I can't talk to you now because I don't have time.
  b I don't ....
  ....
6 a I'll arrange for somebody to contact you with the details.
  b I'll have ....
  ....
7 a The next thing she did was write a book about her experiences.
  b She went ....
  ....
8 a I watch the sunrise while I'm sitting in my chair.
  b I sit ....
  ....
9 a I once spent a month in Antarctica to see what it was like.
  b I once tried ....
  ....
10 a It started getting dark, so we decided to go home.
  b It was starting ....
  ....

MY TURN!

Imagine you live in the Sahara desert or the Amazon jungle. Write a short email telling a friend about your new life. Talk about how you spend your time, what you enjoy seeing and doing, what you hope to do and what you miss.

Delete Reply Reply All Forward Print

....
....
....
....
....
....
....
....
....
....
....
....
....
....
....
....
....
....
....

MY TEST!

Circle the correct option.

1 When I saw Kate's pictures, it .... me want to go to Antarctica too. a forced b urged c made
2 You scored 15 points, which is not bad, ... this is your first game. a considering b noticing c mentioning
3 Her plan .... to the South Pole didn't really work – she had to return to camp after two days.
  a to travel b travel c travelling
4 I regret not .... to the concert – I wish I'd been there. a to going b to go c going
5 I'm looking forward .... a break. a to have b to having c having

My Test! answers: 1c 2a 3a 4c 5b

27 Copular verbs

There are plenty of ways of appearing younger.

Who wants to live forever?

No one likes the idea of **growing** old – **getting** ill, **turning** grey, **going** bald – but is there anything we can do to **keep** ourselves young? Well, there are plenty of ways of **appearing** younger. You could **dye** your grey hair black, go to the gym to try to **stay** fit, or avoid high-risk activities like smoking (which will make you **smell** better and **feel** better as well as **look** younger). And it may **sound** incredible, but some scientists claim that it will soon **become** possible to **remain** young much, much longer. It's no longer **considered** ridiculous to believe that scientific progress will **make** it possible for today's teenagers to live to 150. And it **seems** that there's plenty of money around to pay for research into genetic engineering. Just think of all the millionaires who are **driven** crazy by the idea that they can buy everything except a longer life! Of course, no amount of genetic engineering can help you if you **fall victim** to an accident, so perhaps the idea of living forever will **prove** no more than a dream. But some scientists predict that the first person to live to 1,000 years old is already alive today. You may **find** that hard to believe, but if it **comes true** … perhaps it could **be** you!

?
1 What can you do to appear younger?
2 Why is there so much money for anti-ageing research?

Answers: 1 Dye your grey hair (black), go to the gym, avoid high-risk activities like smoking. 2 A lot of millionaires want to be able to buy a longer life.

Copular verbs

1 Copular verbs are usually followed by an adjective (describing the subject of the sentence).
*Her parents are slowly growing **old**.*
*She looks **nice** today.*

2 Important copular verbs include:
– *be*
*They **are** very healthy for their age.*
– sense verbs, e.g. *look, sound, feel, smell* and *taste*
*... which will make you **smell** better and **feel** better as well as **look** younger.*

TIP

We can use *sound* to describe statements, not just noises.
*It may **sound** incredible, but ...*

– verbs describing changes, e.g. *become, end up, turn, get* and *grow*
*No one likes the idea of **growing** old – **getting** ill, **turning** grey, **going** bald.*

– verbs describing no change, e.g. *stay, remain* and *keep*
*You can go to the gym to try to **stay** fit.*

– verbs describing impressions or results, e.g. *seem, appear, prove* and *turn out*
*And it **seems** that there's plenty of money around ...*

Some fixed expressions with copular verbs + adjectives include: *go crazy / mad, go wrong, go bald, come true, come alive, fall asleep* and *fall ill*.
*Be careful what you wish for – it might **come true**.*
*The town really **comes alive** in the summer.*

3 **Many verbs have a copular and non-copular meaning.**

copular	non-copular
The flowers **smell** lovely.	Why are you **smelling** the flowers?
Her car **looks** expensive.	Can I **look** at your new car?
It **feels** quite cold tonight.	It was so cold that I couldn't **feel** my toes.
That bell **sounds** really loud.	The bell **sounds** every hour.
He **appears** quite confident.	The magician made a rabbit **appear** from nowhere.
This coffee **tastes** strange.	Can I **taste** your coffee?
The weather **turned** bad.	I can't **turn** this key – it's stuck.
The journey **proved** difficult.	The police **proved** that he was the murderer.

4 **Copular verbs are often used with particular adjectives.**

Use *go* for changes of colour; use *turn* to emphasise gradual changes.
*Jenny's face **went** red when everyone laughed at her.*
*In the autumn, I love watching the leaves slowly **turning** red.*
OR ... ***going*** *red.*

Use *get* for changes in skills, health / appearance, temperature / weather / time, emotional states and quality.
*You've **got** a lot taller since I last saw you.*
*We went home when it started **getting** dark.*

Use *remain* in formal English and *stay* / *keep* in less formal English to describe no change.
*Temperatures will **remain** high all week.*
***Stay** calm – there's no reason to panic.*

Use *grow* to emphasise slow, natural processes.
*Nobody likes the idea of **growing** old.*

Use *turn out, end up* or *prove* to describe unexpected outcomes. *Prove* is more formal.
*The film **turned out** / **proved** (to be) better than we expected.*

5 **Some copular verbs can be followed by a noun or pronoun which refers to the same person / thing as the subject, e.g. *be, become, prove* and *remain*.**
*Perhaps it could **be** you.*
*The idea of living forever will **prove** no more than a dream.*

6 **Some verbs can be followed by an object and an adjective (describing the object), e.g. *make, paint, dye, turn, keep, find, consider* and *call*.**
*You could **dye your grey hair black**.*
*Put the pizza in the fridge to **keep it fresh**.*
***Call me crazy**, but I'm going for a swim in the sea.*
*I **find it hard** to concentrate with all this noise.*

When someone is accused of a crime, a court might *find them innocent* or *guilty*.

*The court **found him guilty** of stealing the money, and sent him to prison.*

We often use the passive with these verbs.
*It **is** no longer **considered** ridiculous ...*
*Millionaires **are driven crazy** by the idea.*

If something or somebody *drives* / *makes you crazy*, you find it / them very frustrating.

*You **drive me crazy** sometimes when you don't listen to what I say.*

7 **Some verbs can be followed by an object and a noun or pronoun. It refers to the same person / thing as the object, e.g. *call, name, vote, elect* and *make*.**
*They **elected him President**.*
*His books have **made him an expert** on the subject.*

We often use the passive with these verbs.
*He **was voted the best new singer**.*

▶ See Unit 28 for other uses of *make somebody something* and *call somebody something*.

Practice

A Match the sentence beginnings to the correct endings.

1 When he was a teenager, he grew very [c]
2 When he won the lottery, it made him [ ]
3 He played so well that they elected him [ ]
4 This food tastes [ ]
5 I felt really cold, so I put on a sweater to keep [ ]
6 I found the exam [ ]
7 This picture looks [ ]
8 The party proved [ ]
9 He was angry because she called him [ ]
10 The leaves look beautiful as they gradually turn [ ]

a warm.
b a disaster – everything went wrong.
c tall very quickly.
d captain of the team.
e red in the autumn.
f normal, but there's something strange about it.
g disgusting. I can't eat it.
i a very rich man.
h an idiot.
j really difficult.

B Write at least two possible adjectives to complete each sentence. Use the words in the box and your own ideas.

angry black blond dangerous ~~delicious~~ difficult dirty disgusting exciting healthy horrible ill impossible modern nice old pink sad ~~salty~~ sick sleepy ~~spicy~~ strong stylish tired tiring tricky upset weak young

1 This soup tastes really *salty / spicy / delicious*.
2 He's dyed his hair ....
3 I'm worried about our dog. She seems very ....
4 A: I'm going to spend a month climbing in the mountains.
B: That sounds really ....
5 When you forgot my birthday, it made me really ....
6 They bought an old house and made it really ....
7 These old clothes smell ....
8 You look so fit. How do you stay so ....
9 A: Could you get me a free ticket to the concert?
B: That could prove ....
10 Can I lie down? I'm feeling a bit ....

C Underline the correct option.

1 Last night I dreamt I had an accident – I hope it doesn't *get* / <u>*come*</u> / *turn* true.

2 Take a map if you don't want to *end up* / *turn up* / *go* lost.
3 This party's too quiet. I hope it *gets* / *becomes* / *comes* alive soon.
4 It's a really important day for me. I hope nothing *turns* / *goes* / *gets* wrong.
5 I'm afraid Julie has *gone* / *turned* / *fallen* ill and can't come today.
6 Make sure you don't *end up* / *fall* / *find* victim to an Internet trick to steal all your money.
7 The apples on the tree are slowly *turning* / *turning out* / *staying* red.
8 Suddenly, the room *went* / *turned up* / *proved* very quiet.
9 I thought the book would be boring, but it *went* / *kept* / *turned out* very interesting.
10 It *makes* / *turns* / *finds* me very sad when you laugh at my work.

D Put the lines of the story in the correct order 1–10.

1	**a** On our first day in Spain, by lunchtime we were really hungry, so we looked for a restaurant that didn't look
	b green when she saw it! But it turned out
	c 'quite nice'!
	d me crazy when people only eat the food they know. She told me last time she ate Spanish food it made
	e a nice little restaurant in a quiet square away from the tourists. It looked
	f her very ill. Anyway, we found
	g too expensive. Jackie said she wanted a burger, but I said we should eat Spanish food in Spain. It drives
	h delicious on the menu. But when it came to our table, it looked awful – lots of shellfish and crabs' legs and things. Jackie's face turned
	i really friendly and nice. We ordered the speciality, paella, which sounded
	j much better than it looked. Even Jackie said she found it

E Complete each sentence b so that it means the same as sentence a, using the word in brackets.

1 a Monica was the best player in the club, and she still is. (remains)
  b Monica ....remains the best player........ in the club.
2 a The other players elected him president of the club. (by)
  b He .... players.
3 a I know it may be hard to believe, but it's true. (find)
  b You ...., but it's true.
4 a It made her angry when they refused to say sorry. (got)
  b She .... they refused to say sorry.
5 a Some people consider it rude to talk and eat at the same time. (considered)
  b It .... to talk and eat at the same time.
6 a You may think I'm crazy, but I've decided to give up my job. (call)
  b You ...., but I've decided to give up my job.
7 a Your trousers are too long. You need to shorten them. (shorter)
  b Your trousers are too long. You need to ....
8 a He was so shocked that his hair went grey. (turned)
  b The ....

MY TURN!

In your notebook, write a list of four things you could do to change your appearance and four things you don't want to change as you get older.

Examples: *I could dye my hair pink. I want to stay fit.*

MY TEST!

Circle the correct option.

1 It's getting .... tonight. a dark quickly b darkly quickly c darkly quick
2 In my opinion, the idea of living to 1,000 .... terrible! a appears b sounds c goes
3 When she said I looked older than I am, I .... really angry. a proved b got c kept
4 I'm going to .... a paint black my room b paint my room in black c paint my room black
5 The man was .... innocent of the crime and sent home. a driven b made c found

My Test! answers: 1a 2b 3b 4c 5c

28 Verbs with two objects

Why do we love to give each other presents?

Why do we love to **give** each other presents? Why are businesspeople so keen to **buy** each other a meal? Why do people **hand** you free food in the supermarket? And what makes us **lend** things **to** our friends?

The answer, in a word, is reciprocity, which means that if you **do** a favour **for** someone, they feel they must - really must - **do** you a favour in return.

Imagine a friend has just **cooked** a meal **for** you. You should be happy, but it might also **give** you a bad feeling that you now **owe** your friend something in return. So when, at the end of the meal, your friend **asks** you a favour, you'll find it very difficult to **refuse** them what they want.

Businesspeople use this technique all the time to **sell** things **to** people. They **offer** customers a special deal, or **promise** them a small gift. Of course, they don't **tell** customers that they need to buy something in return. They don't need to - the feeling that you **owe** somebody something is strong enough.

This should **teach** you an important lesson - when someone **offers** you something for free, they might actually want something from you in return. So **do** yourself a favour and **hand** the free sweets back **to** the nice lady in the shop - unless you feel you're strong enough to resist the power of reciprocity!

?
1 What is reciprocity?
2 Why do people give you free food in a supermarket?

Answers: 1 If you do a favour for someone, they feel they must do you a favour in return. 2 Because they want you to buy something.

Verbs with two objects

1 Ditransitive verbs, e.g. *give, send* and *tell*, have two objects: a direct object and an indirect object. The direct object is usually a thing and the indirect object is usually a person.
What makes us lend ***things*** *to* ***our friends****?*

2 The indirect object (the person) can come before or after the direct object (the thing); if it comes after, then we use *to* or *for* before it.
He read his children ***a poem****.* OR *He read the poem* ***to his children****.*

We usually put longer phrases and clauses last. We usually put pronouns first.

*Why do people hand **you free food**?*
*Hand **them** back to **the nice lady in the shop**.*

If there are two pronouns, we often put the indirect object last, with *to* or *for*.

*Can you pass **it to me**?*
OR *Can you pass **me it**?* (less common)

3 Ditransitive verbs with *to* include:

ask	*owe*	*send*
award	*pass*	*serve*
give	*pay*	*show*
hand	*promise*	*teach*
lend	*read*	*tell*
offer	*sell*	*throw*

*What makes us **lend** things **to** our friends?*
OR *... **lend** our friends things?*

Exception: we use *describe, explain* and *suggest* either with *to* or with no indirect object.

*I **explained** the answer **to him**.*
OR *I **explained** the answer.*
NOT ~~*I explained him the answer.*~~

4 Ditransitive verbs with *for* include:

bake	*cut*	*order*
build	*draw*	*play*
buy	*earn*	*set*
call	*find*	*sing*
cook	*get*	*win*

*Imagine a friend has **cooked** a meal **for** you.*
OR *Imagine a friend has **cooked** you a meal.*

5 Some ditransitive verbs are possible with *to* or *for* but with different meanings.

bring	*make*	*take*
leave	*send*	*write*

*I've **taken** some flowers **to** my grandmother.*
(= I've given them to her.)
*I've **taken** some flowers **for** my grandmother.*
(= because I want to give them to her)
*He **made** an offer / a promise **to** his friend.*
*He **made** dinner / some shelves **for** his friend.*

6 Some ditransitive verbs are not normally used with *to* or *for*. These include:

cause	*cost*	*refuse*
charge	*deny*	*wish*

*They **denied** / **refused** her the chance to spend a year abroad.* NOT ~~*... the chance to her ...*~~

7 Some idiomatic structures with *give* are never used with *to* or *for*, e.g. ***give a hand, give a lift, give a kick, give a ring.***

*If the door won't open, **give** it a kick / a push.*
NOT ~~*... give a kick / push to it.*~~
***Give** me a ring when you get home.* (= phone me)
NOT ~~*Give a ring to me ...*~~
*Can you **give me a hand** with this bag?* (= help me)

TIP
If somebody *gives you a lift*, they take you somewhere in their car.
*She **gave me a lift** to the station.*

8 We usually use ditransitive *do* with *for*.

*I'**m doing** some painting **for** Steve this weekend.*
NOT ~~*I'm doing Steve some painting ...*~~

TIP
The expression *do a favour* can be without *for*.
*Can you **do me a favour**?* OR *Can you **do a favour for me**?*

TIP
The expression *do a deal* uses the preposition *with*, not *to* / *for*.
*I'll **do you a deal**.* OR *I'll **do a deal with you**.*

9 Many ditransitive verbs have two passive forms.

***I was told** this story by a very wise man.*
OR ***This story was told** to me by a very wise man.*

Some other verbs that can have two passive forms are:

ask	*find*	*owe*	*send*
award	*give*	*pay*	*serve*
bring	*grant*	*prescribe*	*set*
buy	*hand*	*promise*	*show*
cause	*leave*	*read*	*teach*
charge	*lend*	*refuse*	*tell*
deny	*offer*	*sell*	*write*

10 With some ditransitive verbs, e.g. ***tell, ask, show, pay*** and ***owe***, you don't need to mention the direct object if it is clear from the context.

A: What does this word mean?
*B: Let's **ask** Paula. She'll be able to **tell** us.*

With most other ditransitive verbs, you must mention the direct object.

A: I haven't got any money.
*B: I'll **lend** you some.* NOT ~~*I'll lend you.*~~

Practice

A Match the sentence beginnings to the correct endings.

1 He baked us
2 He built me
3 She bought me
4 Can you call me
5 They caught us
6 They caused us
7 It cost us
8 Could you cut me
9 I'll draw you
10 This idea could earn us

a a fish in the river.
b a piece of cake?
c some biscuits.
d a present.
e a taxi?
f £20 to get in!
g a model ship.
h a lot of problems.
i a fortune if it works.
j a map.

1 c 2 ...... 3 ...... 4 ...... 5 ......

6 ...... 7 ...... 8 ...... 9 ...... 10 ......

B Rewrite these sentences, using *to* or *for*.

1 Could you pass me the salt, please?
Could you pass the salt to me, please?

2 Can you read us a story?

3 I'll get you a newspaper from the shop.

4 She's always doing her friends favours.

5 Could you order me a pizza?

6 Could you throw us our ball? It's in your garden.

7 The waiter served us our soup ... but it was cold!

8 I'm teaching my little sister English.

9 I lent Sharon my dictionary.

10 Sit down and I'll make you a cup of tea.

C Rewrite these sentences, using the passive. You don't always need to write *by* (someone).

1 My grandfather gave me this watch for my 18th birthday.
I was given this watch (by my grandfather) for my 18th birthday.

2 Laura's dad gave us a lift home.
We ......

3 His parents bought him this guitar for his birthday.
This guitar ......

4 Lots of people owe me money.
I'm ......

5 A famous artist taught me how to paint.
I ......

6 Nobody told me what time to be here.
I ......

7 When I was a child, I used to love people reading stories to me.
When I was a child, I ......

8 My grandmother told me that story.
That story ......

D **Complete the dialogue, using the words in the box in the correct order. Add a preposition if necessary.**

1 ~~a lift / me~~	6 €10 / me
2 any trouble / you	7 €20 / me
3 that book / you	8 it / you
4 it / me	9 everything you owe me / me
5 it / her	

Bob: Hi Andy. Sorry I'm late. I had to wait for my mum to give [1] *me a lift* . I hope I didn't cause [2] ....

Andy: No problem. While I was waiting I found [3] .... you've been looking for.

Bob: Show [4] .... Oh, wow! Thanks! I promised my mum that I'd get it for her. It's her birthday next week.

Andy: So, you'd better buy [5] ...., then.

Bob: Well ... I would, but I haven't got any money. You couldn't lend [6] ...., could you?

Andy: Er ... well, don't you still owe [7] .... from last month? And €15 from the month before? OK, listen. I'll lend [8] .... now, but you've got to pay [9] .... as soon as you get paid.

Bob: Thanks, Andy. You're my hero!

E **Complete the sentences, using appropriate direct and indirect objects.**

1 I've given *him the money I owed him* , so now he's happy.
2 Let's set off early – I'll take .... in case they get hungry.
3 She sent ...., explaining her decision, but they haven't received it yet.
4 He wrote ...., but in the end he was too shy to show it to her.
5 I've brought .... from my garden – you can use them to make some soup.
6 Every night, he told .... before she went to sleep.
7 When she died, she left ...., and he used it to buy a house.
8 Don't eat everything – leave .... !
9 I'll make .... – I'll never do anything to hurt you ever again.
10 Would you like me to lend .... until you get paid?

MY TURN!

In your notebook, write at least seven sentences describing what you could do to make someone owe you a favour. Use ditransitive verbs.

Example: *I could cook her a meal.*

MY TEST!

Circle the correct option.

1 I had to give .... with his homework but in return he has to tidy my room.
  a a hand to my brother **b** a hand my brother **c** my brother a hand
2 I paid .... for the car. **a** the owner £300 **b** to the owner £300 **c** £300 for the owner
3 Can you .... ? Can you pass me that pen? **a** do a favour me **b** do for me a favour **c** do me a favour
4 They denied .... the opportunity to take part. **a** to her **b** her **c** for her
5 .... some free sweets but I refused them. **a** They were offered to me **b** To me were offered **c** I was offered

My Test! answers: 1c 2a 3c 4b 5c

29 Advanced verb structures

I heard a key turn in the lock.

I was **driving** through the forest when suddenly my car **stopped** for no reason. I tried to **start** it again, but nothing happened. I got out, but as I stood up I **dropped** my phone and it **shattered** on the road. I **left** the car by the road and decided to **walk** the two kilometres back through the forest to where I'd noticed a house. As I walked, I **tripped** on a piece of metal that had been left in the road and fell and hurt my ankle. I thought I'd **twisted** it, but although it **hurt**, I could still walk – just about!

Reaching the house, I **rang** the doorbell. I heard it **ring**, but there was no answer. My ankle was **hurting** badly now, and my hands were **shaking**. I **looked** through the kitchen window; a large pan **stood** on the stove with something **boiling** in it, and there was something **baking**, or rather **burning**, in the oven. I pushed the door. It **opened**, and I stepped inside. 'Hello? Anyone home?' I stared at the strange pictures **hanging** on the walls, and the dirty carpet that **lay** on the floor. I **turned** round as the door **slammed** shut behind me. The candles **blew** out. Then I heard a key **turn** in the lock outside. I was trapped!

?
1 What three things went wrong in the forest?
2 Where was the owner of the house waiting?

Answers: 1 The car stopped for no reason; the phone got broken; the person fell and hurt his/her ankle. 2 Outside

Advanced verb structures

1 Verbs like *ring, close* and *stop* can be used in two ways. They can have a subject (usually a person) and an object or they can have only a subject (usually a thing).

*I **rang** the bell. The bell **rang**.*

*Joe **closed** the door. The door **closed**.*

*I **stopped** the car. My car **stopped** for no reason.*

Other verbs that can be used in these two ways include:

begin	*decrease*	*improve*	*stand*
bend	*double*	*increase*	*star*
break	*drop*	*move*	*start*
burn	*dry*	*open*	*stop*
change	*finish*	*ring*	*trip*
close	*grow*	*shake*	*turn*
cook	*hurt*	*sit*	*work*

*The boy **opened** the door. The door **opened**.*

*He **shook** my hand when he came in. My hands were **shaking**.*

*The film **starred** Alex Black. Alex Black **starred** in the film.*

2 **Many phrasal verbs can be used in the same two ways. These include:**

blow up	*melt down*	*spin around*
break up	*move on*	*stand up*
close down	*shut up*	*trip over*
dry off	*sit down*	*turn over*

*We **moved on** after the concert had finished.*
*The policeman **moved** us **on**.*

*Ralph **tripped** Frank **over**.* (= It was Ralph's fault that Frank fell.)
*Ralph **tripped** over.* (= Ralph fell.)

3 **Some pairs of similar verbs work in the same way, e.g. *lay / lie, raise / rise* and *fell / fall*. With the first verb in each pair, a person causes an action to happen; with the second verb, the action just happens.**

*He **laid** the map on the table.*
*The map **lay** on the table.*

*She **raised** her eyes.*
*The sun **rose**.*

*We asked some men to **fell** our old apple tree* (= cut it down) *because we were worried it might **fall** on our house.*

TIP

Don't confuse the irregular verbs *lie* (past: *lay*; past participle: *lain*) and *lay* (past: *laid*; past participle: *laid*).

*... and the filthy carpet that **lay** on the floor.*
*He **laid** the box carefully on the table.*

4 **Some verbs can be transitive (they have an object [usually a thing]) or intransitive (they have no object) with no change of meaning. These include:**

eat	*lose*	*sing*
drink	*play*	*win*
drive	*read*	*write*

*She **sang** a beautiful song.*
*She **sings** beautifully.*

TIP

***Leave* can be used with or without an object, but with a change in meaning. When it has no object, it often means 'leave home' or 'leave this place'.**

*I **left** the car by the road.*
*What time did you **leave**?*

▶ **See Unit 28 for *play, leave, write, read, sing* and *win* + two objects.**

Some verbs, e.g. *go, cry, walk* and *live*, are normally intransitive but can have objects in idioms and fixed collocations.

go the extra mile	*die a death*
go the whole hog	*run / walk / swim,* etc. (+ a distance)
walk a dog	*speak a language*
live (a) life	*want / live / sleep* (+ a time)

*When I ask her for help, she always **goes the extra mile** and does more than she needs to.*
*I **walk** my **dog** every evening.*

TIP

When *run* has an object, it often means 'manage' or 'lead'.

*Who would like to **run** this meeting?*

5 **The verbs *read, sell* and *keep* are normally transitive, but can be intransitive in certain structures.**

*Your essay doesn't **read** well.* (= It doesn't sound natural.)
*Her books always **sell** well.*
*Bananas **keep** longer in the fridge.* (= They last longer.)

6 **The verbs *meet, marry* and *divorce* are normally transitive, but we can omit the object if it is *each other*.**

*They **met** when they were 17, **married** at 18 and **divorced** when they were 19.*

Practice

A Rewrite each sentence, using the word in brackets as the subject.

1 Some bread was baking in the oven. (I)
I was baking some bread in the oven.
2 The weather was starting to worry me. (I)
3 He was moving his arms and legs in time with the music. (his arms and legs)
4 These tomatoes grew in my garden. (I)
5 I usually dry my hair in the sunshine. (my hair)
6 When you've melted the butter, you can fry the mushrooms. (the butter)
7 They open their shop at 6 am and close it at 11 pm. (their shop)
8 How do I work this computer? (this computer)
9 Your work needs to improve before you're ready for the exam. (you)
10 The window broke while we were playing football. (we)

B Complete the sentences, using verbs from the box in the past simple form. Use a dictionary if necessary.

bounce dissolve drop halve melt shake shatter ~~slam~~ stretch twist

1 Everyone jumped when the door suddenly slammed.
2 The ice cream quickly .... in the sun.
3 As she spoke she .... her hair around her fingers in a shy, self-conscious way.
4 The cat bit me when I picked it up, so I .... it straight away.
5 Mike walked across the sports hall and .... a basketball on the floor.
6 I .... the tablet in a glass of water, then drank it all in one go.
7 Suzie .... the elastic too much, causing it to break.
8 The plate .... when it fell, leaving small pieces all over the floor.
9 In the sales, they .... the price of the ring from €100 to only €50.
10 His hands .... as he nervously tried to turn the key in the lock.

C Complete the description of the graph, using verbs from the box in the past simple. Use each verb no more than twice. Sometimes there is more than one possible answer.

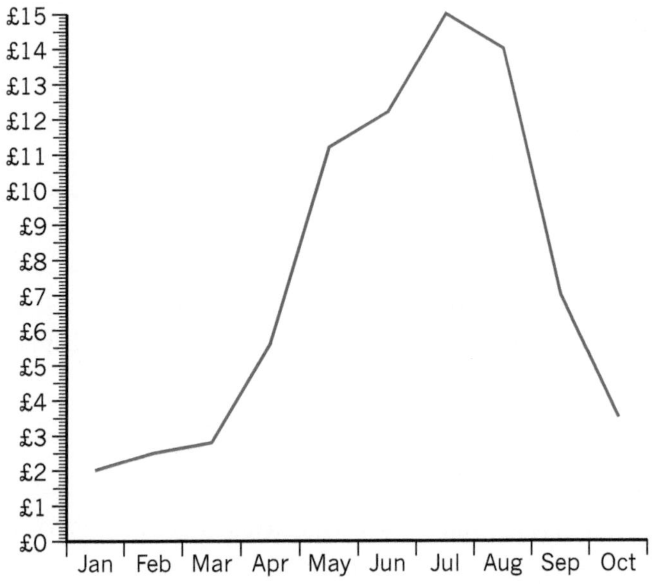

decrease double drop fall halve increase raise rise ~~stand~~

In January, the price of a ticket to the swimming pool [1] stood at £2. In February it [2] .... slightly to £2.50. They [3] .... it again in March, to £2.80. In April, it [4] ...., to £5.60. They [5] .... it again in May, to £11.20. It [6] .... again slightly in June, but only by £1. They [7] .... it to £15 in July. Then in August, they [8] .... the price by £1. In September the price [9] .... to £7. Finally, they [10] .... it again, to £3.50, in October.

D Complete each sentence b so that it has a similar meaning to sentence a, using the word in brackets.

1 a Someone had laid some old clothes on the bed. (lay)
  b Some ....old clothes lay on the bed.... .
2 a The star of the film was Frank Ellis. (starred)
  b The ....
3 a The little dog ran in front of David and tripped him up. (over)
  b ....
  when it ran in front of him.
4 a I went for a 10 km run this morning. (ran)
  b I ....
5 a We had to cut down our old tree. (fell)
  b We ....
6 a Don't keep this juice for more than two days after you open it. (keep)
  b This juice ....
  ....
7 a No one will ever buy these new machines – they're too expensive. (sell)
  b These new machines ....
  – they're too expensive.
8 a I want to live a long time and die peacefully when I'm old. (life)
  b I ....
  death, when I'm very old.

E Tick the sentence that has a different meaning.

1 a I landed at 8 pm.
  b My plane landed at 8 pm.
  c I landed my plane at 8 pm. ✓
2 a We met last year.
  b We had a meeting last year.
  c We met each other last year.
3 a His car drove 5 km.
  b He drove his car 5 km.
  c He drove 5 km.
4 a I worry about you.
  b You worry.
  c You worry me.
5 a The party starts at 7. What time do you want to leave home?
  b The party starts at 7. What time do you want to leave it?
  c The party starts at 7. What time do you want to leave?
6 a Alan tripped over the other player.
  b Alan tripped over.
  c Alan tripped the other player over.
7 a Liliana walks her dog twice every day.
  b Liliana takes her dog for a walk twice a day.
  c Liliana's dog goes for a walk two times every day.
8 a An invention like this won't sell itself.
  b An invention like this won't sell at all.
  c We won't be able to sell an invention like this.

MY TURN!

Write the next part of the story from page 124 in your notebook. Try to use at least five of the verbs from this unit.

MY TEST!

Circle the correct option.

1 On the way back to my car I accidentally .... my keys. a fell b felled c dropped
2 After our swim, we lay in the sun to .... a melt down b dry off c trip over
3 An enormous dog .... sleeping on the floor in the corner of the kitchen. a laid b lay c lied
4 How long do these yoghurts .... ? a keep b stay c remain
5 The balloon filled with air and gradually .... into the sky. a raised b increased c rose

My Test! answers: 1c 2b 3b 4a 5c

R4 Review: phrasal verbs; verbs with infinitive or *-ing*; copular verbs; verbs with two objects; advanced verb structures

A Circle the correct option

Delete Reply Reply All Forward Print

Hi Alex,
You'll be surprised to hear that yesterday I ran my first half marathon – that's 21 kilometres! No, I'm not [1]… – I really did do it. I spent about five months training for it, mainly running round my local park six days a week. A half marathon is a long race and, unless you're naturally very fit, you've got to take it seriously - you can't [2]… . Most days I trained with Chiara. She lives near me and I get [3]… . The first time we went for a run, we set [4]… too quickly and I [5]… breath after about 10 minutes. I had to walk [6]… home feeling terrible. I nearly [7]… at that point because I thought I'd never be able to run very far but Chiara persuaded me to [8]… on trying. We worked [9]… a sensible training programme, starting with short, slow runs and then gradually doing more. This really helped and I got fitter. Running six days a week is hard and I had to [10]… up with aches and pains in my ankles and my knees, but generally it was nice to feel fit. Then Chiara [11]… the idea of entering the half marathon. In the weeks before the race, both of us got really excited and, luckily, the day [12]… our expectations. There were about 5,000 other runners and Chiara and me [13]… up finishing in a time of just under two hours, which is pretty good for a first try.
OK, that's all for now. Perhaps you could let me know what you've been [14]… recently.
All the best
Julie

1 a making up it b backing it up ©c making it up d backing up it
2 a put off b run down c get up d mess around
3 a on with b on well with her c well with her d on her well
4 a off b up c down d forward
5 a got away with b broke up with c ran out of d came out of
6 a to b for c on d back
7 a let down b shut up c went down d gave up
8 a get b take c keep d move
9 a out b in c up d off
10 a come b pick c set d put
11 a got on with b put up with c came up with d went on with
12 a lived up to b stood up with c looked up to d ran up with
13 a got b ended c took d stayed
14 a on about b up to c down to d in with

B Complete the sentences using TWO of the verbs in brackets in the correct forms: *to*-infinitive, infinitive without *to*, or *-ing*.

1 ....To tell.......... the truth, I don't remember ....seeing.......... Peter at school yesterday. (~~see~~ / say / ~~tell~~)
2 Frankly .... , I'm not looking forward to .... the situation to Laura. (talk / speak / explain)
3 I lay on the sofa .... through a magazine and then decided .... something to eat. (look / let / have)
4 There's not much .... in this area in the evenings, so I suggest .... to the city centre for a while. (go / spend / do)
5 Stefan wanted to do something .... his spoken English, so he tried .... a conversation class and he said it helped. (join / know / improve)
6 Our Science teacher never lets us .... in class and he always makes us .... extra homework. (relax / do / give)
7 .... to the gym is good for my self-confidence, not .... my health. (mention / use / go)
8 They spent two weeks .... around Greece and then stopped for a few days in Athens .... the historical monuments. (meet / see / travel)
9 I can't imagine .... a lot of money, but I wouldn't mind .... a bit richer than now. (do / be / have)
10 It's always been my dad's ambition .... in the countryside, but my mum's worried about not .... any family or friends there. (come / have / live)

C Complete both sentences, using the same verb. Use the same tense.

1 It .....got..... really cold last night, didn't it?
I .....got..... eight books for my birthday – it's a good thing I like reading!
2 My computer is always crashing – it .... me absolutely mad.
My dad .... a much smaller car than he used to.

3 Is this fish OK? It doesn't .... very nice.
Can you .... something burning?

4 Patricia .... asleep on the train and missed her bus.
My brother .... off his bike this morning but he didn't hurt himself.

5 Lubna suddenly heard a noise behind her and .... round quickly.
The air was cold and the sky .... a dark grey colour, so we all went inside.

6 Amanda's an actress and she used to .... quite often on TV.
Dimitri didn't .... very surprised at the news of his brother's problems.

7 The security guard .... the alarm and the firefighters were at the building within 10 minutes.
That programme about the Arctic .... interesting – I wish I'd seen it.

8 I didn't think Katia was very good at chess but when we played at the weekend she .... to be much better than I'd expected.
The evidence finally .... that Fabrice was innocent.

9 Imran was so annoying – he .... interrupting me all the time.
Julia didn't want anyone to know about her visit so we .... quiet about it.

10 The court .... Jack Downing innocent, so he went home a free man.
When she was looking through some old papers, my mum .... a funny photo of herself as a student.

D Make sentences by putting the words in the correct order.

1 you / favour / a / I / owe
I owe you a favour.

2 you / a / could / hand? / me / give
....

3 her / Jaime / described / to / it
....

4 far / charged / they / much / too / us
....

5 the / was / father / I / taught / my / by / piano
....

6 by / the / waiter / we / French / served / a / were / food
....

7 to / who / dinner / you / for / is / going / cook?
....

8 for / pizza / ordered / we / everyone
....

9 friends / us / luck / wished / Tony's / good
....

10 job / sister / offered / been / my / interesting / has / an
....

E Complete the questions and replies with the verbs from the boxes, then match the questions to the correct replies.

fall hang ~~hurt~~ lose melt open play sell

blow out dry finish keep raise rise ~~stand up~~ win

Questions 1–8

1 Do those shoes ....hurt.... you?
2 Do you think these games will .... well?
3 Are your brothers going to .... football tomorrow?
4 Won't these strawberries .... their flavour in the fridge?
5 Do you think temperatures are going to .... soon?
6 Should I .... these wet clothes on the washing line?
7 Do you mind if I .... the window a little?
8 Won't those chocolates .... in the sun?

Replies a–h

a Maybe, but they'll .... longer.
b Only if I have to ....stand up.... in them for a long time.
c No, they'll .... better by the radiator.
d The problem is, the candles might .... in the draught.
e Yes, and they think they'll .... quite easily again.
f Yes, so let's .... them all now before they do.
g Not if the shops .... the prices too much.
h Probably, but then they'll start to .... again.

1 ..b.. 2 ...... 3 ...... 4 ......
5 ...... 6 ...... 7 ...... 8 ......

F Cross out the underlined words if the sentence is still grammatically correct without them. Put a tick if the words have to stay.

1 My sister's studying ~~medicine~~ at university.
2 We met <u>each other</u> about six years ago.
3 I enjoyed <u>the meal</u> very much. ✓
4 He shook <u>his head</u> as he walked out of the room.
5 At the end of the talk, several people raised <u>their hands</u> to ask a question.
6 You need to change <u>your clothes</u> before you go to the interview.
7 Rashida tripped over <u>a cable</u> and hurt her ankle.
8 I first met <u>Hiroko</u> six years ago.
9 The company closed down <u>two shops</u> last year.
10 Annie starts <u>work</u> at 8 o'clock.
11 I rang <u>the bell</u> but no one came to open the door.
12 Before we started to paint, we laid <u>old newspapers</u> on the floor.

30 Prefixes and suffixes

The fines for homelessness are inevitably unaffordable.

The San Francisco Police Department recently gave 32 police officers a new job. With murders at a 10-year high, you might expect that they have been sent to stop more **senseless** killings or to investigate the **considerable** number of **unsolved** murders. But you'd be wrong. These 32 officers have joined the fight against ... **homeless** people! It is now a crime to sleep on the streets, and the **unfortunate** people who do so have to pay a fine or go to prison.

What's wrong with this? For a start, it **distorts** the idea of a 'justice' system to **criminalise** homeless people – who, by **definition**, have no place to live – for living outside. This simply feels **immoral**. It's also a waste of time and money. First, there's the money to pay a **monthly** salary to the new officers. Then, because the fines for **homelessness** are **inevitably unaffordable**, the homeless people have to be **imprisoned**, another **costly** result. In the end, the homeless person is back on the street (but now **re-labelled** a 'criminal') and the **overworked** and **underfunded** police go back to the beginning. Nothing is achieved.

Common sense tells us that criminalising homelessness is **counter-productive**, making it harder for homeless people to find a **solution** to their problems. If the **disadvantages outweigh** the advantages, perhaps this **unfair**, **wasteful** and **pointless** new **decision** should be **overturned**.

1 What does the writer think the new police officers should be doing?
2 Does the writer present both sides of the argument or only one side?

Answers: 1 Stopping more senseless killings and investigating unsolved murders 2 Only one side

Prefixes and suffixes

1 Prefixes are attached to the beginning of words; suffixes are attached to the end of words.

In general, prefixes tell us something about the meaning of a word (e.g. *re-* = again, as in *re-labelled*), while suffixes show us which class a word belongs to (e.g. *-ous* = adjective, as in *dangerous*). But many suffixes also carry meaning (e.g. *-able* / *-ible* and *-less*, as in *usable, useless*).

The prefix *a-* can change verbs like *float* or *sleep* into adjectives (*afloat, asleep*); *en-* can change nouns like *courage* or *trap* into verbs (*encourage, entrap*).

Prefixes

2 Some useful prefixes are:

a- (= without) ***a**moral, **a**symmetric*
anti- (= against) ***anti**perspirant*
auto- (= self) ***auto**matic, **auto**biography*
co-, con- (= together, with) ***co**-organise, **con**nect, **com**munity, **col**league, **cor**respond*
counter- (= the opposite) ***counter**productive, **counter**argument*
cyber- (= Internet, computer) ***cyber**space, **cyber**criminal*
de- (= reverse action) ***de**-friend, **de**motivate*
down- (= lower, worse) ***down**market, **down**play*
e- (= electronic) ***e**mail, **e**-commerce*
ex- (= out of) ***ex**it, **ex**tract*
ex- (= former) ***ex**-boss*
fore- (= front, before) ***fore**legs, **fore**cast*
in- (= not, opposite) ***in**complete*
inter- (= between) ***inter**cultural*
mega- (= great, a million) ***mega**star, **mega**byte*
micro- (= very small, one millionth) ***micro**scope, **micro**second*
mid- (= middle) ***mid**-life*
mini- (= small) ***mini**ature*
mono-, bi-, tri-, multi- (= one, two, three, many) ***mono**lingual, **bi**lingual, **tri**lingual, **multi**lingual*
non- (= not) ***non**-fattening, **non**-verbal*
out- (= be better / more than) ***out**weigh, **out**number*
over- (= too much) ***over**charge, **over**sensitive*
post- (= after) ***post**pone, **post**-graduate*

pre- (= before) ***pre**-date, **pre**view*
pro- (= for, in favour of) ***pro**-European, **pro**posal*
pseudo- (= false) ***pseudo**nym*
self- (= self) ***self**-confident, **self**-conscious*
semi- (= half) ***semi**-final*
sub- (= below) ***sub**-zero, **sub**way*
super- (= above, more than) ***super**visor, **super**market*
tele- (= distant) ***tele**portation*
trans- (= through, across) ***trans**port, **trans**national*
under- (= not enough) ***under**cook, **under**sized*
up- (= better, higher) ***up**grade, **up**lifting*

TIP

***Unlike* is a preposition; *dislike* is a verb.**

*I really **dislike** rap music. **Unlike** my sister, who loves it.*

TIP

in-* is spelt *im-* if it comes before *p, b* or *m, ir-* if it comes before *r* and *il-* if it comes before *l*: *impossible, irrelevant, illegal.

The same applies to *con-* (*com-, cor-, col-*): *community, correspond, collect.*

TIP

***in-* and *im-* aren't always negative. In words like *imprison, import, inflammable* and *insert*, the prefix just means 'in'.**

*... the homeless people have to be **imprisoned.***
(= put in prison)

TIP

***Oversee, overlook, overhear* and *overturn* work in a different way. *Oversee* means 'be in charge of something'; *overlook* means 'forget to do something' or 'ignore something'; *overhear* means 'hear by accident'; *overturn* means 'cancel'.**

Suffixes

3 **Common suffixes for making adjectives include:**

noun + suffix ➜ *adjective*

*-al: magic**al***
*-ful: beauti**ful***
*-ic: hero**ic***
*-ish: child**ish***
*-less: pain**less***
*-ly: friend**ly***
*-ous: danger**ous***
*-y: nois**y***

verb + suffix ➜ adjective

*-able: read**able***
*-ive: attract**ive***
*-ing: charm**ing***

TIP

The suffix *-ish* can be added to adjectives to mean 'more or less', especially in informal English.

*Her hair is short**ish** / long**ish** / dark**ish.***

4 **Common suffixes for making nouns include:**

verb + suffix ➜ noun

*-ance: appear**ance***
*-ence: differ**ence***
*-er: play**er***
*-ery: brib**ery***
*-or: act**or***
*-ant: defend**ant***
*-ent: recipi**ent***
*-ment: encourage**ment***
*-y: discover**y***
*-tion: protec**tion***
*-sion: deci**sion***
*-ee: train**ee***
*-al: withdraw**al***
*-ing: paint**ing***

adjective + suffix ➜ noun

*-ness: kind**ness***
*-ity: modern**ity***

concrete noun + suffix ➜ abstract or collective noun

*-age: bagg**age***
*-hood: man**hood***
*-ism: protection**ism***
*-ship: relation**ship***

noun + suffix ➜ noun

*-ist: violin**ist***
*-ess: princ**ess***

TIP

Use *-er* and *-or* for the subject of the verb (e.g. a *trainer* is a person who *trains*; an *interviewer* is a person who *interviews*); use *-ee* for the object (e.g. a *trainee* is the person who is *trained*; an *interviewee* is a person who is *interviewed*).

5 **Common suffixes for making verbs include:**

adjective + suffix ➜ verb

*-ise / -ize: real**ise***
*-en: sadd**en***
*-ify: solid**ify***

noun + suffix ➜ verb

*-ise / -ize: critic**ise***
*-en: fright**en***
*-ify: horr**ify***

TIP

The verb suffix *-ise* is used mainly in British English; *-ize* is more common in American English, but is becoming increasingly common in Britain and other English-speaking countries.

*... a 'justice' system to **criminalise** homeless people.*
OR ... to ***criminalize*** ...

Practice

A Look back at the text on page 130. Where possible, take away the prefixes and suffixes from the words in bold. Which words are left?

Paragraph 1: senseless → sense
considerable → consider unsolved → solved
....

Paragraph 2: ....
....
....
....

Paragraph 3: ....
....

B Match the underlined words in 1–10 to explanations a–j.

1 The plan to criminalise homelessness will be counterproductive. [f]
2 If we pre-book the tickets, the price will be much lower. [ ]
3 Sorry about that – it was a simple misunderstanding. [ ]
4 We overestimated the number of people that would come. [ ]
5 I thought I played chess well, but she completely outmanoeuvred me. [ ]
6 They undercharged us in the restaurant. [ ]
7 The poem was really uplifting. [ ]
8 She discouraged me from giving up college. [ ]
9 I overheard Mr Wallis talking about your test results. [ ]
10 My father is semi-retired. [ ]

a I thought you meant 8 am, not pm.
b It made everyone feel much better.
c Every move I made, she made a better move.
d They forgot to include our desserts in the bill.
e She persuaded me it was a bad idea.
f It will have the opposite result from the one they planned.
g He only works a few hours a week now.
h We were expecting hundreds, but there were only about 30.
i We will pay less if we order them in advance.
j He didn't know I was listening.

C Circle the correct option.

1 Be careful – the river is very danger......... .
a ing b (ous) c ed d ly
2 I didn't understand the explanation the first time I read it. I'll have to ....read it.
a over b counter- c re- d up
3 I feel fine when the boat isn't moving, but I feel sick when it's ....float
a a b im c en d en
4 Although she's only nine, she's already a brilliant pian......... .
a o b ist c izer d er
5 The boss was so ill we had to ....pone the meeting.
a post b sub c re d de
6 He always ....spells my name. He writes Migeul instead of Miguel.
a un b mis c counter- d dis
7 I ....slept and missed my train. My alarm clock didn't wake me up.
a over b under c out d up
8 In my class, girls ....number boys. There are 20 girls and only 6 boys.
a mis b over c out d up
9 Her paintings are very attract......... They look really good.
a ful b some c ing d ive
10 This soup is too salt......... – I can't eat it.
a y b ed c ised d ened

D Complete the dialogues, using verbs made from one of the nouns or adjectives in the box.

broad dark fright sad sharp short straight strength sweet ~~wide~~

1 A: The road's too narrow.
B: Yes, they really should ....widen.... it.
2 A: This picture on the TV's too bright.
B: Just a minute – I'll .... it.
3 A: The mirror's hanging too much to the left.
B: Would you like me to .... it?
4 A: Did you put any sugar in this tea?
B: Ah no ... I forgot to .... it.
5 A: This pencil's blunt.
B: I'll .... it.
6 A: I'm going to jump out and scare the children.
B: No, don't .... them.
7 A: These trousers are too long.
B: I'll .... them.
8 A: You should see more of the world.
B: Yes, I need to .... my horizons.
9 A: Were you angry that she was so rude?
B: No, but it .... me.
10 A: This bridge is too weak.
B: Yes, they need to .... it.

E **Make one sentence from each group of sentences by changing the underlined words.**

1 Some people don't have a home. This problem has been treated as a crime. The writer does not consider this to be moral.
The writer considers the ...criminalisation... of ...homelessness... to be ...immoral... .

2 You solved the problem. I can't accept the way you did it.
I think your .... is ....

3 She decided to leave. This was not popular. This made her feel very unhappy.
The .... of her .... to leave caused her considerable ....

4 He didn't relate to his brother as a friend. This made him sad.
He was .... by his .... with his brother.

5 I calculated the money incorrectly. This was because when I estimated the costs, I made them too low.
My .... of the money resulted from an .... of the costs.

6 One person decided not to compete and withdrew. This happened because they discovered he had not been behaving properly.
The .... of one of the .... from the .... followed the .... of his ....

7 After he robbed the bank, the person who was defending himself in court dramatically altered the way he appeared. He claimed this was an accident.
The .... claimed that the dramatic .... of his .... after the bank .... had been ....

8 The performance of the main woman who acted in the play was full of charm. Some people might be critical of the plot. The number who enjoyed the play was certainly higher than the number who didn't.
The main .... gave a .... performance. Although some people might .... the plot, those who enjoyed the play certainly .... those who didn't.

MY TURN!

Make as many new words as you can from each of these words. Use a dictionary if you wish.

1 destroy: *destructive, destructible, indestructible, destroyer, destruct, destruction*
2 produce: ....
3 popular: ....
4 fresh: ....
5 sense: ....

Now write five sentences about yourself, each using one word from each group.

Example: *My little brother has so much energy – he's almost indestructible!*

....
....
....
....
....

MY TEST!

Circle the correct option.

1 When I come home from a holiday, I hate .... a unpacking b repacking c outpacking
2 This steak is a bit .... You cooked it too long. a outdone b underdone c overdone
3 We can't hear you. Is your .... phone switched on? a cyber b mini c micro
4 The twins are almost identical, although Josie has got .... hair, and Kim's is a bit darker. a blondy b blondish c blondness
5 At my job interview, the .... asked me some really difficult questions. a interviewee b interviewing c interviewer

My Test! answers: 1a 2c 3c 4b 5c

31 Compounding

You're sunbathing on the beach, enjoying an ice cream.

You know the feeling:

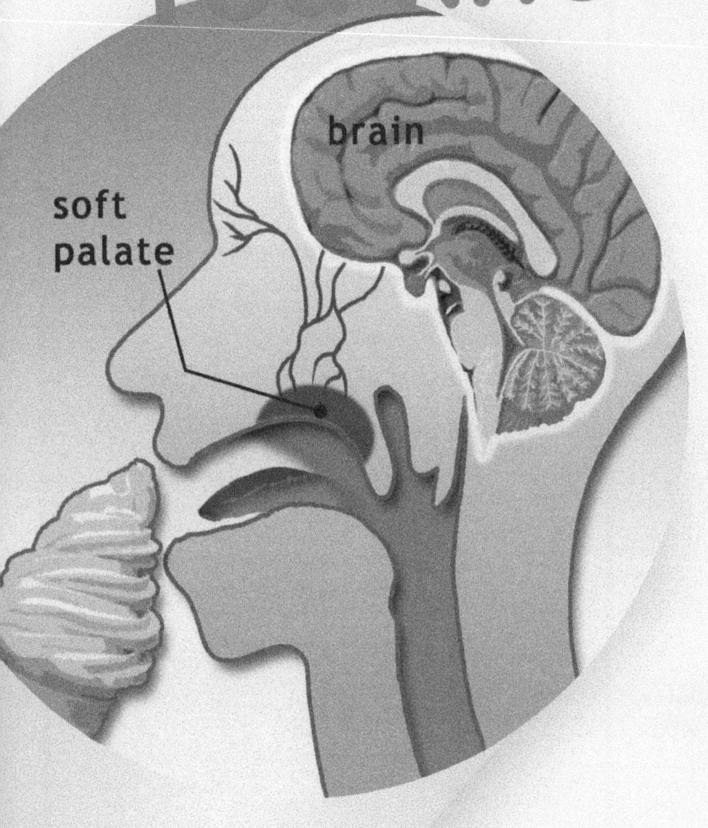

you're **sunbathing** on the beach, enjoying an **ice cream** or having a **well-deserved** break in a **fast-food restaurant** with an **ice-cold milkshake**, and then suddenly … you feel a **head-splitting** pain between your eyes! You've just suffered from **brain freeze** – an **ice-cream headache**. You groan and hold your head in agony, and **bystanders** think you're **play-acting**, but the pain is real enough. Fortunately, after a **twenty-** or **thirty-second** period, the pain disappears, and there's no **long-lasting** damage. But what causes **ice-cream headaches**? Basically, when something cold touches your soft palate, a **nerve centre** above the roof of your mouth sends a **warning signal** that your brain is freezing. This causes **blood vessels** to become suddenly wider so that the blood can heat up your brain. This sudden change can make even the most **cool-headed**, **mild-mannered** person cry out in pain. But the thing is, because the nerves above your mouth are also connected to nerves in your face, the pain feels like it's coming from your **forehead**, not from inside your mouth. What can you do if you love **ice cream** but don't want to get **brain freeze**? Well, it's simple – eat your **ice cream** slowly, and only one **teaspoonful** at a time!

1 Are ice-cream headaches dangerous?
2 Why do you feel the pain between your eyes?

Answers: 1 No. 2 Because the nerves above your mouth are also connected to nerves in your face.

Compounding

1 **Compounding involves putting two or more words together to make a new word.**

Compound nouns include: *headache, bathroom* and *toothpaste.*

Compound adjectives include: *long-lasting, well-built* and *broad-minded.*

Compound verbs include: *daydream, water-ski* and *sunbathe.*

2 **We write compounds as one or two words (e.g. *armchair, living room*) or with a hyphen (e.g. *south-west*).**

We can join compounds and other words to make new compounds, e.g. *science-fiction writer* or *fast-food restaurant.*

We can also use words like *in* or *and* in compounds with hyphens, e.g. my *mother-in-law*, a *black-and-white* film.

3 In general, the last part of a compound tells us what sort of thing it is, e.g. ***handbag*** (a type of ***bag***) and ***video camera*** (a type of ***camera***).

▶ See Unit 32 for compounds formed from phrasal verbs.

Compound nouns

4 Usually, the first part of a compound noun is not plural, even when the plural is more logical.

shoe shop NOT ~~*shoes shop*~~
car factory NOT ~~*cars factory*~~

Some nouns have a different meaning in the plural, so we use a plural in a compound to avoid misunderstanding.

*an **art critic** comments on art* (= paintings, sculpture)
*an **arts critic** comments on the arts* (= art, music, literature, theatre, film, etc.)
*a **sale price*** (= the price during a *sale*)
sales figures (= the number of products sold)

The same rule works with compound adjectives.

*I've just bought a **hands-free** phone.* (= a phone which leaves both hands free)

Sports is always plural in compounds, e.g. ***sportswear, sportswoman, sports car.***

5 Writers often invent compound nouns for ideas related to science, technology, business, etc.

*You've just suffered from **brain freeze.***

6 Many compound nouns end in verb + *-er* and refer to a person / thing that does the action, e.g. ***pencil sharpener, dishwasher.***

7 Many compound nouns are made from verb + *-ing* + noun and refer to something used for the activity, e.g. ***warning signal, swimming pool.***

8 Many compound nouns are made from noun + verb + *-ing* and refer to activities that involve the noun, e.g. ***letter-writing, marathon running.***

9 In a compound noun, the stress is usually on the first word. This helps listeners to hear the difference between compounds and simple word combinations.

*I don't like **<u>writing</u> tests.*** (= I don't like tests of writing skills.)
*I don't like writing **<u>tests</u>**.* (= I don't like the activity of preparing tests.)

Compound adjectives

10 Many compound adjectives are formed from nouns, e.g. ***five-star, full-length.*** Use a hyphen when the compound adjective comes before the noun, but not when it comes after ***be*** or another copular verb (see Unit 27).

*We watched a **full-length** film.* OR *The film we watched was **full length.***

11 The last part of a compound adjective may be an adjective, e.g. ***navy blue, ice cold.***

12 Compound adjectives often describe ages / distances / times, using a number + singular noun.

*She's six years old → She's a **six-year-old** child.*
NOT ~~*... a six-years-old child.*~~
*We walked 12 kilometres → It was a **12-kilometre** walk.* NOT ~~*... a 12-kilometres walk.*~~

13 Many compound adjectives use an adverb + past participle, e.g. ***highly paid, well-built.***

14 Many compound adjectives use a number or an adjective + noun + *-ed* to describe what a person or thing has, e.g. a ***blue-eyed*** girl has blue eyes, a ***cool-headed*** person has a cool head.

> **TIP**
> You don't need to repeat nouns that are the same in two compound adjectives.
> *After a **twenty-** or **thirty-second** period, the pain disappears.*

15 Many compound adjectives use an *-ing* form, e.g. ***long-standing, heart-breaking.***

16 Some compound adjectives have prepositions, e.g. ***well-off*** (= ***rich***), ***hard up*** (= ***poor***), ***fed up*** (= ***bored*** / ***unhappy***).

> **TIP**
> ***Everyday*** (one word) is a compound adjective. Use it before a noun. ***Every day*** (two words) is an adverb. Use it at the beginning or end of a sentence.
> *It's an **everyday** event.* (= It's normal.)
> *I see her **every day**. / **Every day** I see her.*

Compound verbs

17 Some compound verbs are formed from noun + verb, e.g. ***sunbathe, water-ski, daydream.***

18 Some compound verbs are formed from two verbs, e.g. ***play-act, sleep walk.***

19 Verbs often combine with words like ***after, up*** and ***under*** to form prepositional verbs (e.g. ***to look after***), phrasal verbs (e.g. ***to wake up***) and prefixed verbs (e.g. ***to underline***).

▶ See Unit 20 for prepositional verbs.
▶ See Unit 25 for phrasal verbs.
▶ See Unit 30 for verbs with prefixes.

Practice

A Complete the sentences with compound nouns made from the underlined words.

1 I swim in this pool. It's a swimming pool.
2 We play pool on this table. It's a ....
3 This is the top part of a table. It's a ....
4 You can buy hats in this shop. It's a ....
5 There are two assistants in the shop. They're both ....
6 He is a manager who is the main manager's assistant. He's the ....
7 This is a small hill made by a mole. It's a ....
8 I love walking in the hills. My hobby is ....
9 In this race, you have to walk fast. It's a ....
10 This horse takes part in races. It's a ....

B Make compound nouns and adjectives from the underlined words. Be careful with plurals.

1 This shop sells toys. a toyshop
2 This hotel has five stars. a .... hotel
3 We were on holiday for two weeks. a .... holiday
4 This hall is used for sports. a ....
5 This is a place where cars park. a ....
6 This person is an expert in art. an ....
7 This person is manager of the sales department. a ....
8 This man is 20 years old. a .... man
9 You wear these bands on your arms when you're learning to swim. ....
10 We'll go there for two days. a .... visit

C Match the sentence beginnings to the correct endings.

1 The film has a heart-
2 She sits next to a blond-
3 He only made a half-
4 You have to be very thick-
5 An octagon is an eight-
6 They're a very well-
7 He's rather shy and quietly-
8 They had a long-
9 We all sat down together and had a round-
10 I can't believe he got angry. He's normally so mild-

a skinned if you want to be a politician.
b matched couple.
c spoken.
d hearted effort to help.
e table discussion.
f breaking story.
g mannered.
h sided shape.
i standing agreement to help each other.
j haired boy.

1 f 2 ...... 3 ...... 4 ...... 5 ......
6 ...... 7 ...... 8 ...... 9 ...... 10 ......

D Circle the correct option. Use a dictionary if necessary.

1 You shouldn't wake someone up when they're ...walking.
(a) sleep b night c dream
2 It used to be an ...day experience to go to the post office, but these days people do it much less often.
a each b every c all
3 I often sit and day... instead of concentrating on what people are saying.
a nap b sleep c dream
4 She told me she comes from a hard-... family, but they're actually very well-off.
a up b off c away
5 After a half-hour workout in the gym, I always have a ...-earned break.
a good b nicely c well
6 He's such a know-... . He thinks he's an expert on everything!
a it b all c everything
7 He did a lot of pains... research for this book, but it was worth the effort.
a giving b making c taking
8 Don't pay any attention to her – there's nothing wrong with her, she's just ...-acting.
a play b game c drama
9 We stopped at a drive-... restaurant on the way, but we didn't go inside – we wanted to keep driving.
a by b away c through
10 She played her guitar in the street, and soon there was a large group of by-... watching her.
a watchers b standers c lookers

E Complete the sentences, using compound nouns made from the words in the box.

air bee bottle clean climb design fabric freshen keep mountain open ~~pencil~~ play ~~sharpen~~ soften tennis time vacuum waste web

1 I can't write with this – it's too blunt. Have you got a ……*pencil sharpener*…… that I can borrow?
2 Phew – it smells terrible in here! Have we got any …………………………………………?
3 Mmm! My brother gave me this home-made honey – he's an amateur …………………………………………… .

4 Before turning the washing machine on, remember to add some …………………………………………… as well as detergent.
5 My new multi-tool has got everything: a knife, scissors, a screwdriver, and even a …………………………………… !
6 I can't believe how dirty your carpet is! Haven't you got a …………………………………………………?
7 My little brother loves the Internet and he's very artistic, so he wants to be a ……………………………………… .
8 My sister is a …………………………………………… in her free time; last year she went on an expedition to Mount Everest, but unfortunately she didn't get all the way to the top.
9 You seem to spend hours lying on the sofa and you never seem to do anything! I don't understand how you can be such a …………………………………… !
10 Julie's a really keen …………………………………… . Ever since she first picked up a racket when she was about five, it's as if she's always been holding one!

MY TURN!

Use a dictionary to find at least three compound nouns and three compound adjectives that are not in this unit. Can you find any compound verbs?

……………………………………………………………………………………
……………………………………………………………………………………
……………………………………………………………………………………
……………………………………………………………………………………
……………………………………………………………………………………
……………………………………………………………………………………

MY TEST!

Circle the correct option.

1 He works in a …………… . They make the screens for computers.
a screen computer factory b factory screen computer c computer screen factory
2 Eating too many sweets can give you really bad …………… . a toothache b teethache c tooth-pain
3 His hobby is …………… . a climbing mountain b mountains climbing c mountain climbing
4 They've got an …………… baby. a eight-week-old b eight weeks old c eight-weeks-old
5 I used to love ice cream but I got fed …………… with getting headaches! a off b up c out

My Test! answers: 1c 2a 3c 4a 5b

32 Word formation 1: conversion

Go for a stroll to help clear your head and calm your nerves.

You've applied for your first job, and they're going to **interview** you. But how can you **increase** your chances? Our **list** of interview **'dos and don'ts'** might help!

Dos

1. Find out as much as possible about the **ins and outs** of the job.
2. **Get a good night's sleep** before the interview.
3. Take a **copy** of your application with you and **have a read** through it before the interview to **fine-tune** your thoughts.
4. Arrive early, so you can **get a feel for** the place and **orientate** yourself. And before the **start** of the interview, **go for a stroll** to help **clear** your head and **calm** your nerves.
5. At the **end** of the interview, be ready to **question** the interviewer.

Don'ts

1. Don't forget to **practise. The well-prepared** always do better in interviews.
2. Don't try to **mask** your weaknesses. And don't **make claims** about your achievements unless you can **back them up** with evidence.
3. Don't **position** yourself too near the interviewer – you might make them feel uncomfortable.
4. Don't try to **manipulate** the interview. Good interviewers will give you plenty of opportunities to show what you're really like.
5. When it's **your turn** to ask questions, don't **corner** the interviewer by asking about money. You can always **phone** or **email** them to ask about salary after you're offered the job!

?

1 Why should you take a copy of your application to the interview?

2 Why shouldn't you sit too near the interviewer?

Answers: 1 So that you can read it and fine-tune your thoughts. 2 You might make them feel uncomfortable.

Word formation 1

Nouns used as verbs

1 **We can use many nouns as verbs, e.g.** ***champion, experience, film, interview, party, speed*** **and** ***video.***

*They're going to **interview** you.*
*She's always **partying**.*

Some such verbs refer to the action performed by the noun, e.g. ***alarm, cycle, brake, mask, mirror, motor, pen, pencil (in), question*** **and** ***ship.***

*Don't try to **mask** your weaknesses.*
*Be ready to **question** the interviewer.*

Some such verbs refer to functions that are metaphorically associated with parts of the body, e.g. ***back, elbow, eye, finger, hand, head, mouth, nose, shoulder*** **and** ***stomach.***

*I find her selfish attitude really hard to **stomach**.*

Some such verbs refer to the action of applying something to something else, e.g. ***air, butter, carpet, glue, grease, oil, paint, paper, polish, shampoo*** **and** ***water.***

*We've just had our lounge **carpeted**.*

Some such verbs refer to the action of changing the position or state of something, e.g. ***bank, bin, bottle, cash, corner, file, group, pocket*** **and** ***position.***

*Don't **position** yourself too near the interviewer.*
*Don't **corner** the interviewer.*

Some such verbs refer to the action performed by a person, e.g. ***baby, boss, coach, mother, nurse*** **and** ***pilot.***

*The athlete was **coached** by his father.*

Some nouns connected with information technology are often used as verbs, e.g. ***blog, email, fax, input, network, phone, program*** and ***text***.

*You can always **phone** or **email** them.*

Many two-syllable nouns and verbs have the same written form, but are pronounced with different stress, e.g. ***contrast, decrease, export, import, increase, object, produce*** and ***subject***.

How can you in<u>crease</u> your chances?
There has been an <u>in</u>crease in unemployment.

2 Some verbs are formed by making nouns shorter, e.g. ***burgle, edit, evaluate, legislate, liaise, manipulate, obsess, sculpt*** and ***televise***.

3 Some nouns combine with verbs to form compound verbs, e.g. ***babysit, shoplift, sightsee*** and ***proofread***.

Other compound verbs are formed with verb + verb (e.g. ***sleepwalk***), adjective + verb (e.g. ***dry clean, fine-tune***) or noun + noun (e.g. ***moonlight***).

▶ See Unit 31 for compounding.

Adjectives used as verbs

4 We use some adjectives as verbs, e.g. ***calm, clear, clean, dry, empty, narrow, smooth, thin, tidy, warm*** and ***wet***.

*... to help **clear** your head and **calm** your nerves.*
*You can't go out until you've **tidied** your room.*

Verbs used as nouns

5 We use some verbs as nouns, e.g. ***concern, dislike, feel*** and ***hate***.

*Arrive early, so you can get a **feel** for the place.*

Some fixed noun phrases include examples of verbs used as nouns, e.g. ***dos and don'ts, haves and have nots*** and ***likes and dislikes***.

Some nouns were originally verbs which describe events or activities, e.g. ***catch, claim, fall, play, search, smile, throw*** and ***visit***.

*Don't make **claims** about your skills and experience ...*

In more informal situations, many of these nouns are often used in expressions with the verbs ***have, go for, give, get*** and ***be***.

***have** a go / laugh / listen / look / read / rest / think*
***go for** a run / stroll / swim / walk*
***give** something a go / kick / push / pull / try*
***get** a good night's sleep or rest / a feel for something*

*Have a **read** through it before the interview.*
*The door gets stuck, so you'll need to give it a **push** or a **kick**.*

The nouns ***go*** and ***turn*** don't mean the same as the corresponding verbs.

*It's your **go** / your **turn**.* (= You are the next person to take part, during a game or process.)
*I'm going to **have a go at** fixing the car.* (= I'm going to try to fix it.)

Some nouns refer to the result of an action, e.g. ***copy, clone, find*** and ***plan***.

*Take a **copy** of your application with you.*

Some nouns perform the function of the verb, e.g. ***answer, cover, divide, end, help, lift*** and ***start***.

*Before the **start** of the interview ...*
*... and the best **answers** to give.*

Some nouns refer to people who do the action described by the verb, e.g. ***cheat, cook, judge*** and ***spy***.

6 Some nouns are formed from phrasal verbs, e.g. ***dropout, fallout, hangover, takeaway, take-off*** and ***washing-up***. Some of these nouns usually appear with hyphens (e.g. ***fall-back***), some without hyphens (e.g. ***getaway***). Sometimes, both versions are possible (e.g. ***dropout*** or ***drop-out***).

*He was a college **dropout**.* (= He dropped out of college.)

Adjectives used as nouns

7 We can use adjectives as nouns in some situations.

*Sitting around watching TV all day won't do your health any **good**!*
*Parents teach their children about **right** and **wrong**.*

We sometimes use ***the*** + adjective as plural nouns to refer to a group of people with a certain characteristic, e.g. ***the blind, the deaf, the old, the poor, the rich, the young*** and ***the unemployed***.

We use ***the*** + some adjectives as plural nouns describing nationalities, e.g. ***the British, the Chinese, the Dutch, the English, the French, the Irish, the Japanese*** and ***the Spanish***.

▶ See Unit 21 for nouns used as adjectives.

We use some prepositions and conjunctions as nouns in fixed expressions such as ***a big if, ifs and buts, ins and outs*** and ***ups and downs***.

*Find out as much as possible about **the ins and outs** of the job.*
*If I get the job, and it's **a big if**, I'll buy a new car.*

Practice

A Match the sentence beginnings to the correct endings.

1 Police are carrying out
2 You don't have to decide now. Have
3 I know I'm not perfect but I don't like being called
4 The discovery of the lost treasure is
5 Sandra and her mother are so similar, they're like
6 Let me know if you need
7 My grandmother's in hospital because she had
8 Our car wouldn't start this morning – we had to give

a a think about it and let me know tomorrow.
b a fall and broke her leg.
c a detailed search of the area.
d a very significant historical find.
e it a push to get it going!
f any help with your homework.
g clones of each other.
h a cheat and a liar!

B Complete the sentences with the nouns used as verbs from the box. Use a dictionary if necessary.

air boss brake grease network pocket ship ~~shoulder~~ text water

1 I'm not prepared to ......shoulder...... all the blame for the accident because it wasn't really my fault.
2 It hasn't rained for ages, so Dad asked me to .... the garden this afternoon.
3 Why do you have to .... me around all the time? Let me do things my way for once!
4 Charlie doesn't know what time his train arrives, so he's going to .... me when he finds out.
5 It's important to .... the tin before pouring in the mixture, otherwise the cake will stick.
6 If Mum and Dad decide to move to Australia it will be expensive to .... all our things there.
7 With profits high this year, the directors of the company are likely to .... a record bonus.
8 It's dangerous to .... suddenly if there is ice on the roads, so don't drive too fast.
9 This conference is a great opportunity for us to .... with people and find useful contacts.
10 It's a bit hot in here – do you mind if I open the window to .... the room a bit?

C Underline the correct option. Use a dictionary if necessary.

1 Do you want to go out for a meal tonight or shall we just have a *getaway* / *takeaway* instead?
2 There was a really good *turnout* / *dropout* for the meeting – more than two hundred people came.
3 Did you see the match last night? 7–1! It was a complete *takeover* / *walkover*, wasn't it?
4 Unfortunately our car was so badly damaged in the accident that it's a *write-off* / *take-off*.
5 The policeman realised he couldn't deal with the situation on his own, so he radioed for *backup* / *wind-up*.
6 Having to go back to work after such a great holiday was a real *comedown* / *putdown*.
7 The *fallout* / *blackout* from this scandal will have serious consequences for the government.
8 People in our area have started a protest against the building of a new *flyover* / *hangover*.
9 There have been significant changes in the *make-up* / *pick-up* of the company in the last few years.
10 Boxing legend Jack Tyson has announced that he is making a *fallback* / *comeback* at the age of 42.

D Complete the email, using the correct form of the expressions in the box.

be a good laugh get a feel get a good night's sleep ~~go for a swim~~ go on a visit have a go have a look have a listen have a rest have a stroll

Dear Maria,

I'm having a great time here. There isn't much to do apart from sunbathe, [1] ......go for a swim...... in the sea or [2] .... along the beach, but it means I can [3] .... after such a busy year. Oh, you can go surfing too. I haven't tried it yet but I definitely want to [4] .... before I go home! Actually, yesterday we [5] .... to the island's capital, to try and [6] .... for the local culture, and we [7] .... around the markets. I bought some clothes and a CD of traditional music, which is really beautiful – you can [8] .... when we get home! At night it's different. There are cafés and clubs everywhere – last night we stayed out dancing and telling jokes all night, which [9] .... ! I think I'll go to bed early tonight though, because if I don't [10] ....
I'll be exhausted tomorrow. See you soon!

Love, Alicia x

E Complete each sentence b, using a verb formed from the underlined adjective in sentence a, so that it means the same.

1 a Before eating this bread, get it warm in the oven for 10 minutes.
  b Before eating this bread, ...warm it........ in the oven for 10 minutes.
2 a Wash the mushrooms, then get them dry using a paper towel.
  b Wash the mushrooms, then .... using a paper towel.
3 a Because of the economic problems, the shops were empty of customers.
  b The economic problems .... of customers.
4 a Make sure your teeth are clean after every meal.
  b .... after every meal.
5 a Since her heart attack, my mother takes tablets to make her blood thinner.
  b Since her heart attack, my mother takes tablets ....
6 a Diplomats will meet next week to try to make the path towards peace smoother.
  b Diplomats will meet next week to try ....
7 a Statistics suggest that the gap between rich and poor is getting narrower.
  b Statistics suggest that the gap between rich and poor ....
8 a The lid of the pie will stick better if you make the pastry wet with a little milk.
  b The lid of the pie will stick better if you .... with a little milk.
9 a You can't go out until you've made your room tidier.
  b You can't go out until ....
10 a The roads are always busy now but they are usually clear by 10 o'clock.
  b The roads are always busy now but they .... by 10 o'clock.

MY TURN!

Try to work out the meaning of the underlined verbs in these headlines, then check in a dictionary.

UNIVERSITIES SHELVE PLANS TO INCREASE COST OF COURSES

COACH AXED AFTER SHOCK CUP EXIT

PARENTS BLAST PHONE COMPANY OVER TEENAGER AD CAMPAIGN

UNITED MUSCLE THEIR WAY PAST LOCAL RIVALS

STUDENTS CLASH WITH TEACHERS OVER EXAM PLANS

SCHOOLS TO PILOT NEW TEST

Now invent two or three of your own headlines, using some of these verbs.

....
....
....
....
....

MY TEST!

Circle the correct option.

1 I'll .... the job interview in for Tuesday and we can confirm it later. a pen b pencil c note
2 You can't wash this jacket in the washing machine – you need to get it ....
  a dry cleaned b spin-dried c spring-cleaned
3 You must be freezing – why don't you sit by the fire and .... up a bit. a heat b hot c warm
4 It'll be difficult to get the job but I'm going to give it .... a a try b a test c an attempt
5 This government has helped .... much more than the poorer members of society. a rich b riches c the rich

My Test! answers: 1b 2a 3c 4a 5c

Word formation 2: other sources

Did you know *penguin* is a Welsh word?

fjord

rucksack

jacuzzi

sushi

Radio Presenter: Today's guest, Professor Terry Sands, is an expert on words. So, Professor, where do English words come from?

Professor: Well, many are borrowed from other languages, like **rucksack** from German and **shampoo** from Hindi. Others don't even look English, like the German **kindergarten**, or **fjord**, from Norwegian. Even Latin expressions, like **et cetera**, and many words from French, like **café**, don't even sound English!

Presenter: But don't some topic areas use more non-English words than others? Food, for example …

Professor: Yes. **Croissant** and **pizza**, for instance. Plus Asian food words, like **sushi** and **kebab**. In sport, we have **judo** and **karate**, of course. And many animal names, too: **kangaroo**'s obviously an Australian word, say. But did you know **penguin** is a Welsh word, meaning 'white head'?

Presenter: Amazing! Where else do our words come from?

Professor: Well, often from people or places. **Sandwich** and **jacuzzi** were both people, and **bungalow** and **jeans** come from place names – Bengal and Genoa. Even English words are always changing. We shorten many, like *gymnasium* to **gym,** or *advertisement* to **advert** or **ad**. Others mix two separate words, like **brunch**, combining *breakfast* and *lunch*. New words appear every day, as do words which are really just sounds, like **bang** or **squeak**. We're very good at finding ways to put our thoughts into words!

1 Which language does the phrase *et cetera* come from?
2 Which item of clothing takes its name from the Italian city of Genoa?

Answers: 1 Latin 2 Jeans

Word formation 2

Borrowing

1 **English has always used words taken from other languages. We now view many of these as English words.**

apostrophe (Greek)
cotton (Arabic)
landscape (Dutch)
piano (Italian)
potato (Spanish)
pyjamas (Persian)
rucksack (German)
shampoo (Hindi)

2 **Other words and expressions are still usually recognised as non-English, often because of their spelling or how they are used.**

anorak (Inuit languages)
bravado (Spanish)
et cetera (Latin)
etiquette (French)
fjord (Norwegian)
futon (Japanese)
graffiti (Italian)
kindergarten (German)
sauna (Finnish)

The word *wiki*, a Hawaiian adjective meaning 'fast', is now used as a noun in English to refer to a collaborative website.

3 **Some areas of English vocabulary have an especially high number of words taken from other languages.**

Food, cooking, e.g. *curry* (Tamil); *kebab* (Armenian); *cappuccino, pizza* and *spaghetti* (Italian); *paella* and *vanilla* (Spanish); *sushi* (Japanese); *biscuit, café, chef, pâté* and *restaurant* (French).

Sports, pastimes, e.g. *judo, karaoke* and *karate* (Chinese / Japanese); *ski* (Scandinavian languages).

Music, dance, e.g. *samba* and *salsa* (Spanish / Portuguese); *concert, orchestra* and *solo* (Italian).

Politics, law, warfare, e.g. *ballot* and *manifesto* (Italian); *apparatchik* and *glasnost* (Russian); *ombudsman* (Swedish); *guerrilla* (Spanish).

Animals, birds, e.g. *kangaroo* and *koala* (Australian Aboriginal languages); *chimpanzee* and *zebra* (African languages); *wildebeest* (Afrikaans); *giraffe* (Arabic); *cockatoo* and *orang-utan* (Malay); *hippopotamus* and *elephant* (Greek); *penguin* (Welsh).

4 We form the plural of most countable nouns taken from other languages by adding *s*, as with most English ones. However, a few usually keep their original plural form.

singular noun	usual plural	less usual plural
appendix	appendixes	appendices
bureau	bureaux	bureaus
cactus	cacti	cactuses
formula	formulas	formulae
forum	forums	fora
fungus	fungi	funguses
medium	media	mediums
nucleus	nucleuses	nuclei
stadium	stadiums	stadia

TIP

We can use *data* as an uncountable noun (*We don't have much data*), or as the plural of *datum* (*We do not have many data*), but the uncountable form is becoming more common.

5 A few plural nouns from other languages are usually used as singular or uncountable nouns in English, e.g. *agenda, graffiti, opera, spaghetti* and *trivia*.

▶ See Unit 16 for more on the formation of plural nouns.

6 Some words in English are formed from the names of places associated with them.

armageddon *bikini* *bohemian* *bungalow* *china* *denim* *dollar* *hamburger* *jeans* *marathon* *spa*

7 Many English words are taken from the names of people, but are used as common nouns without capital letters.

atlas *boycott* *diesel* *guillotine* *guy* *jacuzzi* *pilates* *sandwich* *teddy* (*bear*) *volt* *watt*

We often add the suffixes *-esque, -ic, -ial* or *-ian* / *-an* to the names of real or fictional people to form adjectives meaning 'in the style of' the named person. These sometimes begin with capital letters.

chauvinistic *Dickensian* *herculean* *Freudian* *Kafkaesque* *Keynesian* *Machiavellian* *martial* *quixotic* *Shakespearean* *titanic*

Abbreviation

8 We cut syllables from the ends of some words / phrases, especially in informal situations.

advert / *ad* (*advertisement*)
bike (*bicycle*)
decaf (*decaffeinated coffee*)
exam (*examination*)
fax (*facsimile*)
gym (*gymnasium*)
lab (*laboratory*)
mobile (*mobile phone*)
sci-fi (*science fiction*)
typo (*typographical error*)

Some other words / phrases are often shortened in other ways.

burger (*hamburger*)
flu (*influenza*)
fridge (*refrigerator*)
paper (*newspaper*)
phone (*telephone*)
plane (*aeroplane*)

A few shortened words are particularly common in US English.

cell (*cell* / *cellular phone*)
deli (*delicatessen*)
dorm (*dormitory*)
gas (*gasoline*)
limo (*limousine*)

The word *mathematics* is shortened to *maths* in British English, but *math* in American English.

9 We form some words by putting parts of two different words together.

brunch *camcorder* *cyborg* *electrocute* *fanzine* *heliport* *moped* *motel* *netiquette* *smog* *telethon* *travelogue*

10 We sometimes combine letters from a group of words to form a new noun which we pronounce as one word (called an acronym), e.g. *AIDS, laser, NASA, NATO, radar, scuba* and *sonar*.

We often use the initials of a group of words as a separate word, with the letters pronounced separately, e.g. *BBC, FAQ, SMS, MP3, PC, PDF, UK, UN, US* / *USA* and *VIP*.

We use *an*, not *a*, before words like these if the first letter starts with a vowel sound, e.g. *an MP3 player* and *an SMS*.

Other kinds of word formation

11 Some nouns sound like what they describe, e.g. *bang, beep, buzz, click, crash, groan, hum, mumble, smash, snore, pop, sizzle, thud* and *yawn*. We can use these nouns as verbs.

Most words for the sounds which animals make are like this.

bark (dogs) *buzz* (bees) *chirp* (birds) *hiss* (snakes) *miaow* (cats) *moo* (cows) *neigh* (horses) *roar* (lions) *squeak* (mice)

Practice

A Put the words in the box next to the correct headings in the table, then check in a dictionary.

bungalow (Bengali)	serenade (Italian)
budgerigar (Australian Aboriginal languages)	~~slalom~~ (from Scandinavian languages)
chalet (French)	taekwondo (Korean)
gazelle (Arabic)	tango (Spanish)
propaganda (Italian)	tapas (Spanish)
samosa (Indian languages)	veto (Latin)

food and cooking	....
sports and pastimes	slalom, ...
music and dance	....
houses and living spaces	....
politics and law	....
animals and birds	....

Without looking back at the unit, can you think of any more words for each topic?

B Combine each pair of words to form a new word that matches each definition. Try to make at least six words. Use a dictionary if necessary.

1 breakfast / lunch
A meal you eat in the middle of the morning. brunch
2 camera / recorder
A portable machine for making video films. ....
3 motor / hotel
A place where drivers can stop to spend the night in the middle of a long journey. ....
4 helicopter / port
A place to land a helicopter. ....
5 Internet / etiquette
A set of rules for how to communicate with people online.
....
6 smoke / fog
A form of air pollution which makes it difficult for people to breathe.
....
7 cybernetic / organism
A kind of machine which has some natural parts as well as artificial ones. ....
8 fans / magazine
An unofficial newsletter for people who like a famous person or sports team. ....
9 travel / monologue
A documentary or journal in which someone describes a journey.
....
10 television / marathon
A television programme lasting several hours which tries to raise money for good causes. ....

C Complete each sentence, using an adjective formed from the name in brackets. Use a dictionary if necessary.

1 The shop lights and the snow on the ground gave the street an almost ....Dickensian........ appearance. (Charles Dickens)
2 The President was a .... leader, who used every possible trick in order to try to hold on to power. (Niccolò Machiavelli)
3 My family history contains so much greed and dishonesty it's like a .... tragedy. (William Shakespeare)
4 I was so embarrassed at school today – I called my teacher 'Dad' by mistake! It was a real .... slip! (Sigmund Freud)
5 To complete the building in only eight months has been a .... task, but all our hard work has been worth the effort. (Hercules)
6 Gary's not a very practical person. In fact his behaviour is almost .... sometimes. (Don Quixote de la Mancha)
7 Her new novel is a .... nightmare in which the main character loses control of his life. (Franz Kafka)
8 The government's latest plan represents a return to the .... economic policies of the 1950s. (John Maynard Keynes)

D Complete each sentence, using an abbreviated form of one of the words or phrases in the box.

~~decaffeinated coffee~~	mobile phone
facsimile	newspaper
gymnasium	refrigerator
influenza	science fiction
mathematics	typographical error

1 I'd like a ....decaf.......... with milk to take away, please.
2 There was a really interesting article in the .... this morning.
3 I'm terrible at subjects like .... or Science – I prefer History.
4 I like all kinds of films, but I particularly enjoy fantasy and ....
5 Before you print your assignment, use the spell check to look for ....
6 I've decided to get fit by going to the .... twice a week.
7 To confirm your reservation, please send a .... to 0207 374885.
8 Sorry, Kelly's not here, but call her on her ....
9 Poor Tom – he spent all weekend in bed with the ....
10 Is there any milk in the .... ?

E Complete each sentence with the most appropriate plural form of the word in brackets. Use a dictionary if necessary.

1 A crowd of ....paparazzi.......... were waiting to photograph the actress as she left her hotel. (paparazzi)
2 My parents are planning to go to France to visit the .... of the Loire. (château)
3 This new coffee machine of yours makes amazing .... ! (cappuccino)
4 The .... on the building made it look really ugly. (graffiti)
5 There have been four attempted .... in this country in the last ten years. (coup)
6 *La Traviata* and *Tosca* are two of my favourite .... (opera)
7 We'd like two .... with salad, please. (lasagna)
8 The .... clearly proved that our theory was correct. (data)
9 Climate change may cause unusual weather .... (phenomenon)
10 She is a talented director in a wide range of film .... (genre)

MY TURN!

Write a list of 20 words borrowed from English that are used in your own language.

....
....
....
....

MY TEST!

Circle the correct option.

1 I've decided to buy a .... instead of a bed, because I can also use it to sit on . **a** sauna **b** anorak **c** futon
2 It's considered .... to write an email in CAPITAL LETTERS.
a bad netiquette **b** bad propaganda **c** a bad typo
3 We didn't need our old car any more, so we put an .... in the paper to try to sell it.
a advertising **b** advert **c** advertise
4 I couldn't sleep on the plane because the man next to me was .... **a** sizzling **b** thudding **c** snoring
5 I'm going to stay at university and study for an .... **a** MBA **b** PhD **c** BA

My Test! answers: 1c 2a 3b 4c 5a

Conditional clauses

If it hadn't been for Percy, who knows what could have happened?

ANTI-CRIME CAMERA BREAKS THE LAW

If the police **had asked** for a safety licence for their new flying camera, it **would have been** a major crime-fighting success. Unfortunately they didn't, and as a result the young man they filmed stealing a car might go free. '**As long as** you have a licence, there is no problem using these machines,' said a lawyer. '**Had** they used a properly licensed camera, it **would have been** fine.' **Should** the police lose their appeal, the court **may** decide the film can't be used as evidence and the thief **might** walk free. **If** that **happens**, the police **are going to feel** rather silly.

Today's headline | Most read

PERCY THE HERO

'**If it hadn't been for** Percy, who knows **what could have happened**?' said 78-year-old Maureen Thomas. Maureen knows that if her parrot **hadn't woken** her after a fire started in her kitchen, she **might** not **be** alive today. 'I always leave Percy's cage door open **in case** he **wants** to fly around,' explained Maureen. Seeing the fire, Percy flew into Maureen's bedroom and started squawking. '**If** Percy **squawks**, everyone in the street **hears** him,' Maureen added, 'so I woke up straight away.' One firefighter added: '**If** Percy **weren't** so noisy, Maureen **might** not **have woken** up in time. **If** we **gave** medals to pets, Percy **would** definitely **get** one!'

?
1 What should the police have done before using their flying camera?
2 Why does Percy the parrot deserve a medal?

Answers: 1 Asked for a safety licence. 2 Because he woke his owner when a fire started in her kitchen.

Conditional clauses

Real conditional clauses

1 If we are referring to something that is generally true, we use the same tense (present or past) in both the *if*-clause and the main clause (zero conditional).

*If Percy **squawks**, everyone in the street **hears** him.*
*When I was a child, **if** I **was** naughty my parents **sent** me to bed early.*

2 If we are referring to something that may happen in the future, we use the present tense in the *if*-clause and a future form in the main clause (first conditional).

*Be careful on that wall! **If** you **fall**, you'**ll hurt** yourself.*

We can often use the present perfect or the present simple, with a time expression, in the *if*-clause.

***If** they **haven't arrived by 3.30**, we'll have to leave without them.* OR ***If** they **don't arrive** ...*

We can use ***might, may, could, can / be able to, should, had better*** or ***be going to*** in the main clause instead of ***will***.

***If** that **happens**, the police **are going to feel** rather silly.*

We can use ***unless*** in real conditional clauses to mean ***if ... not***.

***Unless** it **rains**, we're going to have a picnic this afternoon.* OR ***If** it **doesn't rain**, we're ...*

The main clause can be an imperative or a request.

__Listen__ carefully __if__ you __want__ to know what to do.

We don't usually use *will* in the *if*-clause.

__If__ the bus __doesn't come__ soon, I'll start walking. NOT ~~*If the bus won't come soon ...*~~

▶ See Unit 35 for situations when we do use *will* in the *if*-clause.

3 If we want to express present or future responses to something that happened in the past, we can use the past tense or present perfect in the *if*-clause.

__If__ you __didn't sleep__ well last night, I'm not surprised you're tired.

__If__ you__'ve broken__ my computer, I'll be very angry!

Unreal conditional clauses

4 If we are referring to imaginary or untrue present situations or unlikely future situations, we usually use a past tense in the *if*-clause and *would* + *to*-infinitive in the main clause (second conditional).

__If__ we __gave__ medals to pets, Percy __would__ definitely __get__ one.

TIP

We often use *were* instead of *was* in unreal conditional clauses, especially in more formal situations.

If Percy __weren't__ so noisy ... OR *If Percy __wasn't__ ...*

We don't normally use *would* in the *if*-clause.

I would take a day off work today __if__ I __didn't have__ an important meeting. NOT ~~*... if I wouldn't have ...*~~

▶ See Unit 35 for situations when we do use *would* in the *if*-clause.

We can use *might* or *could* in the main clause instead of *would*.

__If__ she __paid__ more attention in class, she __might understand__ the lessons a bit better.

We can use *were* + *to*-infinitive in the *if*-clause to suggest that something is particularly unlikely.

__If__ the factory __were to close__, hundreds of people __would lose__ their jobs.

5 If we are referring to imaginary past situations, we usually use the past perfect in the *if*-clause and *would have* + past participle of the verb in the main clause (third conditional).

__If__ the police __had asked__ for a licence, they __would have had__ no problem.

Instead of *would have*, we can use *might have* or *could have* in the main clause.

6 We can sometimes mix these two different types of unreal conditional clause.

__If__ her parrot __hadn't woken__ her during the night, she __might not be__ alive today.

__If__ Percy __weren't__ so noisy, Maureen __might not have woken up__ in time.

7 We sometimes use *if it was* / *were not for* + noun phrase or *if it had not been for* + noun phrase.

__If it hadn't been for__ Percy, who knows what __could have happened__?

Alternatives to *if*

8 Instead of *if*, we can use *provided* / *providing, given, assuming, suppose* / *supposing, imagine, as long as, on condition that* and *even if*.

__As long as__ you __have__ a licence, ...

__Assuming__ the police __lose__ their appeal, ...

We use *in case* (+ present tense) to mean 'because ... might'.

I leave his door open __in case__ he __wants__ to fly around. (= *... because he might want ...*)

TIP

We use *in case of* + noun to mean *if there is* / *are*.

__In case of fire__, call the fire brigade.

9 In formal language we sometimes invert *had*, *were* or *should* and the subject, and leave out *if*.

__Had__ they __used__ it to catch the thief, ... OR *__If__ they __had used__ it ...*

__Were__ they __to close__ the factory, ... OR *__If__ they __were to__ close the factory, ...*

__Should__ the police __lose__ their appeal, ... OR *__If__ the police __lost__ their appeal, ...*

▶ See Unit 40 for more information on inversion.

10 In informal situations, we can use an imperative phrase + *and* / *or* instead of an *if*-clause.

__Do__ that again __and I'll call__ the police. OR *__If__ you __do__ that again, ...*

__Finish__ your dinner __or__ you __can't watch__ TV. OR *__If__ you __don't finish__ your dinner, ...*

Short conditional expressions

11 We often use expressions like *if so, if not, otherwise, in which case* or *in that case* to refer back to the previous sentence or clause.

The court may decide the film cannot be used as evidence, __in which case__ the thief __will be__ released.

12 We often leave out the verb *to be* with adjectives such as *applicable, appropriate, necessary* and *possible*, and in expressions such as *if asked, if known* and *if in doubt*.

Please complete Section 3 (Reasons for Leaving your Last Job), __if applicable__. OR *... if this section applies to you.*

Practice

A Match the sentence beginnings to the correct endings.

1 If I drink coffee at night,
2 The teacher sometimes let us go home early
3 If we don't hurry up,
4 I'll be very surprised
5 If you haven't tidied your room by dinnertime,
6 Wear lots of warm clothes
7 Could you help me with my homework
8 If they got up so early this morning,
9 If Gloria wants to pass her exam,
10 Irene's going to have an accident

a we're going to miss the train!
b she'd better start studying very soon.
c unless you want to freeze to death.
d if you have time?
e they must be exhausted by now.
f I find it difficult to get to sleep.
g if Paula's still working here six months from now.
h unless she learns to drive more carefully.
i if we worked hard during the lesson.
j you won't be allowed to have any ice cream.

1 ...f... 2 .... 3 .... 4 .... 5 ....
6 .... 7 .... 8 .... 9 .... 10 ....

B Underline the correct option.

1 If it <u>*wasn't*</u> / *wouldn't be* so windy outside at the moment, it would be nice to go for a walk.
2 If you helped round the house a bit more, I *allow* / *might allow* you to have a bit more pocket money.
3 I *won't* / *wouldn't* mind about Lisa coming home late if she just phoned to let me know she was OK.
4 *If* / *Unless* the company were to reduce its costs, profits would increase.
5 My brother *stays* / *would stay* in bed all day if he didn't have to go to school.
6 If I *know* / *had known* you were such a gossip, I wouldn't have trusted you with such personal information.
7 Sandra would have given up her course by now, if it *hadn't been* / *wouldn't have been* for her teacher's encouragement.
8 If we found someone else to go with us, it *had been* / *would be* cheaper to rent a car.
9 If it hadn't been for losing our suitcases on the way home, it *will* / *would* have been a perfect holiday!
10 We could have invited more people to the party if we *lived* / *would live* in a bigger house.

C Complete the sentences with the expressions from the box. Sometimes more than one answer is possible.

if applicable	if asked	if in doubt	if known
if necessary	if not	if possible	if so
in that case	in which case		

1 If the weather is good we can have a barbecue, but ......if not...... we'll have to eat indoors instead.
2 Make sure you know what time your lessons start in the morning. ...., ask your teacher.
3 The train tickets might be too expensive, ... we'll need to go by bus.
4 Ideally, everyone will be here on time, but .... we can wait a little bit longer.
5 I'd like to change this shirt for a larger size, ...
6 Are you going to see Nicky today? ...., can you give her a message, please?
7 Felipe might not be able to help us move house, and .... we'll have to do everything ourselves.
8 .... to recommend one thing for a visitor to your town to see, what would you choose?
9 Please include the full name of your last employer, ...
10 Write your full address, including your postcode (..................).

D Complete each sentence b so that it means the same as sentence a, using the words in brackets.

1 a If we assume the traffic isn't too heavy, it should take us about four hours to get there. (assuming)
  b ...Assuming the traffic isn't too heavy..., it should take us about four hours to get there.
2 a If the main door is locked, please use the side exit. (which)
  b The main door might be locked, ..., please use the side exit.
3 a If you tell anyone about this, I'll never speak to you again! (and)
  b .... I'll never speak to you again!
4 a Please do not hesitate to contact me if you require any assistance. (should)
  b Please do not hesitate to contact me ....
5 a Having a salary of a million dollars still wouldn't make me want to do your job! (even if)
  b .... I still wouldn't want to do your job!

6 a Take a sandwich with you because you might feel hungry later. (case)
 b Take a sandwich with you ....
 ....

7 a If you don't buy your ticket for the concert today, there won't be any left. (or)
 b ....
 there won't be any left.

8 a If I hadn't been here to help you, what would you have done? (supposing)
 b .... ,
 what would you have done?

9 a You may leave unless you need a certificate, in which case please come to my desk. (otherwise)
 b Please come to my desk if you need a certificate.
 ....

10 a Given good weather, a boat trip on the river is a great way to spend an afternoon. (long)
 b .... good, a boat trip on the river is a great way to spend an afternoon.

MY TURN!

Complete the sentences so that they are true for you.

1 If I have made some mistakes with these exercises, *I'll go back and do them again*.
2 Had I been better prepared, ...
 ....
3 If I have enough time later today, ...
 ....
4 If it hadn't been for ....
 ....
5 Unless I ....
 ....
6 Even if ...., I wouldn't
 ....
7 If I had ....
 ....
8 If one of my friends were to ....
 ....
9 As long as ....
 ....
10 I might ...., in which case
 ....

E Complete the news story with one word in each space.

A PRISONER IN HIS OWN OFFICE

Primary school headteacher Tom Ellis might [1] *have* .... taken more care with the keys to his office last Wednesday, [2] .... he known what his students were planning. The nine-year-olds, angry at the bad quality of the school food, locked him in his office and said they would only let him out on [3] .... that he agreed to order takeaway pizzas for them. 'If I [4] .... said OK, I don't know what they [5] .... have done. They might have left me in there, in which [6] .... I would have had to phone for help,' said Mr Ellis. 'I admit the school food is terrible, so I can understand why they complained. I [7] .... want to eat it [8] .... if I was starving!' Mr Ellis has promised to try to improve the quality of the food. 'I told them that if it hasn't improved in a month's time, I [9] .... personally pay for another pizza for everyone. I really hope we can do something to improve the food by then. If [10] ...., it's going to cost me a fortune!'

MY TEST!

Circle the correct option.

1 If you're still sitting reading the newspaper when I come back in five minutes, I .... very angry.
 a am b 'll be c 'd be
2 We'd all be much happier if we .... about money all the time.
 a aren't worrying b wouldn't worry c weren't worrying
3 If .... here earlier, you would have met my friend Andrea. a you'd been b you'd be c you're
4 You should install a smoke detector in your house .... there's another fire.
 a in case b in case of c in which case
5 I might see you tonight, but .... I'll give you a ring tomorrow instead. a if no b if not c if it's not

My Test! answers: 1b 2c 3a 4a 5b

35 Other conditional forms

If you would just wait here for a moment.

Shop assistant: Can I help you?
Customer: Yes, I bought this phone here yesterday and it doesn't work.
Shop assistant: I see. What exactly is the problem?
Customer: It's simple. If I press 'On', nothing happens! It was very cheap, and actually **I wish I'd bought a more expensive one**!
Shop assistant: OK. **If you would just wait here for a moment**, I'll find a technician ...

Technician: So you're having phone problems, sir? **If you'll let me have a quick look** ...
Customer: Sure, here it is.
Technician: Right, I'm afraid **this looks as if water has got into the phone**. It's quite common, actually. I always think, 'Well, **if you will use your phone while you're in the bath**!'
Customer: Water? But it was like this when I opened it.
Technician: Maybe it was already broken. Do you have the receipt?
Customer: Actually, no. I've lost it. I'm terrible with these things. **If only someone else would look after them for me**!
Technician: Well, **I wish I could help you**, but without the receipt ... . We can give you a discount on another phone, **if that will help at all**.
Customer: Well ... OK, I suppose.
Technician: Right, I'll show you what we've got. Keep this one, though, and **if you should happen to find the receipt by any chance**, bring it in and we'll give you a refund ...

1 What is the problem with the customer's new phone?
2 Why can't the shop give the customer a refund?

Answers: 1 If he presses 'On', nothing happens. 2 Because he has lost the receipt.

Other conditional forms

Wish and *if only*

1 We can use *wish* or *if only* to express a desire for an alternative present situation. We usually use the past simple or past continuous form of the verb.

*I **wish** I **could** help you.*
***If only** we **were sitting** in a warm car instead of standing in the rain.*

2 We can use *wish* or *if only* to express a desire for an imaginary past situation. We usually use the past perfect form of the verb.

*I **wish** I'**d bought** a more expensive one.*
***If only** you **had told** us you were going to be in town!*

3 We can use *wish* or *if only* with *would / wouldn't* to express a desire for a hypothetical change in general behaviour.

*I **wish** you **wouldn't make** so much noise when you come home late.*
***If only** he **wouldn't lose** his temper so easily!*

We can sometimes use the past simple instead of *would / wouldn't*.

***If only** someone else **looked after** ...* OR ***If only** someone else **would look after** them for me!*

We usually use the past simple, not *would / wouldn't*, with *wish* or *if only* to refer to ourselves.

*I **wish** I **didn't fall asleep** as soon as I started watching a film!* NOT ~~*I wish I wouldn't fall ...*~~
*Sometimes I **wish** I **had** more time.*

If ... will / would in conditional clauses

4 We sometimes use *will* or *would* in an *if*-clause to refer to the result of an action in the main clause.

*We can give you a small discount on a different phone, though, **if** that **will help** at all.*
*I can meet you at 7 instead of 6, **if** that **would be** more convenient for you.*

We can use *will* or *would* in an *if*-clause to talk about promises. Note the difference:

***If** you'**ll wash** the car, you can borrow it.* (= You can borrow it if you promise to wash it afterwards.)
***If** you **wash** the car, you can borrow it.* (= You can borrow it if you wash it first.)

5 We sometimes use *will / can* or *would / could* in an *if*-clause, often with *just*, to make a request sound more polite. *Would / could* are more polite than *will / can*.

***If** you **would just wait** here for a moment, I'll ...*
***If** you'**ll let** me have a quick look ...*

If we stress *will* in a spoken *if*-clause, it suggests that we disapprove of someone's behaviour.

*If you <u>**will**</u> **use** your phone while you're in the bath!*

If ... should / happen to / should happen to

6 We sometimes use *if ... should ...*, *if ... happen to ...*, or *if ... should happen to ...* to refer to events which are possible but not very likely.

***If** the train **should be** / **happens to be** late, I'll text you to let you know.*

We sometimes use the phrase *by any chance* in real conditional sentences to emphasise that we think something is unlikely to happen.

***If** you **should happen to find** the receipt **by any chance**, bring it in ...*

It will / would be ... if ...

7 We sometimes use expressions like noun phrase + *will / would / might be* + adjective + *if ...* at the beginning of a clause to make an opinion, suggestion, request, etc. sound less direct.

***It will be great if** you can let me know by the end of the day.*
***I'd be grateful if** you didn't mention this conversation to anyone.*

As if and *as though*

8 We can use *as if* or *as though* after verbs like *seem, look, sound, feel, act* or *behave* followed by a verb in the present or present perfect to make comparisons which we see as real.

*This **looks as if** water **has got** into the phone.*

9 We can use *as if* or *as though* with the same verbs followed by a verb in a past tense to make comparisons which we see as unreal or imaginary.

*My brother often behaves **as though** he **was** eight years old, rather than 18!*

▶ See Unit 37 for more information on adverbial clauses of comparison.

Practice

A Match the sentence beginnings to the correct endings.

1 We
2 If there
3 If I
4 We all wish there
5 If only we
6 I wish they
7 I wish you
8 If you
9 If Jake
10 It

a had set off a bit earlier, we might have avoided the rush hour.
b wouldn't play your music so loud!
c happens to call while I'm out, can you take a message?
d might be a good idea to book a table in advance.
e could spell that for me, please.
f is anything I can do to help, let me know.
g had phoned to say they were going to be late, then I wouldn't have been so worried.
h would be much more relaxed if we knew you weren't going to be on your own.
i should happen to find your keys, I'll give them to you tomorrow.
j was a better solution.

1 ...h... 2 ...... 3 ...... 4 ...... 5 ...... 6 ...... 7 ...... 8 ...... 9 ...... 10 ......

B Match requests 1–10 to speakers a–j.

1 If you can all gather round me, please. [a]
2 If I could see some form of identification. [ ]
3 If you will just hold the line while I put you through. [ ]
4 If you can just print out this report for me. [ ]
5 If you could spend a few minutes reading through the safety instructions. [ ]
6 If we can make it a bit later, say around 4. [ ]
7 If you would like to take a seat in the waiting room. [ ]
8 If you could just lift your bags onto here, please. [ ]
9 If you would just send us an email confirming those dates. [ ]
10 If I could have your attention, please. [ ]

a A tour guide explaining something to a party of tourists.
b An airport worker checking in a passenger's luggage.
c A teacher talking to a class full of noisy students.
d A boss speaking to her secretary.
e A hotel receptionist taking a reservation for a guest.
f A call centre worker taking a call from a customer.
g A man arranging a game of tennis with a friend.
h A health centre receptionist welcoming a patient.
i A bank clerk dealing with a customer.
j A flight attendant giving instructions to his passengers.

C Complete the dialogues by putting the words in brackets in the correct order.

1 A: I can't come out tonight – I haven't got any money.
B: I could lend you some, ...if that would help... .
(help / if / would / that)

2 A: Please can I have a cat for my birthday?
B: OK. On one condition: ....
(it / look after / if / you'll)

3 A: I can't believe how much work I have to do!
B: ....
(all the time / complain / wish / I / wouldn't / you)

4 A: I feel really tired this morning – I just want to stay in bed.
B: Well, ... !
(you / watching / TV / will stay up / if / half the night)

5 A: I'd love to come with you but I just haven't got time.
B: Oh well. But ...., give me a ring.
(by any chance / you / if / change your mind / happen to)

6 A: I've had bad stomach pains the last few days.
B: Right, well, ... (lie down / if / just/ you /on the bed / could)

7 A: I don't really feel like going to Jenny's party tonight.
B: No, I don't either. .... not to go!
(of / we / a good excuse / only / if / could think)

8 A: Now you have a new car, will you sell your old one?
B: No, ..., I might need it again.
(the new one / I / have / to / any problems / if / happen / with / should)

9 A: I can't believe you broke my phone! Why don't you take more care with other people's things?
B: ...., you won't be so angry!
(me / explain / if / let / you'll)

10 A: Georgia's been thrown out of school!
B: I know! She must really wish .... (her exam / cheated / hadn't / she / in)

D Complete each sentence with one appropriate word.

1 If you should ......happen...... to see Andrew, ask him to call.
2 She looks terrible, ... though she hasn't slept for days.
3 Don't you sometimes wish you .... go and live on a tropical island?
4 .... would be helpful if you could tell us by Friday.
5 Please contact us if you .... need any more help.
6 If .... there was an earlier train, we'd be able to get there in time.
7 We'd prefer it .... you took a taxi instead of walking.
8 I .... you wouldn't come in the house in those muddy boots!

E Complete the sentence for each picture, using an appropriate structure from this unit.

1 If only ...you'd remembered to fill it up with petrol...!
2 I wish I ....
3 Well, if you ....!
4 I wish ....
5 This feels ....
6 It ....!
7 I bet you wish ....
8 If only ....!

MY TURN!

If you had six wishes which could change your past, present or future, what would you wish for?

I wish I were ......a better singer.......
If only I hadn't ....
I wish I could ....
If only .... would ....
I wish I didn't have to ....
I wish I had ....

MY TEST!

Circle the correct option.

1 I really wish you .... with us, but I understand how busy you both are. **a** came **b** can come **c** could come
2 If only you .... the receipt, we would have been able to help you. **a** kept **b** had kept **c** would have kept
3 If it .... things easier for everyone, let's meet at my house. **a** can make **b** will make **c** had made
4 If Laura .... to call, tell her I'll be back at 10. **a** happens **b** will happen **c** would happen
5 If your mobile phone .... to get water in it, it'll stop working.
a will happen **b** should happen **c** would happen

My Test! answers: 1c 2b 3b 4a 5b

36 Relative clauses

It has Andean mountains, many of which rise to over 4,500 metres.

Venezuela

There are not many countries [illegible] of landscapes as Venezuela. It has Andean mountains, **many of which rise to over 4,**[illegible], **fertile plains**, a desert, a jungle, and the world's highest waterfall. This waterfall – Salto Angel, **named after Jim**[illegible], an American pilot and **the first person to fly over** [illegible] – is nearly 1,000 metres high.

Under Venezuela there is oil, **the reason why the country was South America's strongest economy from the 19**[illegible] **19**[illegible]. This economic **prosperity** goes back to 1922, **the year in which oil was discovered** [illegible]**aibo**. After that, engineers **drill**[illegible] **for oil** seemed to find it **wherever they looked**. The political problems **which hit the country in the late 19**[illegible] meant the amount of oil **being produced** then fell significantly. However, given the enormous supply of oil **available** and enough other countries **keen** to buy it, Venezuela is a country **wh**[illegible] **future should be secure**.

Venezuela, **not somewhere most people think of** [illegible] **for a holi**[illegible], actually has many tourist attractions. Its **coastline**, **which stretches for nearly** [illegible], is more Caribbean than South American. And because it has a climate **that varies little du**[illegible], with temperatures **averaging** 25–30°C in most of the country, holidaymakers can be confident of having good weather. All in all, Venezuela is a country **anyone should enjoy vi**[illegible].

?
1 What is special about Salto Angel?
2 Why should Venezuela's economic future be secure?

Answers: 1 It's the world's highest waterfall.
2 Because it has a lot of oil.

Relative clauses

Defining and non-defining relative clauses

1 A defining relative clause gives necessary information about a noun.

*There are not many countries **which have such a variety of landscapes as Venezuela**.*

We can usually leave out the relative pronoun in defining relative clauses when it refers to the object of the clause.

Venezuela is a country anyone should enjoy visiting.
OR *... a country **which** / **that** anyone ...*

2 A non-defining relative clause gives extra information, separated from the main clause by commas.

*Its coastline, **which stretches for nearly 3,000 kilometres**, is more Caribbean than South American.*

We can't leave out the relative pronoun in non-defining relative clauses.

*My brother, **who** you will meet at the party, is a teacher.*
NOT ~~*My brother, you will meet ...*~~

Relative pronouns: *which*, *that* and *who*

3 We can use *which* and *who* in defining and non-defining relative clauses.

*The political problems **which hit the country in the late 1990s** ...*

TIP

Don't use *which* to refer to people.

*The people **who live next door** are from France.*
NOT ~~*... people which ...*~~

In defining relative clauses we can use *that* instead of *which* or *who* in more informal situations, but not in non-defining relative clauses.

*The man **that** you met ...* OR *... who you met ...*
*My sister, **who** lives in Australia, is staying with us at the moment.* NOT ~~*..., that lives in Australia, ...*~~

In very formal language we sometimes use *whom* as the object form of *who*.

*Alice Wallis, **whom** many see as the country's best writer, will be giving a talk tonight.*

We usually use *which* or *whom*, not *that* or *who*, after a preposition.

*My mother is someone **to whom** I will always be grateful.* NOT ~~*... to who I will always ...*~~

In less formal language, we can use *that*, *who* or no pronoun if we put the preposition at the end.

*My mother is someone **who** / **that** I will always be grateful **to**.* OR *... someone I will always be grateful to.*

4 **In non-defining relative clauses we can use *of which* or *of whom* after words like *some, any, none, all, both, many* and *few*, or after numbers and superlative adjectives.**

*The company has three offices, **one of which** / **the largest of which** is in Moscow.*

5 **We can use *which* as a non-defining relative pronoun to refer back to the entire main clause.**

*I've got lots of homework to do, **which** means I can't go out tonight.*

We can also use phrases like *in which case, by which time* and *at which time* / *point* in a similar way.

*The restaurant might be fully booked, **in which case** we'll have to go somewhere else.*

***In which case* has a meaning similar to *if so* (see Unit 34).**

Other kinds of relative clause

6 **We can use *when* or *in* / *at* / *on which* to refer to a noun of time, like *day, year,* etc.**

*... to 1922, **the year in which** oil was discovered at Maracaibo.* OR *... **the year** (**when**) ...*

We can leave out such words after the words *day, year, moment* and *time*.

*Stefan was born in 1989, **the year** (**when**) the Berlin Wall came down.*

7 **We can use *where* or *in* / *at which* after a place noun, or after words like *case, example, point* and *situation*.**

*This is the kind of situation **where** there's no easy solution.*

We can leave out *where* after *somewhere, anywhere, everywhere* and *nowhere* and sometimes *place*.

*Venezuela, **not somewhere** / **not a place** most people think of going ...*

8 **After *reason*, we can use *why* or sometimes *that* or no conjunction.**

*Under Venezuela there is oil, **the reason why** / **that** it was South America's strongest economy ...*

9 **We use *whose* + noun as an alternative to *of whom* or *of which*.**

*Venezuela is a country **whose** economic future / the economic future **of which** should be secure.*

10 **We sometimes use *what or who* in a way similar to a relative pronoun, to mean 'the thing which' or 'the person who'.**

*The traffic is **what** I hate about living in a big city.* OR *The traffic is **the thing** (**which**) I hate ...*

> **TIP**
> **We can't use *what* in this way after a noun.**
> *The main thing that I liked about the film was the script.* NOT ~~*The main thing what I liked ...*~~

We can use *when, where* and *why* in the same way.

*My childhood was **when** I was happiest.*
*This town is **where** I lived.*
*That's **why** it's so nice to be back.*

Shortened relative clauses

11 **We sometimes use only present participles or past participles to make relative clauses shorter.**

*Salto Angel, **named** after Jimmie Angel ...*
*... engineers **drilling** for oil ...*

12 **We can use a *to*-infinitive after a superlative, *the first* / *second*, etc., *the next* / *last* / *only* and *the one*.**

*... the first (person) **to fly** over it.*
*The Venezuelan team is the one **to watch** this year.*

13 **We can use adjectives on their own to make relative clauses shorter. Often these have prepositions or *to*-infinitives after them.**

*... other countries **keen** to buy **it** ...* OR *... other countries **which are keen** ...*

We can use some adjectives, e.g. *affected, available, concerned, involved, present, responsible* and *necessary*, alone after a noun as a shortened relative clause.

*Given the enormous supply of oil **available** ...*
*I didn't know any of the people **present**.*

▶ See Unit 21 for more information on the position of adjectives.

14 **We can use prepositional phrases after a noun to make relative clauses shorter.**

*Can you pass me that book **on the table**?* OR *... that book **which is on** ...*

Practice

A Circle the correct option.

1 My mobile phone, ... I got for my birthday last year, is my most important possession.
a what (b) which c that
2 My brother is the only person in the world for ... I would do anything.
a who b which c whom
3 The company ... I used to work has closed down.
a which b where c –
4 By the time you get here I might have gone to bed, in ... case I'll leave the door unlocked.
a – b that c which
5 Pasta is probably the kind of food ... I like best.
a where b what c which
6 My mother's cooking was ... I missed most when I left home for the first time.
a which b that c what
7 Sara still hasn't replied to my email about Friday's party, ... suggests she's not very keen on the idea.
a that b which c –
8 Is Natasha the girl ... mother is an English teacher?
a who b her c whose
9 There aren't many cases ... people find their perfect job as soon as they leave school or university.
a where b why c that
10 The only reason ... Neil doesn't like Liam is because Liam always gets better marks at school.
a for b if c why

B Complete each sentence with a relative pronoun.

1 The town ....*where*.......... I grew up has changed a lot in the last few years.
2 Luca, ... goes to school with my sister, is a really good tennis player.
3 Spring is the time of year .... I like best.
4 We finally arrived home at nearly 2 in the morning, by .... time we were all exhausted.
5 The audience consisted of about 20 people, most of .... left before the end of the play.
6 The relaxed atmosphere is .... I like best about living here.
7 Jessica told everyone what had happened, which is .... I don't trust her.
8 We were back home by 9.30, the time at .... many people were just going out.
9 That's Marco, ... brother is in my class at school.
10 I usually get home at 6.30 in the morning, ... many people are just getting up.

C Make the relative clauses shorter by crossing out any unnecessary words.

1 We are determined to do everything ~~that is~~ necessary to find a solution to this problem.
2 Google, which was started by Larry Page and Sergey Brin in 1996, is the world's best-known internet search engine.
3 Most of the people who had been present at our first concert also came to our second one.
4 The motorway which is being built at the moment will make the journey between the cities much faster.
5 All the people who were waiting for the bus were complaining about how late it was.
6 Look at this old school photo – do you recognise the girl who is in the middle of the back row?
7 The company has apologised to everyone who has been affected by the problem.
8 If you call our Helpline tomorrow morning, there'll be someone who'll be available to advise you.
9 Children who are under the age of 12 can travel free.
10 This suitcase is the only one which is big enough to fit everything in.

D Join the sentences, using relative clauses and the words in brackets.

1 I bought some shoes last week. The shoes were very expensive. (that)
The shoes that I bought last week were very expensive.

2 My cousin's name is Jeff. He works for a big American bank. (whose)

3 One of Joe's brothers lives in Canada. He is a singer in a rock band. (who)

4 I'd like to thank my family. I wouldn't have been able to win this award without my family. (whom)

5 A new shopping centre is being built in the city centre. The new shopping centre will open in two years' time. (which)

6 We always go on holiday at the end of September. Flights are cheaper at the end of September. (when)

7 Kevin is my new boss. I introduced you to Kevin this morning. (who)

8 I fell asleep during the lesson. This happened because I was very tired. (why)

9 The lights suddenly went out. I started to feel frightened at that point. (which)

10 My favourite city is San Sebastian. I've been to San Sebastian many times. (where)

E Complete each sentence in an appropriate way, starting with a relative clause.

1 The woman *who is standing in the corner is a famous actress*.

2 This time of year, ...

3 The train didn't arrive until 10.30, by ....

4 At the back of the cupboard ....

5 President Jones, for ....

6 In 1998, the year ....

7 The percentage of people ....

8 There were only seven passengers on the bus, few of ....

9 It was a really difficult week, at the end of ....

10 Maurizio, ...

MY TURN!

Choose at least five of the items in the box and write a true sentence about each one in your notebook. Include at least one relative clause or shortened relative clause in each sentence.

your best friend   an interesting place in your country an important year in your life   a singer you like a popular meal or food in your country your favourite film   a hobby you enjoy a plan or ambition   a memorable experience

Example: *My best friend, whose name is Melissa, is a very good tennis player.*

MY TEST!

Circle the correct option.

1 The new Italian restaurant, ... looks very nice, is also quite cheap. **a** which **b** that **c** what

2 The woman .... lives next door always plays her music really loud at night. **a** – **b** who **c** whom

3 Next weekend I'm going to Caracas, ... I used to live. **a** that **b** which **c** where

4 3 August 1998, the day on .... my sister was born, is the first day I remember. **a** when **b** which **c** that

5 The only person .... me when I lived in Venezuela was my brother. **a** visited **b** what visited **c** to visit

My Test! answers: 1a 2b 3c 4b 5c

Adverbial clauses

Effort is only effort when it begins to hurt.

If you don't want to work, you have to work to earn enough money **so that you won't have to work**. (Ogden Nash, poet)

Effort is only effort **when it begins to hurt**. (Jose Ortega y Gasset, philosopher)

By the time a man realises that his father was right, he usually has a son who thinks he's wrong. (Charles Wadsworth, pianist)

A lie can travel half way around the world **while the truth is just putting on its shoes**. (Mark Twain, author)

The brain starts working when you get up in the morning, and doesn't stop **until you get to the office**. (Robert Frost, poet)

Everything is funny **as long as it is happening to somebody else**. (Will Rogers, comedian)

We don't stop playing **because we grow old**. We grow old **because we stop playing**. (George Bernard Shaw, writer)

I don't know the key to success, **but the key to failure is trying to** please **everybody**. (Bill Cosby, comedian)

No matter what side of the argument you are on, you always find people on your side that you wish were on the other. (Jascha Heifetz, violinist)

1 Which quote talks about family relationships?
2 What will happen if you try to make everybody happy?

Answers: 1 Charles Wadsworth's 2 You won't succeed.

Adverbial clauses

1 Adverbial clauses give extra information about a main clause. If they come before the main clause, they are usually followed by a comma.

If you don't want to work, you have to ...
Effort is only effort ***when it begins to hurt.***

Adverbial clauses starting with *since, as* and *while* can give more than one kind of information.

You'd better go ***since / as*** *it's getting late.*
(*since / as = because*)
You've grown ***since*** *I last saw you!*
I watched ***while / as*** *the procession went past.*
(*while / as = at the same time as*)
While *it's not the best hotel, it's comfortable enough.*
(*while = although*)

2 Adverbial time clauses tell us when something happens and start with words like *when, now, as long as, as soon as, until* and *while.*

A lie can travel half way around the world ***while the truth is just putting on its shoes.***

TIP

We use an affirmative verb after *until.*

... doesn't stop ***until you get to the office.***
NOT ~~*... until you don't get ...*~~

We can sometimes use *hardly / scarcely* (+ past perfect) + *before / when* or *no sooner* (+ past perfect) + *than / when* with a similar meaning to *as soon as.*

We had ***hardly*** *moved into our house* ***when ...***
OR *We had* ***no sooner*** *moved into our house* ***than ...***

In adverbial time clauses which refer to the future, we usually use the present simple, not the future.

Give me a ring ***when you decide what you're going to do.*** NOT ~~*... when you will decide ...*~~

But in certain contexts, we can use a future form after *when* in a relative clause. Note the difference:

Jacob will retire next March, ***when he'll be 65.***
(a relative clause, referring to *next March*)
Jacob will retire ***when he's 65.*** (adverbial clause)
NOT ~~*... retire when he'll be 65.*~~

3 Adverbial clauses of reason explain something in the main clause and usually begin with *because, as, seeing* (*that*) or *since*.

We don't stop playing ***because we grow old****. We grow old* ***because we stop playing****.*

> **TIP**
>
> We can also use *because of* as a preposition to give a reason for something.
>
> ***Because of the bad weather*** *we had to cancel the barbecue.* OR ***Because the weather was bad****, we ...*

4 Adverbial clauses of purpose explain our purpose in doing something described in the main clause and usually begin with *so* (*that*) or, in more formal situations, *in order that*.

If you don't want to work, you have to work to earn enough money ***so that you won't have to work****.*

We can also explain purpose using the *to*-infinitive, *in order to* + infinitive or *so as to* + infinitive.

After driving for four hours we stopped (***in order***) ***to have*** *lunch.*

5 Adverbial clauses of result explain the consequence of an action / situation and usually begin with *so*. They come after the main clause. In more formal situations we can say *with the result that*.

Jamie didn't study very hard, ***so he failed all his exams****.* OR *...,* ***with the result that he failed*** *...*

6 Adverbial clauses of contrast give information which contrasts with the information in the main clause, and begin with *although, though, even though, while, whereas, whilst* and *in spite of / despite the fact that*.

While I like learning new things*, I hate studying!* OR *I hate studying, while I like learning ...*

We can sometimes use *Much as* to mean *Although / Though / While ... very much*.

Much as I like Sue*, I wouldn't want to go on holiday with her!* OR ***Although I like Sue very much****, I ...*

If the subject of the two clauses is the same, we can often use *in spite of / despite* + gerund.

Despite being tired*, I decided to go to the gym.* OR ***Despite the fact that I was tired****, I decided ...*

We can use *no matter* + question word or *whatever / wherever / whoever / whenever / whichever / however* at the start of an adverbial clause to mean 'It doesn't matter what / where / who, etc.'

No matter what side of the argument you are on, ...
Whenever I ring Kevin *he's always out.*

7 Adverbial clauses of place give information about the location of an event or situation in the main clause and usually begin with *where, wherever, anywhere* or *everywhere*.

You can sit (***any***)***where you like****.*

8 Adverbial clauses of comparison with *as, just as, the same as* and (in informal situations) *like* usually come after the main clause and introduce a comparison with something in the main clause.

We're going to Spain for our holidays, ***like we did last year****.* OR *...,* ***as we did last year****.*

▶ See Unit 23 for more comparative forms with *as* and *than*, and for clauses of comparison with *too* and *enough*.

Adverbial clauses with present and past participles

9 We can begin adverbial clauses with present participles (verb + *-ing*) instead of *while / because*.

Not knowing *what else to do, I went home. (= Because I didn't know ...)*

We can use *Having* + past participle in a similar way instead of *after / because*.

Having eaten *all our food, he fell asleep. (= After / Because he had eaten ...)*

We can use past participles in a similar way with a passive meaning.

Spoken *by only a few people, this beautiful language is dying.*

10 We can use participles after words like *after, before, on, once, since, until, when* and *while* to give information about time, or after *by, in, with* and *without* to give information about how something happens.

On arriving*, I noticed a strange smell in the room.*
Will ran home ***without stopping****.*

11 We can use a noun or certain pronouns (e.g. *there, everyone*) before participles.

There being *nothing in the fridge, I ordered a pizza.*

Shortened adverbial clauses

12 In more formal situations, we can use participles instead of normal verb forms in adverbial clauses.

When speaking in public*, always make sure you've got some water to drink. (= When you are speaking ...)*

If the verb in the adverbial clause is *be*, we sometimes leave it out completely.

Though not really hungry*, I made myself a sandwich.* OR ***Though I wasn't really hungry****, I ...*

Practice

A **Underline the correct option.**

1 I'm much more relaxed *before* / *now* I've done all my exams.
2 *When* / *While* I broke my leg, I had to spend three days in hospital.
3 *Although* / *But* we really wanted to see the film, the tickets were a bit too expensive.
4 I will have to take the bus to school *if* / *until* I fix my bike.
5 *Since* / *Whereas* we had a few hours before our flight, we decided to explore the city.
6 Mikael and Martin are coming to stay with us during the summer, the same *as* / *like* they always do.
7 *As soon as* / *As long as* it started raining we picked up our things and ran inside.
8 *While* / *Because* I love going to the theatre, I find opera really boring.
9 I'd no sooner switched my phone on *before* / *than* it rang.
10 *Despite* / *Even though* Dan has been studying Spanish for years, he still can't speak it very well.

B **Complete sentences a and b, using the same word.**

1 a I want to go and live in France for a year ......because...... I think that's the best way to learn French.
  b ......Because...... of her poor attitude, Jessica has never done very well at school.
2 a People still go swimming in the river .... knowing that it's dangerous.
  b .... the fact that it rains a lot there, it's a great place to have a holiday.
3 a .... we couldn't afford to stay in hotels, we took a tent and camped instead.
  b I haven't had a holiday .... the summer before last.
4 a .... I don't think you'll get the job, I still think you should apply for it.
  b Would you like a drink .... you're waiting?
5 a .... I'd finished everything I needed to do, I decided to go home early.
  b Isabella offered to cook dinner for us, just .... I knew she would.
6 a The restaurant is very popular in the evening, ... you may need to book a table in advance.
  b Please arrive at the airport two hours before your flight .... as to allow plenty of time to check in.
7 a They had no sooner fallen asleep .... their baby started crying and woke them up.
  b The view from the top of the mountain is more beautiful .... any other view I've ever seen.
8 a Amy was really excited .... she heard your news this morning.
  b Give me a ring .... your train gets in and I'll come and pick you up.
9 a .... possible, I avoid walking on my own at night.
  b I always have my camera with me .... I go, in case I see something interesting to photograph.
10 a We can't buy the tickets .... Cristina has decided if she wants to come with us or not.
  b After landing, passengers should stay seated .... given permission to leave by a flight attendant.

C **Complete each sentence with an appropriate participle (present or past) of the verb in brackets. Sometimes more than one answer is possible.**

1 As the train pulled into the station I saw Paula ......standing...... on the platform. (stand)
2 .... the painting from the City Museum last year, the thief was finally caught yesterday. (steal)
3 .... using only the best ingredients, our food is known for its high quality. (prepare)
4 He slowly opened the front door, ... hard not to make any noise. (try)
5 Steve felt sick, ... too much chocolate. (eat)
6 .... his parents to be worried, he phoned to tell them he was going to be late. (not want)
7 Our cakes are particularly delicious .... with ice cream. (serve)
8 .... for a bus for nearly an hour, we eventually gave up and decided to walk. (wait)
9 Rafael had to borrow money from his friend, ... his wallet some time during the journey. (lose)
10 .... by an earthquake in the 18th century, the city has been completely rebuilt. (destroy)

D **Complete each sentence b so that it means the same as sentence a, using only TWO words.**

1 a It felt like we'd hardly arrived when we had to leave again.
  b It felt like we had to leave almost .... as we'd arrived. as soon
2 a During his attempt to walk to the North Pole, the adventurer Pierre Marchant fell and broke his ankle.
  b .... to walk to the North Pole, the adventurer Pierre Marchant fell and broke his ankle.

3 a Celine organised a party because she wanted to celebrate passing her exams.
b Celine organised a party in .... celebrate passing her exams.

4 a It's not necessary to leave a deposit when you make a reservation.
b It's possible to make a reservation .... a deposit

5 a As he didn't know any of the other guests, Alex didn't enjoy the party very much.
b .... any of the other guests, Alex didn't enjoy the party very much.

6 a There are lots of potential advantages, in the same way that there are lots of things that could go wrong.
b .... there are lots of things that could go wrong, there are also lots of potential advantages.

7 a You could set off earlier but I don't think it will make any difference.
b .... how early you set off, I don't think it will make any difference.

8 a It wouldn't matter how many people wanted to go, there would be plenty of room for everyone.
b .... people wanted to go, there would be plenty of room for everyone.

9 a Don't worry about giving me back the CD. Keep it until you've finished with it.
b Don't worry about giving me back the CD. Keep it as .... you want.

10 a Because there were four people who were interested in going on the trip, it was cheaper to take a taxi.
b .... four people were interested in going on the trip, it was cheaper to take a taxi.

E Complete the sentences by adding appropriate words to the underlined adverbial clauses.

1 It had already got dark by the time ....*we got home*.... .
2 I wouldn't want to play tennis every day, much as ....
3 The Royale isn't as nice a hotel as ....
4 My brother and I still go fishing together every weekend, just like ....
5 People always seem to panic whenever ....
6 There is so much traffic on the roads these days that ....
7 All flights have been cancelled because ....
8 My parents won't let anyone leave the dinner table until ....
9 The match had hardly started when ....
10 Painting the kitchen took a lot longer than ....

MY TURN!

Complete at least five of the following sentences so that they are true for you, your town, or people you know. Include an adverbial or participle clause in each one.

1 *I had to stand on the school bus this morning* since there ....*were no empty seats*.... .
2 No sooner had ....
3 I .... whenever someone ....
4 By the time I ....
5 .... while ....
6 Being ....
7 I ...., not wanting ....
8 After going ....
9 I ...., everyone having ....
10 It ....

MY TEST!

Circle the correct option.

1 I was watching television .... I heard a loud bang outside my house. a when b as c while
2 .... there were only two people in the band, they were incredibly loud. a Although b Despite c But
3 Much .... we enjoy films, we both found this one a bit long and boring. a if b like c as
4 Since .... Rome on a school trip when she was 12, Leanne has really wanted to live there. a visit b have visited c visiting
5 Once ...., this product should be kept in a cool, dark place. a opening b opened c having opened

My Test! answers: 1a 2a 3c 4c 5b

38 Question forms

Why is the kitchen covered in bubbles, do you think?

Sue: **Whatever's going on here?**
Matt: Oh, hi. I was just doing a chemistry experiment.
Sue: **You were doing a what?**
Matt: I wanted to make carbon dioxide.
Sue: And **what went wrong?**
Matt: Nothing. It worked perfectly.
Sue: **You think so, do you? Then why is the kitchen covered in bubbles, do you think?**
Matt: Er ... that's the experiment. It's called a lemon volcano. You have to mix lemon juice with baking soda and washing-up liquid. And I added some green food colouring.
Sue: Sorry, **what did you say it was called? A lemon what?**
Matt: Volcano.
Sue: Right ... **don't you think you used a bit too much washing-up liquid?**
Matt: Yeah, I suppose so.
Sue: And **what happens next? Who do you think's going to clear up the mess?**
Matt: **I am, aren't I?**
Sue: I certainly hope so. But I'll give you a hand ... **let's get started, shall we? Pass me a towel, will you?**

1 What was Matt trying to make?
2 What ingredients did he use?

Answers: 1 Carbon dioxide 2 Lemon juice, baking soda, washing-up liquid and green food colouring

Question forms

Word order

1 Questions in English are normally formed with auxiliary verbs (*be, have, do*) or modals (e.g. *can, must*) before the subject.

*What **did you** say?*

If we use *what, which, who* or *whose* as the subject, we use the same word order as in a statement.

What went wrong?

▶ See Unit 39 for word order in indirect questions.

Question words

2 Question words include *what, when, which, why, where, who, whose, how* and *whom*. Question phrases with *how* include *How long ...?, How far ...?* and *How much / many ...?* Question phrases with *what* include *What time ...?* and *What kind / type / sort (of) ...?*

TIP

We sometimes use *ever* or *on earth* after *what, who, when, why, where* and *how* to show surprise or disbelief.

***Whatever's / What on earth**'s going on here?*

▶ See Unit 37 for adverbial clauses with *whatever, wherever*, etc.

3 We can use *How* or *What ... like?* to ask for a general opinion about something.

***How** was your weekend?* OR ***What** was your weekend **like**?*

4 We can use *What about ...?* or *How about ...?* to make a suggestion.

***What / How about** going for a walk this afternoon?*

5 We usually use a singular verb in questions where we use *who, what* or *which* as subjects, even when we expect a plural answer.

*Who **wants** one of these biscuits?* NOT ~~*Who want ...?*~~

6 **If there is a preposition, it usually goes at the end. In very formal questions, it may go at the beginning.**
*What was she talking **about** this morning?*
(More formal: ***About what** was she talking ...?*)

7 **In formal situations, we sometimes use *whom* instead of *who* when it is the object of the verb, or after a preposition. In this case the preposition goes at the beginning of the sentence.**
***To whom** was the woman speaking?*
OR ***Who** was the woman speaking **to**?*

8 **We usually use *which*, not *what* or *who*, when we refer to a limited range of possible answers.**
*There are trains every 30 minutes. **Which** do you want to take?* NOT ~~*What do you want ...?*~~

9 **We use *whose* before a noun phrase or *be*.**
***Whose shoes** are these?* OR ***Whose are** these shoes?*

TIP

Note the difference in spelling between *whose* ('of whom') and *who's* ('who is' or 'who has').
***Whose** car is that?* (= Who does the car belong to?)
***Who's** coming with me?* (= Who is ...?)

Negative questions

10 **We use negative questions if we expect a positive answer, or to express surprise.**
***Don't you know** Lucy? I thought you went to school with her?*

Question tags

11 **We usually use a negative question tag with an affirmative verb, expecting the answer 'Yes', and an affirmative question tag with a negative verb, expecting the answer 'No'.**
*It's cold, **isn't it**?*
*I should**n't** have done that, **should I?***

12 **A rising intonation on a question tag usually expresses more doubt, and a falling intonation usually expresses more certainty.**
*You're Emma's friend, **aren't you?***
(= I'm not really sure, so I would like you to confirm.)

*It was really cold today, **wasn't it?***
(= I'm sure, and I'm inviting you to agree.)

13 **Some question tags have an irregular form, e.g. *aren't I?* and *shall I / we?***
I'm** going to clear up, **aren't I?
Let's** get started, **shall we?

14 **We can use an affirmative question tag with an affirmative verb to express surprise.**
*You **think** so, **do** you?*

We sometimes use affirmative question tags to turn a statement into a request.
***You couldn't** help me to move this table, **could you**?*

15 **We can use question tags with *will, would, can* and *could* to make imperatives sound less direct.**
*Pass me a towel, **will you**?*

Short answers

16 **We often respond to yes / no questions by using short answers.**
A: These apples aren't very good, are they?
*B: **No, they're not**.*

If we are not sure of the answer, we can use verbs such as *think, imagine, guess, suppose* and *hope* with *so* (for affirmative answers) and *not* (for negative answers). *Think* is different.
*Yeah, I **suppose so**. / No, I **suppose not**.*
*I **think so**. / No, I **don't think so**.*

▶ **See Unit 43 for more information on short answers, ellipsis (missing nouns / verbs) and substitution.**

Echoing

17 **We can use echo questions or statements in informal situations to show interest or express surprise.**
*A: He's got a new car. B: **Has he? / He has?***
*A: I didn't like him. B: **Didn't you? / You didn't?***

We can repeat a sentence with a question word, to show we don't understand part of it.
A: I was just doing a chemistry experiment.
*B: You were doing a **what**?*

In informal conversation, we can make questions with short phrases such as *How come?, Like what?* and *So what?*
A: I'm afraid I can't come to the meeting.
*B: **How come?** Are you too busy?*

Complex questions

18 **We often use *is it?, was it?* or question forms like *do you think / feel / imagine / suppose?, did you say?* to ask for opinions or information**
***What was it** (that) you liked about the book?*
*Who **do you think**'s going to clear up the mess?*
*What **did you say** it was called?*
*Why is the kitchen covered in bubbles, **do you think?***

Practice

A Complete the questions with the question words from the box.

How about How long What ~~What time~~ What's up When Where Which Whose Why

1 A: What time is the next train to Dublin?
B: 2.40.
2 A: .... did it take you to do your essay?
B: About four hours in total.
3 A: .... are your new neighbours like?
B: They seem really friendly.
4 A: .... with Andres today?
B: He's got a cold.
5 A: .... couldn't Sandrine and Jean come to your birthday party?
B: They'd gone away for the weekend.
6 A: .... have you put the remote control for the television?
B: I think it's on the table in the kitchen.
7 A: .... did you first fly in a plane?
B: When I was about seven.
8 A: .... books are these?
B: They're mine.
9 A: .... of these dresses do you prefer?
B: The blue one, definitely!
10 A: .... meeting me for a coffee after school?
B: OK, that sounds good.

B Match the sentences to the correct question tags / replies.

1 I'm supposed to be having lunch with Joanna today,
2 Don't say anything to Amanda about this,
3 That's Yvonne,
4 I wouldn't eat in that restaurant if I were you.
5 Where did Natalie get her hair done?
6 Alan's failed his driving test again!
7 I think I saw a ghost last night.
8 So Ian came to the party as well.
9 The 3.30 train always takes hours to get there.
10 Isn't this the street Jorge lives in?

a Yes, I think so.
b Wouldn't you? Why not?
c He hasn't, has he? Oh no!
d Did he? That's unusual for him.
e Does it? Let's get a different one then.
f will you?
g Sorry, where did she what?
h isn't it?
i You saw a what?
j aren't I?

1 j 2 ..... 3 ..... 4 ..... 5 .....
6 ..... 7 ..... 8 ..... 9 ..... 10 .....

C Complete the questions by putting the words in the correct order.

1 in Paris / was / your weekend
How was your weekend in Paris?
2 Liliana / look nice / her new dress / in
Doesn't ....?
3 you / do / that I gave you / the CD / think of
What ....?
4 do / like best / food / sort of / you
What ....?
5 Jane / to her / what / tell you / happened
Did ....?
6 with / go / you / the concert / to / did
Who ....?
7 football / having / of / a game / about
What ....?
8 say / was / your name / you / did
What ....?
9 lives / your cousins / nearest / you / of / to
Which ....?
10 the bus station / a lift / me / give / you / to
Could ....?

D Complete each dialogue with an appropriate short answer, echo or follow-up question.

1 A: Danielle's got a new car.
B: Has she? What make is it?
2 A: Jill doesn't have a mobile phone, does she?
B: Yes, ... She sends me text messages all the time.
3 A: I'm not feeling very well today.
B: ....? Why, what's the matter with you?
4 A: Antonia and Jarek can't come with us.
B: ....? That's a shame. Why not?
5 A: We probably won't be able to get tickets to see the match.
B: No, ... But we can watch it on TV instead.
6 A: Can you lend me some money until tomorrow?
B: .... , I'm afraid. I haven't got any with me.

7 A: We're going to be late. You won't be long, will you?
B: .... I just need to send this email, then I'll be ready.
8 A: It's freezing cold today.
B: .... ? I can hardly feel my hands!
9 A: I'm going to the supermarket.
B: .... ? We have all the food we need.
10 A: I watched a really interesting documentary last night.
B: Oh yes? .... ?
A: It was about volcanoes.

E Write an appropriate question to match each reply.

1 A: *How far is it from your flat to your school* ?
B: About three kilometres.
2 A: .... ?
B: The sports car is my brother's, and the one next to it is my dad's.
3 A: .... ?
B: On foot usually, but occasionally I take the bus.
4 A: .... ?
B: Yes, he is. He's one of the friendliest people I know.
5 A: .... ?
B: Great, thanks! It was my uncle's birthday and we went to a party at his house on Saturday night.
6 A: .... ?
B: Er, I think I'll try the strawberry one, please.
7 A: .... ?
B: I don't really know. It was the first thing that came into my mind. I'm very sorry.
8 A: .... ?
B: Sorry, I didn't realise you were asleep.
9 A: .... ?
B: I'm not sure. Maybe she's just tired.
10 A: .... ?
B: That's a great idea! We haven't been there for ages.

MY TURN!

Think of a famous person you either admire or really dislike. Imagine you are going to interview him / her for a magazine. Complete at least five of the following questions to ask during the interview.

The person I am going to interview is ....

1 What .... ?
2 Did .... ?
3 Why .... ?
4 Would .... ?
5 When .... ?
6 Which .... ?
7 How long .... ?
8 Can .... ?
9 Where .... ?
10 Are .... ?

Example: *1 What advice would you give to someone who wanted to become a successful actor like you?*

What answers do you think the person would give to your questions?

MY TEST!

Circle the correct option.

1 .... of us do you think will be picked to play in the team? a Who b Whom c Which
2 I can't remember what happened at the end of the book. .... the prisoners manage to escape or not? a How b Did c Are
3 We all seem to have a different opinion, so let's let Joey decide, ... ? a do we? b shall we? c will we?
4 .... we do another chemistry experiment instead of going to the science museum? a Couldn't b Could not c Do you think
5 .... you find so interesting about chemistry? I think it's really dull! a Why is it that b How come c What is it that

My Test! answers: 1c 2b 3b 4a 5c

39 Indirect speech

She said she would not take part in the next year's competition.

Billie Jean King was much more than one of the greatest tennis players ever. She was also the loudest voice in the fight for equal rights for sportswomen. She **wanted to know why** female players **were** paid so much less than the men. In 1971, when she was already the world number one, she **persuaded** other women players **to** help her start the Women's Tennis Association to fight for their rights. After winning the 1972 US Open, she **said** she **would** not take part in **the next year's** competition unless the prizes for women **were** the same as for men – and she **didn't think** other women **would** play either. It worked: the organisers **agreed to** pay the women the same as the men. But some men continued to **believe** that it **was** right to pay men more. In 1973, Bobby Riggs, a former men's champion, **claimed** that the men's game **was** so much better than the women's game that he **could** easily beat the best women players. King accepted his challenge. And she beat him 6–4, 6–3, 6–4. 'I **thought** it **would** set us back 50 years if I **didn't** win that match,' she said. By beating Riggs, she **convinced** people that a female athlete **can** win in high-pressure situations and that women **deserve** to be treated fairly.

1 Why did the organisers of the US Open increase the prize money for women in 1973?
2 Why was the match against Riggs so important?

Answers: 1 Because the women players refused to play unless they were paid the same as the men. 2 Because King had to prove that women could play as well as men.

Indirect speech

1 To report what was said, we can focus on the specific words or on their message. Note the difference:

*She **said, 'I won't** take part in **next year's** competition.'* (direct speech – specific words)

*She **said she would not** take part in **the next year's** competition.* (indirect speech – message)

We can also use the same structures to report thoughts, ideas, beliefs, etc.

*He **believed** men **were** much better players than women.*

Backshifting

2 When reporting something that was said or thought in the past, we usually change verbs from present to past and from past to past perfect. This is called backshifting.

*'I **don't** want to go because it's raining.'* →
*He said he **didn't** want to go because it **was** raining.*
*'I'**m** going to win the match.'* →
*He thought he **was** going to win the match.*
*'I **lost** because I **was** tired.'* →
*He claimed he **had lost** because he **had been** tired.*

We usually backshift ***will, can, may*** and ***shall*** to ***would, could, might*** and ***should. Must*** stays the same or changes to ***had to***, and verbs like ***would, could, might*** and ***should*** don't normally change.

*'Jim **won't** / **wouldn't** be at the party.'* →
*She said Jim **wouldn't** be at the party.*
*'I **can** / **could** easily beat her.'* →
*He claimed he **could** easily beat her.*
*'I **must** win this match.'* →
*She knew she **must** / **had to** win the match.*

> **TIP**
>
> **To talk about past ability, we can also change *could* to *had been able to*.**
>
> *He said that in the past, he **had been able to** play much better.* OR *... he **could** play ...*

Many verb structures, e.g. past perfect, second and third conditionals, *would rather* and *should have done*, don't normally backshift in indirect speech.

*'I **had** already **seen** the film.'* →
*She said she **had** already **seen** the film.*
*'It **would** be great if you **could** come.'* →
*She thought it **would** be great if he **could** come.*
*'You **should have** asked me to help you.'* →
*He said we **should have** asked him to help us.*

3 We don't backshift when the reporting verb (e.g. *say, think*, etc.) is in a present tense.

*He still **thinks** he **can** beat me.*
*He's **told** me many times that he **doesn't like** tennis.*

We don't usually backshift when we want to emphasise that something is still true.

*She convinced people that a female athlete **can** win in high-pressure situations.*

4 When we report questions, the word order is the same as in sentences, not questions.

*She wanted to know why **they were** paid less than men.*
NOT ~~*... why were they paid less ...*~~

We use the same word order when a question is part of a sentence or another question.

Direct question: *How much **did she win**?*
Indirect questions: *Do you know how much **she won**? / I wonder how much **she won**.*
NOT ~~*Do you know how much did she win?*~~

We use *if / whether* for yes / no questions.

'Did she win the match?' →
*He asked me **if** / **whether** she had won the match.*

5 When we report advice, orders, instructions, etc., we often use (*not*) *to* + infinitive.

*She **persuaded** other women players **to** start the WTA.*
*They **told** me **not to** worry.*

▶ See Unit 26 for other reporting verbs with *to*-infinitive or verb + *-ing*.

6 Other words also sometimes change, e.g. pronouns and words describing times / places.

here, come, now → *there, go, then*
today, this week, this year → *that day / week / year*
tomorrow, next week, next year → *the next day / week / year* OR *the following day / week / year*
yesterday, last week, last year → *the previous day / week / year* OR *the day / week / year before*

*'I won't play in **next year's** competition.'* →
*She said she wouldn't play in **the next year's** competition.*

When *this, that, these* and *those* are not used to describe time, we often change them to *it, they / them* or *the*.

*'**This** is the biggest match of my life.'* →
*She said **it** was the biggest match of her life.*
*'Where should I put **these** cups?'* →
*He asked me where he should put **the** cups.*

7 Some verbs (e.g. *ask, tell* and *encourage*) have a human object, so we can use the passive.

*They asked **us** what we thought.* →
***We** were asked what we thought.*

With some verbs, we use the passive with dummy *it* to avoid mentioning the speaker.

***Most people** expected that Riggs would win.* →
***It** was expected that Riggs would win.*

> ***To rumour*** **is only possible in the passive.**
>
> *It **was rumoured** that the player had cheated.*
> NOT ~~*People rumoured that the player had cheated.*~~

With some verbs, e.g. *said, thought, rumoured, believed* and *expected*, we can replace dummy *it* with the subject of the *that*-clause.

***Riggs** was expected to win.*
***The player** was rumoured to have cheated.*

▶ See Unit 15 for more information on dummy *it*.

Practice

A Complete the indirect statements.

1 'I don't do any sports.'
He said he ...didn't do... any sports.

2 'I'm going home because I'm feeling terrible.'
He said he .... home because he .... terrible.

3 'I can't find my tennis shoes.'
He said he .... his tennis shoes.

4 'I think it'll be a lovely weekend.'
He said he .... it .... a lovely weekend.

5 'I've played against her five times but I've never won a match.'
He said he .... against her five times but he .... a match.

6 'I didn't have any food at the restaurant because I'd already eaten.'
He said he .... any food at the restaurant because he ....

7 'I was walking home last night when I found a wallet in the street.'
He said he .... home the previous night when he .... a wallet in the street.

8 'If you want to go out, we can go to the park.'
He said if I .... to go out, we .... to the park.

B Use the indirect speech below to write the actual words the speakers used. Change the words if necessary to make them more natural. Sometimes more than one answer is possible. Write in your notebook.

1 Jane asked me if I fancied a game of tennis.
2 I told her I didn't really want to because I was really tired and I had loads of things to do.
3 She asked me what things I had to do.
4 I said that I was going camping the following day with my family, so I needed to pack.
5 She said that it wouldn't take long to pack. She told me to do it later because it would only take half an hour. She ordered me to come and play tennis. She said she'd booked a court and she didn't want to play tennis by herself.
6 I reminded her that, as I had said, I was not feeling good. I said I might just have an early night that night because I had to get up early the following day. I told her that we were leaving at 6.
7 She agreed that I'd better go home. She told me to have a great time camping.
8 I thanked her and told her I'd call her when I got home the following week.

Jane: 1 Do you fancy a game of tennis?
Me: 2 Not really. I'm really tired. I've got loads of things to do.

C Paul is telling his friends about his interview for a job in a shop. Report the questions and imperatives from his interview.

1 'Come in and sit down.'
They told me to come in and sit down.

2 'What's your name?'
....

3 'Are you good at maths?'
....

4 'Please speak clearly so we can hear you.'
....

5 'Do you like helping people?'
....

6 'Why do you want to work here?'
....

7 'Have you ever worked in a shop before?'
....

8 'Would you be able to work at weekends if we needed you?'
....

D Complete the email on the opposite page, using the underlined information from the email below. Think carefully about the dates of the emails.

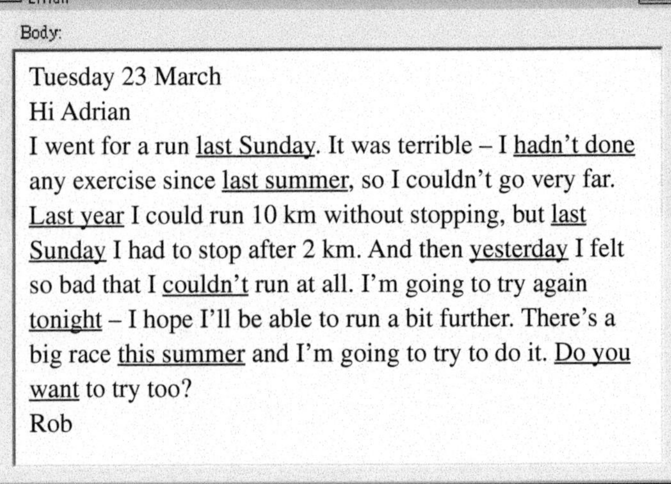
Email

Body:

Tuesday 23 March

Hi Adrian

I went for a run last Sunday. It was terrible – I hadn't done any exercise since last summer, so I couldn't go very far. Last year I could run 10 km without stopping, but last Sunday I had to stop after 2 km. And then yesterday I felt so bad that I couldn't run at all. I'm going to try again tonight – I hope I'll be able to run a bit further. There's a big race this summer and I'm going to try to do it. Do you want to try too?

Rob

File Edit View Insert Format Tools Message Help

Tuesday 30 March
Hi Pete
I got an email last week from Adrian. He said he'd been for a run [1] *the previous Sunday* but it had been terrible – he [2] .... any exercise since [3] .... He said [4] .... he'd been able to run 10 km without stopping, but that [5] .... he'd had to stop after 2 km. And he said that [6] .... he'd felt so bad that he [7] .... run at all! Poor Adrian! Anyway, he said he was going to try again [8] .... and that he hoped he'd be able to run a bit further. He also said there's a big race [9] .... and that he's going to try to do it. He even asked me [10] .... to try too, but I'm not sure if that's a good idea. What do you think?
Rob

E Report this dialogue, using indirect speech. Write in your notebook.

1 Lisa: Do you think the same would happen in another sport?
2 Gary: What do you mean?
3 Lisa: Could a woman runner beat a male runner, for example?
4 Gary: Hmmm ... I don't think so. But don't forget, Riggs was a *former* champion when King beat him. I think he must have been around 50.
5 Lisa: Really? I didn't know that.
6 Gary: Yes, so perhaps a woman runner would be able to beat a 50-year-old.
7 Lisa: You might be right. I've got another question for you. Are women going to catch up with male athletes? I mean, will men always be faster, or will women be just as fast one day?
8 Gary: I don't know. I guess women will get faster, but so will men. I don't think women will ever catch up.

1 *Lisa asked Gary if he thought the same would happen in another sport.*
2 *Gary asked her* ....

MY TURN!

Answer these questions, using indirect speech.

1 Think of a difficult question that somebody asked you. What was the question? What was your reply?
....
....
....
....

2 Think of a question you asked somebody this week. What was your question? What was their reply?
....
....
....
....

3 Think of a time that somebody told you to do something difficult. What did they ask you to do? What was your reply?
....
....
....
....

Example: *My mother asked me if I'd done my homework. I told her I had done it but I hadn't. She didn't believe me anyway!*

MY TEST!

Circle the correct option.

1 She was .... to be the greatest tennis player of all time. **a** told **b** convinced **c** thought
2 I've told you many times that I .... tennis. In fact, I hate it. **a** didn't like **b** don't like **c** haven't liked
3 Could you tell me .... correct? **a** if this is **b** is this **c** if is this
4 I've been .... to organise the school party this year. **a** asked **b** said **c** thought
5 Oh sorry – I didn't know you .... asleep. **a** are **b** were **c** have been

My Test! answers: 1c 2b 3a 4a 5b

40 Emphatic devices

All I did was ask for my money back!

Wendy: Hi, Chloe. Hey – **what a** cool **sweater**! Is it new?
Chloe: Yeah, but **such trouble** it's given me you wouldn't believe. **It was last week** I bought it .... **Wednesday** it was ... but **no sooner had I got** home **than** I realised there was a big hole in the back.
Wendy: You should have tried it on in the shop.
Chloe: I **did try** it on, but **all I could see** in the mirror **was** the front. **It wasn't until** I got home **that** I found the hole.
Wendy: **How annoying**!
Chloe: Yeah, and when I went back to the shop, the shop assistant was **so** unhelpful.
Wendy: **Rude** was she?
Chloe: Yeah. **Not only did she** say it was my own fault for not checking, **but she also** called the security guard.
Wendy: **What a nightmare**! **That's all you needed**!
Chloe: I know. **All I did was** ask for my money back! Maybe I shouted a little, but **it was only** because she didn't listen to me. And then **along comes** this guard and tells me to leave. **It was at that moment that** the manager appeared.
Wendy: Oh no!
Chloe: **What happened was** she took one look at the sweater and told the assistant to get me a new one. It was **so** cool. **Off went the assistant** to get it for me. **All she could do was** give me an angry look. But **never again am I** going back to that shop.

?
1 Why didn't Chloe see the hole when she was in the shop?
2 How did the shop assistant feel?

Answers: 1 Because it was in the back of the sweater. 2 Angry

Emphatic devices

What + *is* / *was* and *all* + *is* / *was*

1 **We can use *what* + clause + *be* to emphasise the part of a sentence that comes next, or the whole sentence.**
I complained about the hole.
→ *What I complained about was* ***the hole.***
→ *What I did was* ***complain*** *about the hole.*
→ *What I did was* ***I complained about the hole.***

What happened was ***she told the assistant to get me a new one.***

2 **We can use *all* + clause + *be* to emphasise that something is 'only' or 'simply'.**
All I could see *in the mirror* ***was the front.*** (= I could only see the front.)

When we use *what* or *all* in this way, we can use the infinitive with or without *to* or we can use a subject with the verb. Sometimes we can use verb + *-ing*.
All I did was (to) ***ask*** *for my money back!* OR *All I did was* ***I asked*** *...*
What I hate is ***having*** *to apologise.* OR *What I hate is when* ***I have to*** *...*
All I'm interested in is ***being*** *treated fairly.* OR *All I'm interested in is that* ***I should be treated*** *fairly.*

It is very common to use *what* and *all* in this way in spoken English.

***What** I think is ...* ***All** you need to do is ...*

What **and** ***all*** **can also be used in this way at the end of a sentence.**

*This sweater is exactly **what** I've been looking for.*

*That's **all** you needed.*

It + is / was + that

3 **We can use** ***it + is / was*** **to emphasise the part of a sentence that comes next. We use a** ***that*****-clause for the rest of the sentence.**

*I bought **this sweater** last week.*

→ *It was **this sweater** (that) I bought last week.*

→ *It was **last week** (that) I bought this sweater.*

→ *It was **me** that bought this sweater last week.*

→ *It was **because it was so cheap** that I bought it.*

▶ See Unit 15 for similar uses of *it*.

Inversion

4 **We can emphasise negative words and phrases by putting them at the beginning of a sentence. These items are then followed by an auxiliary verb or modal before the subject.**

At no point	*Never*	*Only once*
Barely	*Never again / before*	*Rarely*
Hardly	*Not once / only*	*Scarcely*
Little	*Not until later*	*Under no circumstances*

***Not only did she** say it was my fault, **but she also** called the security guard.*

***Never again am I** going back to that shop.*

***Under no circumstances may you** use this machine.*

***Little did I** know, **but** they were planning a surprise party for me.*

We can use ***no sooner + than*** **and** ***hardly / scarcely / barely + when*** **with the past perfect in the same way.**

*No sooner **had I got** home **than** I realised there was a big hole in the back.*

*Scarcely **had we arrived when** they told us to leave again.*

We can use inversion after some negative clauses.

*Not until / Only when / Only after I got home **did I** find the hole.*

NOT ~~*Not until did I get home ...*~~

If you're not sure which verb to change, think about the question. The word order is the same.

*A: When **did she find** the hole?*

*B: Not until **she got** home.* → *Not until **she got** home **did she find** the hole.*

5 **In informal conversation, we can use words like** ***up, along, off, out*** **and** ***back*** **before a verb to describe movement. If the subject is a pronoun, it also comes before the verb.**

Along comes this guard.

Along he comes.

NOT ~~*Along comes he.*~~

Other ways of emphasising

6 **We can emphasise nouns, adjectives and adverbs with** ***such*** **and** ***so*****. Use** ***such*** **when there is a noun and** ***so*** **when there is no noun.**

*That's **such** a nice sweater!*

*The shop assistant was **so** unhelpful.*

▶ See Unit 12 for more information on *such* + noun.

7 **In conversation, we can show surprise, shock, etc. by saying** ***What*** **+ noun or** ***How*** **+ adjective.**

***What a shame**! / **What a pity**! / **What a** cool **sweater**! / **What** lovely **weather**!*

***How annoying**! / **How sad**. / **How funny**!*

8 **We can use** ***do / does / did*** **+ infinitive to emphasise an affirmative sentence in the present or past simple, especially when we want to show a contrast with what another person thinks.**

*Thanks for your help. I **do appreciate** it.*

A: You should have tried it on.

*B: I **did try** it on.*

9 **In conversation, we sometimes start a sentence or question with the most important word and then say the rest. But we can't normally do this in writing.**

***Such trouble** it's given me you wouldn't believe.*

***Wednesday** it was.*

***Rude** was she?*

Practice

A Make these sentences simpler. More than one answer may be possible.

1 It was because I was angry that I left the shop.
I left the shop because I was angry.
2 What I need is a good night's sleep.
....
3 All I bought was a T-shirt. (Use *only*)
....
4 Never in my life have I been so angry!
....
5 What you should have done was complain to the manager.
....
6 Not only were the clothes expensive, but they were also badly made.
....
....
7 All I'm saying is that you ought to be a bit more careful. (Use *only*)
....
....
8 Under no circumstances may you open this door.
....
9 Was it you that wrote this email?
....
10 Not until you have paid for the sweater can you take it home.
....

B Match the sentences to the correct replies. Complete the replies with *what*, *how*, *so* or *such*.

1 My uncle bought me a new bike.
2 I didn't get the job.
3 I'm going on safari!
4 You don't look very well.
5 I'm sure she'll win the competition.
6 It's going to rain all weekend.
7 He told me to get out of the shop!
8 This is a great restaurant.
9 We were worried, but then he phoned to say he was OK.
10 How was your holiday?

a Again? .... terrible weather we've had this summer!
b Yes, I didn't sleep last night. I'm .... tired.
c Amazing! We had .... fun!
d Oh no. That's .... a shame!
e .... rude!
f Yes, she's .... a great dancer.
g What a nice guy!
h .... a relief!
i .... exciting!
j Yes, it was .... lucky they had a free table.

1 g 2 ...... 3 ...... 4 ...... 5 ......
6 ...... 7 ...... 8 ...... 9 ...... 10 ......

C Correct these mistakes (<u>underlined</u>) about the dialogue on page 170. Write full sentences using emphatic devices.

1 <u>Wendy</u> bought the sweater.
No. It was Chloe that bought the sweater.
2 Chloe <u>didn't take</u> it back to the shop.
No. She did take it back.
3 Chloe bought it <u>about a month ago</u>.
No, ...
4 <u>The manager</u> was really unhelpful.
No, ...
5 Chloe asked the shop assistant for <u>a new sweater</u>.
No, ...
....
6 She got angry <u>because the shop assistant walked away</u>.
No, ...
....
7 The manager <u>didn't help</u> her.
No, ...
8 <u>Wendy</u> is never going back to the shop.
No, ...
9 Chloe found <u>a dirty mark</u> on the sweater.
No, ...
10 <u>The security guard</u> is wearing the sweater now.
No, ...

D Complete the sentences, using the words in brackets in the correct order. Use one word in each space.

1 When everyone was on the bus, off we drove. (drove / we)
2 Only .... about something in a shop. (complained / have / once / I)
3 Little ...., ... I had the book on my table at home. (know / did / I / but)
4 She said I didn't clean my shoes, but ....! Then they got dirty again. (did / them / I / clean)
5 No sooner .... it started to rain. (we / than / had / down / sat)
6 I waited half an hour for the bus and then along .... the same time. (came / at / three)
7 Not since .... seen this film. (have / young / was / I / I)
8 Not .... me there, but they also gave me a lift home at the end. (did / they / only / drive)
9 We were sitting quietly watching TV when into .... (the / the / ran / room / children)
10 Not until .... open your presents. (can / I / you / you / tell)

E **Rewrite these sentences in two different ways to emphasise the underlined words.**

1 I'm simply trying to explain what happened.
All I'm trying to do is explain what happened.
What I'm trying to do is simply explain what happened.

2 I had hardly opened my mouth to speak when she interrupted me.
Hardly ....
....
No sooner ....
....

3 We haven't visited them since February.
It was in ....
....
Not since ....
....

4 They didn't stop talking until the film finished.
Not until ....
....
It wasn't ....
....

5 I just feel like sitting and reading my book.
What ....
....
All ....
....

6 While we were watching, a fox came out of its hole.
Out ....
....
What happened ....
....

7 When we first met, I didn't know we'd still be friends 10 years later.
Little ....
....
What I ....
....

8 That match was very boring.
What a ....
.... !
It was such ....
.... !

MY TURN!

Write five sentences about a problem you have had while shopping. Use these ideas or your own and emphatic devices from this unit.

1 Last time I went shopping, what I wanted to buy was ....
....

2 All I said was ....
....

3 What happened was ....
....

4 Not only ....
....

5 Never again ....
....

MY TEST!

Circle the correct option.

1 I'm sorry – .... made the hole in your sweater. **a** it was me that **b** I was it who **c** what I did was
2 Scarcely .... down to watch TV when the phone rang. **a** I had sat **b** did I sit **c** had I sat
3 It's really easy. .... you need to do is explain everything to the shop manager. **a** All what **b** Only thing **c** All
4 Suddenly, ... a helicopter. **a** over the hill flew **b** it flew over the hill **c** flew over the hill
5 What a shame about your exam. But I know .... **a** did you try **b** you did try **c** tried you

My Test! answers: 1a 2c 3c 4a 5b

R5 Review: word formation; conditionals; relative and adverbial clauses; question forms; indirect speech; emphatic devices

A Complete the dialogues. Use words from Box A for part A of each dialogue and prefixes or suffixes from Box B for part B of each dialogue.

A

fed five heart kilometre one paid play ~~sharpener~~ well

B

dis ish ment mis ness ~~over~~ out ship un

1 A: That seems a lot to pay for a pencil ......sharpener...... .
B: Yes, I think we've been ...over...charged.............. .
2 A: Eric looks really .... up today.
B: Yes, he seems to feel he's been ....treated.............. in some way.
3 A: The last James Brook film got ....-star reviews, you know.
B: Maybe it did, but I found it completely ....watchable.............. myself.
4 A: It must have been ....-breaking for Selina when Amir died.
B: Yes it was. They had a very close ....relation.............. .
5 A: Some people think they'll be able to go into a highly-............................ job as soon as they leave university.
B: Yes, they have no ....aware.............. of how hard it is to find that kind of work these days.
6 A: I hear Pam's taking part in a 10-............................ race this Saturday.
B: That's right. I told her I'd go and watch and give her some ....encourage.............. .
7 A: Jake's tall for his age but he isn't very ....-behaved, is he?
B: No, he's not. He's actually rather ....child.............. .
8 A: I'm not sure if Pablo's really in pain. I think he might be ....-acting.
B: Oh no. I think he's in severe ....comfort.............. .
9 A: I thought the match between Brazil and England was very ....-sided, didn't you?
B: Oh yes. Brazil completely ....classed.............. England.

B Circle the correct option.

1 If you want to manipulate the image on screen, just ... here with your mouse.
a beep (b) click c buzz
2 When we were in Buxton, we paid a ... to the old spa.
a claim b search c visit
3 These days so much of the media seems obsessed with ... about the private lives of actors and footballers.
a agenda b trivia c formulas
4 He was ... at the Dickensian conditions that the families were living in.
a alarmed b masked c questioned
5 I'd like to have a go at one of the ... arts like judo or karate.
a titanic b herculean c martial
6 As I'd been sitting down all day, I decided to ... for the gym.
a head b eye c nose
7 It's obvious that no one's proofread the text carefully because it's full of ... .
a ads b typos c decafs
8 Adam's always eating burgers, even though he knows they don't do him any ... .
a right b time c good

C Cross out ONE incorrect option.

1 I'd come and see you later today
a if I had a bit more time.
b ~~if I wouldn't be so busy.~~
c if I wasn't feeling so tired.
2 The bus should get us to the cinema by 7.30 pm
a assuming it comes on time.
b unless the roads are very crowded.
c in case the traffic's not too heavy.
3 a If only
b Given
c I wish
you'd warned me about this earlier.
4 You can always send me an email
a if known.
b if necessary.
c if in doubt.

5 a Had you needed any help
b If you happen to need any help
c Should you need any help
please don't hesitate to ask me.

6 If we'd saved a bit more money
a we could afford a better computer.
b we'd afforded a better computer.
c we might have bought a better computer.

7 a I'd be grateful
b It would be great
c It would be glad
if you could contact me as soon as possible.

8 I may be out of the office,
a in which case one of my colleagues can help you.
b otherwise one of my colleagues can help you.
c and if so, one of my colleagues can help you.

D **Underline** the correct option.

I'm the unusual one in my family. [1] *While* / *As* my wife and children are all mad about sport, I'm not at all interested in it. [2] *So as* / *Much as* I enjoy walking from one place to another, I can't see the fun in doing hard physical exercise. Actually, I was quite sporty [3] *until* / *as long as* I was about 14, but then I broke my leg playing football. [4] *Despite* / *Although* having three operations, each of [5] *them* / *which* was quite lengthy, the bone didn't mend properly and for a long time I needed a walking stick. Then, three years ago, [6] *having* / *after* married and had two children, I had another operation, [7] *this* / *which* was very successful and meant I didn't need to use a stick any more. The funny thing is, [8] *now* / *once* that I can move freely, I've lost interest in sport. [9] *That* / *What* I really like nowadays is my work designing computer games. It's something I can do [10] *however* / *wherever* I am and [11] *no matter* / *whenever* what time of the day or night it is. My wife Diana, [12] *whose* / *her* great passion is volleyball, is determined that our two children will follow her example rather than mine. That's the reason [13] *why* / *for* my son and daughter go to gymnastics, karate, football, tennis and swimming clubs.

E Complete each sentence b so that it has a similar meaning to sentence(s) a, using three to six words including the word in brackets.

1 a Look. Why don't we try again? (let)
b Look. ......Let's try again, shall...... we?

2 a Who does that car belong to? Do you know? (whose)
b Do you know .... ?

3 a There were rumours that the President had resigned. (rumoured)
b The President ....

4 a Yesterday Hasna said to me: 'Have you seen Salim recently?' (asked)
b Yesterday Hasna ....
.... Salim recently.

5 a What are your brother's main interests? (interested)
b What .... ?

6 a 'Be careful with the plant!' I told her. (warned)
b I ....
the plant.

7 a It was a bad idea for Ian to come, wasn't it? (should)
b Ian ...., ... he?

8 a 'I'll ring Nancy tomorrow,' said Richard. (following)
b Richard said he ....
....

9 a Hanah's dad asked her: 'Where are you?' (wanted)
b Hanah's dad ....
....

10 a 'This may be my last chance to see the world.' That was my idea at the time. (thought)
b At the time, ...
....
my last chance to see the world.

F Complete the sentences by adding the words in brackets in the correct order.

1 Sheila ......is such a wonderful person...... .
(wonderful / a / such / person / is)

2 The situation was getting difficult ....
.... Jack to calm things down again. (stepped / when / up)

3 .... we could go to the seaside. (that / was / what / thought / I)

4 ....
.... she was planning to leave.
(point / that / Michelle / no / tell / at / did / us)

5 ....
you've done for me. (appreciate / do / everything / I)

6 ....
....
she also knows how to put them into practice.
(good / Catherine / only / but / does / ideas / not / have)

7 ....
the file for a few minutes. (did / borrow / I / to / all / was)

8 No ....
.... it started to pour with rain.
(we / beach / than / the / sooner / got / had / to)

9 ....
we went to see the photography exhibition.
(recommended / because / it / you / that / it / was)

10 Not .... the recognition he deserved. (Mike / once / given / was)

41 Linking words

Within five days, a five-metre gap had opened up.

In September 2005, the Rift Valley at Afar, Ethiopia, began splitting apart. **Within** five days, a five-metre gap had opened up. **According to** geologists, it was like a huge zip opening in the middle **and then** tearing 60 km along the whole length of the rift. **At the time**, some experts believed it was the beginning of a new ocean which would one day split Africa in two. Many others, **on the other hand**, were not convinced. Recent studies of deep-sea rifts, **however**, have confirmed that the events were **indeed** the beginning of a new ocean. Geologists have known for decades that the continents are **either** pulling apart to form rift valleys **or** colliding to form mountain ranges. **However**, **although** they have studied rifts **before**, the rifts have always been under the sea and **therefore** difficult to observe. **That was why** the Afar events were so exciting. **Using** data from earthquakes, experts think the rift opened suddenly, **rather than** in a series of small movements. **And thanks to** this knowledge, they believe Ethiopia will continue to be pulled apart. There's no need to panic, **though**, **because** there's no danger of the rift opening very much **during** our lifetimes. **In fact**, geologists predict it could **still** take 10 million years for Africa to split.

?

1 What is the connection between the pictures?
2 Why is the opening of the rift in Afar different from others that have been studied?

Answers: 1 The rift valley splitting is like a zip opening in the middle and then tearing along its length. 2 It is on dry land; the others were under the sea.

Linking words

1 Linking words show relationships between words, phrases, clauses, sentences and other pieces of text. They can be conjunctions, prepositions and adverbials.

Conjunctions

2 Conjunctions join two statements and express relationships like time, addition, reason, condition and purpose. Examples include:

although	*as soon as*	*for*	*so*	*while*
and	*but*	*in case*	*until*	*yet*
as long as	*because*	*since*		

TIP

When the subject is the same in both parts of a sentence, we sometimes omit the subject and *be* after *although* (see Unit 37).

Although tired, I couldn't fall asleep. (= *Although I was tired ...*)

When we use *yet* (or *and yet*) as a conjunction, it means *but*.

*I was tired, (**and**) **yet** I knew I had to keep walking.*

3 **Most conjunctions can come either before or between the two parts they connect.**

*There is no need to panic **because** it will take millions of years.*
OR ***Because** it will take millions of years, there is no need to panic.*

The conjunctions *and, but, yet, for, or, nor* and *so* can only come between the two parts they connect. Sometimes they can start new sentences.

*The rift opened under the ocean, **so** it was difficult to study.*
OR *The rift opened under the ocean. **So** it was difficult to study.*

TIP

We sometimes use *for* as a conjunction meaning *because*.

4 **We can use *and, or, nor, but* and *yet* to join words or phrases as well as clauses.**

*The rift is 60 km long **but** / **yet** only 5 m wide.*

Linking prepositions

5 **Common linking prepositions include:**

according to	*during*
as well as	*in spite of*
because of	*instead of*
by	*rather than*
despite	*thanks to*
due to	

***According to** geologists, it was like ...*
***Thanks to** this knowledge, they believe ...*

6 **Prepositions can also express reason, time, purpose, etc. When the prepositional phrase comes at the beginning of a sentence, use a comma.**

***During our holiday**, it rained every day.*
OR *It rained every day **during our holiday**.*

7 **Linking prepositions are often followed by verb + *-ing* or *the fact that* + clause (most common after *despite*).**

***Instead of reading** the book ...*
***Despite knowing** very little / **Despite the fact that I knew** very little ...*

8 ***Since, before* and *after* can be both conjunctions and prepositions.**

*We were very worried **before** / **after** we had taken the exam.* (conjunction)
*We were very worried **before** / **after** the exam.* (preposition)

Linking adverbs

9 **We can use linking adverbs to join sentences / paragraphs. They are normally separated from the rest of the sentence with commas (see Unit 24 for exceptions).**

*Geologists have known for decades that .... **However**, they have always ...*
*... the whole length of the rift. **At the time**, some experts believed that ...*

Common linking adverbs include:

also	*in addition*	*nevertheless*
alternatively	*in fact*	*on the other hand*
finally	*instead*	*therefore*
however	*moreover*	*though*

▶ See Unit 37 for more information on adverbial clauses.

We can use some adverbs, e.g. *therefore, also, in fact* and *even*, with *and* / *or* / *but* to join clauses in a sentence.

*The rifts have always been under the sea **and therefore** difficult to observe.*

10 **We can use linking adverbs as 'discourse markers' (to introduce new topics, give examples, etc.), e.g. *incidentally, indeed, in other words, namely, say, well, by the way, for instance, or rather, that is* and *to put it another way*.**

***Incidentally**, have you finished that book you borrowed from me?*

Pairs of linking words

11 **Some linking words come in pairs, e.g. *on the one hand ... on the other, for one thing ... for another, so ... that, either ... or, both ... and, neither ... nor, not only ... but also*.**

*It was **both** stupid **and** dangerous.*
*I've seen **neither** an earthquake **nor** a volcano.*
*We were **so** excited **that** we couldn't sleep.*

▶ See Unit 13 for *both, either* and *neither* + noun.
▶ See Unit 40 for *so* / *such* for emphasis.

Practice

A Match the sentence beginnings to the correct endings.

1 I'm hungry because
2 I'm going to buy a car as soon as
3 I love to be active when I'm on holiday, while
4 You can have some ice cream since
5 Please don't start watching the DVD until
6 Rachel was heartbroken for
7 I could communicate quite well even though
8 You can borrow my book as long as
9 We'd better go home in a minute as
10 Please be quiet in case

a it's getting late.
b you ate all your dinner.
c I haven't eaten all day.
d I don't speak the language.
e you wake the neighbours.
f I've saved enough money.
g you don't write in it.
h my friends prefer just lying in the sunshine.
i I've finished washing up.
j she knew her dream would never come true.

1 c 2 ...... 3 ...... 4 ...... 5 ......
6 ...... 7 ...... 8 ...... 9 ...... 10 ......

B All these sentences mean the same. Complete them using the linking words from the box. Use each word / expression once only.

although ~~but~~ despite even though however in spite though yet

1 I'm interested in geology ....but.... I don't want to study it.
2 I'm interested in geology. ...., I don't want to study it.
3 I'm interested in geology. I don't want to study it, ...
4 .... of being interested in geology, I don't want to study it.
5 I'm interested in geology, and .... I don't want to study it.
6 .... interested in geology, I don't want to study it.
7 .... I'm interested in geology, I don't want to study it.
8 .... my interest in geology, I don't want to study it.

C Complete the sentences, using one word in each space. The underlined words will help you.

1 The earthquake was both sudden ....and.... powerful. It was incredible.
2 It was such a beautiful day .... we decided to go to the beach.
3 I can think of lots of reasons not to go. For one thing, I'm tired. ...., it's much too late.
4 We can .... stay here or we can go home. Which would you prefer?
5 There were .... many people that we couldn't find anywhere to sit.
6 I can't make up my mind. On the one hand, I know it's a great opportunity. ...., I don't really want to leave home yet.
7 Your story was .... very well written, but also really exciting.
8 We couldn't get any money. There was .... a bank nor even a cash machine in the town.

D Join the sentences, using the prepositions given. Sometimes more than one answer is possible.

1 Peter told me. Ruth's not going to the party.
According to Peter, Ruth's not going to the party.
2 The weather has been terrible. The match is cancelled.
Due to ....
3 You helped me a lot. I finished on time.
Without ....
4 Their prices are too high. No one can afford to eat there.
Because of ....
5 The film was too long. Otherwise, it was perfect.
Except for ....
6 You shouldn't watch TV all the time. You should go out in the sunshine.
Rather than ....
7 My sister is right-handed. Everyone else in my family is left-handed.
Apart from ....
8 Don't drink fizzy drinks. Drink some water.
Instead of ....
9 She is a brilliant pianist. She's also very nice.
As well as ....
10 I was wearing my lucky shoes. So I won the game.
Thanks to ....

E Complete this text, using the linking words in the box.

by the way   for instance   indeed   in other words namely   or rather   say   ~~so to speak~~ to put it another way   well

Geology is often considered to be a dull and unimportant subject, [1] *so to speak*. What could be more boring than looking at rocks all the time? [2] ...., reading books about rocks that other people have looked at. [3] ...., of course there's much more to geology than that. [4] ...., it's thanks to geology that we are starting to understand how our climate is changing. [5] ...., if we want to save our planet from disaster, we need advice from experts, [6] .... geologists. And that's not all. Have you ever wondered, [7] ...., how they find oil under the sea? Or how they build, [8] .... the world's tallest towers, the longest bridges or the deepest tunnels, or [9] .... the building you're in now? [10] ...., can you imagine a world without geologists?

MY TURN!

Complete the first sentence about your plans or dreams for the future. Then complete at least five of the other sentences so they are true for you.

I'd really like to ....

Example: *I'd really like to study at university.*

However, ...

That's why ....

In fact, ...

On the other hand, ...

In addition, ...

In other words, ...

Alternatively, ...

Apart from this, ...

MY TEST!

Circle the correct option.

1 Scientists were excited, ... it was unusual for rifts to appear on land.   a since   b although   c so
2 They didn't see the last event, ... are they likely to see the next one.   a neither   b nor   c yet
3 Everyone was there .... from David.   a apart   b instead   c except
4 The rift will continue to open. ...., it may even form a new ocean.   a Even though   b Or even   c In fact
5 Thanks for the meal. ...., how's your brother getting on?
a For example   b By the way   c To put it another way

My Test! answers: 1a 2b 3a 4c 5b

42 Reference techniques

It happened when he was just 16.

Her paintings have been shown around the world, but Lisa Fittipaldi is no ordinary **painter**. This remarkable **artist** has been completely blind since 1995, and only took up painting two years later.

For Lisa, painting is a way of connecting with the visual world **she** once knew. **She** realised **this** after years of listening to tapes and analysing techniques.

When **she** started, **Lisa** used **a** system of lines on **the** canvas to help **her**, but her mental pictures are so strong **now** that she **no longer** needs **these**. **She** has even taught **herself** to feel different colours with **her** fingers.

It happened when **he** was just 16. **They** were just six young men having fun in **a** fast car. Michael Monaco doesn't remember much about **the** accident that left **him** paralysed from the neck down.

Unable to use **his** hands or feet, Michael learnt to hold **a** pen in **his** mouth. **It** took **him** months of practice. **Later, the** pen was replaced by **a** paintbrush – and **he** discovered **his** amazing artistic talent. **That** was over 30 years ago. Since **then**, Michael has travelled around the world with **his** paintings.

But like many disabled artists – **those** who paint with **their** mouths or **their** feet, or **those** who are blind or autistic – **he** doesn't want people to be amazed at how **his** paintings were created. **He** wants people to love **them** for what **they** are – beautiful pieces of art.

1 How does Lisa know which colours to use?
2 What is special about the way Michael paints?

Answers: 1 She can feel different colours with her fingers.
2 He holds the paintbrush in his mouth.

Reference techniques

1 **Reference words such as articles (*a* / *an, the*) and pronouns (e.g. *it, they, this*) show the reader or listener whether we are telling them something completely new (often indicated by *a* / *an*) or talking about something they already know (often indicated by *the* or pronouns).**

Lisa (known) *used **a** system* (new) *of lines* (new) *on **the** canvas* (known) *to help **her*** (known), *but **her** mental pictures* (known) *are so strong now that **she*** (known) *no longer needs **these*** (known = *the lines*).

We usually start sentences with known information such as a person's name, a pronoun or a noun with *the*, and then put new information (e.g. a noun with *a* / *an*) later in the sentence. Often new information in one sentence becomes known information in the next sentence.

***Michael** learnt to hold **a pen** in his mouth. A few years later, **the pen** was replaced by **a paintbrush**.*

Sometimes we do the opposite: we can start with information presented as 'known' that the reader or listener in fact doesn't yet know, and explain it later. We do this to involve the reader in the story and make it feel more interesting.

***It** happened when **he** was just 16. **They** were just six **young men** having fun in a fast car. **Michael Monaco** doesn't remember much about **the accident** ...*

TIP

To refer to someone who might be male or female, use *he* / *she, his* / *her,* etc., or *they* / *them* / *their.*

A student will learn better if ***he*** / ***she*** *does* ***his*** / ***her*** *homework regularly.*
OR ... *if* ***they*** *do* ***their*** *homework regularly.*

2 We can use either *it, they* / *them, this, that, these, those* or *one* / *ones* to refer back to things mentioned earlier.

It / *they* usually refer back to the last or most obvious noun that they could logically refer to.

He doesn't want people to look at ***his paintings*** *and be amazed at how* ***they*** *were painted. He wants people to love* ***them*** *for what* ***they*** *are.*

Use *this* / *that* / *these* / *those* to draw special attention to a noun that was mentioned earlier.

I'll never forget ***the painting*** *she did for me.* ***This*** / ***That*** *was the best birthday present I've ever received.*

TIP

This / *That* may refer to a whole topic rather than simply the last noun.

Painting is a way of connecting with the visual world she once knew. She realised ***this*** *after years of study.* (*this* = that painting was a way of *connecting with the world*)

That / *those* may refer to things that happened long ago or far away, or things that are no longer true or that we disagree with.

... and he discovered he had an amazing artistic talent. ***That*** *was over 30 years ago.*
Some people describe their work as disabled art, but ***that*** *is far from the truth.*

One / *ones* refer back to a noun mentioned earlier, but not the same actual object / person.

I was going to buy the large painting, but then I decided to buy the small ***one****.*

▶ See Unit 12 for more information on *this* / *that*.
▶ See Unit 14 for more information on *it* and *one* / *ones*.

3 Some words refer to things outside the text. Words like *today, now, here, come* and *bring* refer to the time and place of writing / speaking. Words like *then, there, go* / *take* and *away* refer to a situation different from the time and place of writing / speaking.

We can also use these words to refer to things inside the text: *now, here, come* and *bring* can refer to the time and place of the current topic; *then, there, go* and *take* can refer to other times and places.

Michael learnt to sign his name. ***Now*** *he was ready to start painting.*

4 Many other words show connections with something mentioned earlier. For example:

alternatively, equally
at the same time
eventually, earlier, later
firstly, secondly, finally
however, on the other hand
other / *another, more, again*
the same, similarly, in the same way
so, therefore, that's why
the former, the latter
there, then

Lisa and Michael are both amazing painters. ***The former*** *is blind while* ***the latter*** *paints using his mouth.*

5 Some common words and phrases refer to something mentioned earlier or later in a text, a presentation, a speech, etc.

As discussed / *mentioned earlier*
As previously discussed / *mentioned*
See above / *below for*
... is / *are as follows*
the following
In the previous / *following section*

6 Other techniques for showing connections include:

– repetition (using the same word again)

The accident *happened when he was just 16. ... He doesn't remember much about* ***the accident****.*

– synonyms (words which have similar meaning to refer to the same thing)

Lisa Fittipaldi is no ordinary ***painter****. This remarkable* ***artist*** *...*

– tenses to show that something happened earlier or later

*He woke up in hospital. He'****d had*** *a terrible accident.*
He woke up in hospital. He ***would never remember*** *what had happened ...*

– echoing (using the same pattern of words)

He doesn't want people to *be amazed at how they were painted.* ***He wants people to*** *love them for what they are.*

– ellipsis (missing out repeated words)

She has been blind since 1995, and (she) took up painting two years later.

▶ See Unit 43 for more information on ellipsis.

Practice

A What do the underlined words in the blog refer to?

1 they = my art-loving friends
2 it = ...
3 this one = ...
4 the others = ...
5 It = ...
6 This = ...
7 them = ...
8 they = ...
9 there = ...
10 the whole thing = ...

[1] They told me [2] it would be amazing, but I never imagined *how* amazing. I don't normally go to art galleries, but my art-loving friends told me [3] this one was different from all [4] the others. [5] It showed the work of artists with disabilities. [6] This sounded interesting, so I decided to go. I wasn't expecting [7] them to be especially good – perhaps better than I could do with my eyes closed or with my mouth – but in fact the paintings I saw there were incredible. [8] They were both beautiful and powerful. I ended up spending the whole afternoon [9] there, and I want to go back and see [10] the whole thing again tonight.

B Look again at the underlined words in the email in Exercise A. Which refer forwards (→)? Which refer backwards (←)?

1 they →
2 ....
3 ....
4 ....
5 ....
6 ....
7 ....
8 ....
9 ....
10 ....

C Match the sentences. The underlined words will help you.

1 Some people are born with artistic talent. f
2 The painting was really expensive. ....
3 Art includes not only paintings but also sculptures. ....
4 The following artists have influenced her work. ....
5 I really enjoyed the exhibition. ....
6 He stared at the money in his hand. ....
7 I don't paint what I see with my eyes. ....
8 She usually paints pictures of wildlife in her garden. ....
9 The details of the exhibition are as follows. ....
10 For the first two hours, I was alone at the exhibition of my paintings. ....

a It was one of the best shows I've seen this year.
b She collects the former, but not the latter.
c It runs from 4 April to 11 May and it costs £8 to get in.
d He had sold his first painting.
e I paint what I feel in my heart.
f Others have to work much harder.
g Firstly, Dali, whose paintings she first saw as a child.
h Eventually, however, the first visitors arrived.
i On the other hand, it'll probably be worth even more in a few years.
j She's been fascinated by animals all her life.

D Match the pairs.

1 I bought this painting for £5. It was — b
2 I bought this painting for £5. That was — a

a over 20 years ago.
b a real bargain.

3 I haven't listened to the radio for months. It's
4 I haven't listened to the radio for months. That's

a broken.
b because it's broken.

5 These are my lucky shoes. They've brought me
6 These are my lucky shoes. They've taken me

a around the world.
b lots of luck.

7 She didn't get the job. It was
8 She didn't get the job. That was

a a job she really wanted.
b a real shame.

9 He's a very successful artist. He's come
10 He's a very talented artist. He's gone

a much further than we ever expected.
b a long way since he started painting.

E Replace the underlined words with pronouns.

[1] ~~The theft~~ It happened at midnight. [2] The thief had hidden in a cupboard in the gallery earlier that afternoon. Eventually, after six hours sitting [3] in the cupboard in silence, [4] the thief opened the door and looked around. The gallery was empty. The guard was asleep in her chair. Next to [5] the guard was an empty bag of sweets, which the thief had given to [6] the guard earlier, to send her off to sleep. The guard had eaten the whole pack. The thief crept along the corridor, past valuable works of art. And then he saw [7] the masterpiece, the picture he had come to steal. [8] The thief had planned this break-in very carefully. Many other criminals had tried to steal this painting. [9] The thief had tried to steal [10] the picture himself a few years ago – that robbery had been a disaster. But [11] this robbery would be different. [12] The thief was the first burglar to work out how to switch off the alarm and the cameras and send the guard to sleep. Very quietly, ...

Find one or more synonyms in the story for the words below. Can you think of any more? Use a dictionary of synonyms or a thesaurus.

a robbery, ...theft, break-in, burglary......
b thief, ...
c bag, ...
d picture, ...

MY TURN!

Write a short paragraph about a person who has done something amazing. It could be a true story or invented.

Use the following techniques to make it more interesting:

- pronouns at the beginning of your story, which you explain later;
- echoing;
- tenses such as past perfect to relate the background events to the main events.

....
....
....
....
....
....
....
....
....
....
....
....

MY TEST!

Circle the correct option.

1 I didn't really like the paintings. .... because I couldn't understand what they showed.
a It is b They were c This was
2 Those chocolates were delicious, but I can't eat any more. Do you want ....? a one b these c it
3 When you .... us a present. a come back, bring b go back, bring c go back, take
4 I love both running and painting. The former keeps me fit, while the .... relaxes me.
a following b latter c later
5 I would like to thank the .... people. First of all, my parents, who ... a next b previous c following

My Test! answers: 1c 2a 3a 4b 5c

43 Ellipsis and substitution

Just because you haven't passed yet, doesn't mean you never will.

news

messages

chat

events

friends

chat

Steve:	**Failed** my driving test. Again :-(.
Mikael:	:-O 3rd time? 4th?
Steve:	5th!
Kevin:	**You** know why?
Steve:	**Not** sure. **Examiner** said I drove faster than I **should have**, and I didn't stop at a red light.
Mikael:	Hmmm … **not** good.
Steve:	I really want to pass, but I'm not sure I can **do it**. Maybe I'll give up.
Kevin:	No, don't! I was going **to** after I failed **mine**, but I'm glad I **didn't**. Just because you haven't passed yet, **doesn't** mean you never **will**. I failed twice **but passed** the third time.
Mikael:	**You** really think **so**? Some people are meant to drive … **some aren't**.
Kevin:	Hey, Mikael! You're supposed to be helping Steve feel better.
Mikael:	I'm trying **to**. What happened with the red light, Steve?
Steve:	It was green **but went** red when I got to it. I tried to stop but I **couldn't**.
Mikael:	Here's a tip: **if in doubt**, slow down.
Steve:	Examiner said that! But the test was so **stressful I** forgot everything.
Mikael:	Listen, I have to go. **Better** not be late.
Steve:	**What for**?
Mikael:	**Got** a driving lesson! **Starts** in 10 min. **Must** go.
Kevin:	OK. **Nice** chatting with you.
Steve:	**See** you later.

?

1 Which of the three friends has / have passed their driving tests?
2 Who is more helpful, Mikael or Kevin?

Answers: 1 Kevin 2 Kevin

Ellipsis and substitution

1 When we leave out a word, we call it ellipsis.
*If you haven't passed your test yet, you never **will**.*
(*... pass your test*)

2 When ellipsis is not possible, we often replace words and phrases with simpler words. This is called substitution.
*I thought I wouldn't fail again, but I **did**.*

3 **In informal conversation, we often omit *that* at the start of *that*-clauses / relative clauses.**

The test was so stressful I forgot everything.
OR ... ***that** I forgot everything.*
There's that guy I was telling you about.
OR ... *that guy **that** I was ...*

▶ See Unit 36 for *that* in relative clauses.

4 **In some fixed expressions and formal English, we sometimes omit the subject and *be* after *if, when, while, although, once, as if* or *as though*.**

If in doubt, slow down. OR *If **you're** in doubt ...*

▶ See Unit 37 for shortened adverbial clauses.

5 **We often omit words after *and, or* or *but* if it is clear what they would be. We often use this technique in very formal English.**

***We have** read your proposal and accepted it.*
OR ... *and **we have** accepted it.*
***I** looked for you but couldn't find you anywhere.*
OR ... *but **I** couldn't find you ...*

When we omit the main verb, we can use auxiliary or modal verbs or *to* as a substitution. If these are not possible, use *do* / *did*.

*I didn't watch the film, but perhaps I **should have**.*
*I didn't want to go but everybody else **did**.*
NOT ~~*... but everybody else*~~.

6 **Don't use ellipsis when the repeated nouns refer to different things. Use *one*.**

*I've got a blue **car** and she's got a red **one**.*
NOT ~~*... and she's got a red*~~.

Don't use ellipsis for the object of a verb / preposition. Use *one* or another pronoun.

*I enjoyed the film, but she hated **it**.*
NOT ~~*... but she hated*~~.

▶ See Units 14 and 42 for more information on pronouns and *one*.

We often omit repeated articles or determiners, especially in fixed expressions.

*Can you pass me **the** salt and pepper?*
NOT ~~*... the salt and the pepper?*~~

We can leave out repeated articles with adjectives. Note the difference:

*You'll recognise me easily – I'll be wearing **a red hat** and **scarf**.* (= a red scarf)
*I'll be wearing **a red hat** and **a scarf**.* (= a scarf of any colour)

7 **In conversations, we often leave out repeated words when we reply to someone.**

*A: Why didn't you **call**?*
B: I was just about to when you called me. (instead of *I was just about to **call** ...*)

TIP

We often omit *at* when we talk about time.
A: ~~At~~ what time did you leave?   B: ~~At~~ 8 o'clock.

8 **We use echo statements to add more, similar, information to what someone has said. These also use ellipsis. Echo statements have three parts:**

So *Neither / Nor*	**modal verb** (*can / will*, etc.) **auxiliary verb** (*am / did*, etc.)	**subject pronoun** (*I, you*, etc.) **possessive pronoun** (*mine / ours*, etc.)

A: I can't drive. B: Neither can I. (= I can't drive either.)
A: Our TV is broken. B: So is theirs. (= Their TV is broken too.)

Several similar common grammar structures use ellipsis and substitution:

– **question tags:** *I'm right, **aren't I**?* NOT ~~*..., aren't I right?*~~
– **short answers:** *A: Am I right?   B: Yes, **you are**.*
NOT ~~*Yes, you are right.*~~
– **echo questions:** *A: I'm right.   B: **Are you**?*
NOT ~~*Are you right?*~~

▶ See Unit 38 for more information on these structures.

9 **In very informal conversation and informal writing like SMS text messages, we often omit words that are usually necessary, such as subjects, auxiliary verbs or articles.**

Must go. (***I** must go*).
You know why? (***Do** you know why?*)
Examiner said I drove faster than ... (***The** examiner ...*)

Not all structures with ellipsis are very informal. The following structures with ellipsis are very common in all types of conversation.

See you later. (***I'll** see you* later.)
Pleased to meet you. (***I'm** pleased ...*)

There is a difference between *Nice to meet you* and *Nice meeting you*.

*Hi. **Nice to meet you**.* (when meeting someone for the first time)
*Goodbye. **Nice meeting you**.* (after talking to someone you've met for the first time)

Practice

A Add the missing words to this online chat.

1 ^ (I've) Just finished my driving lesson. ^ (It was) Terrible.

2 Why ^?

3 ^ Couldn't do anything right. ^ Nearly crashed twice.

4 ^ Told you. Some people are meant to drive.

Some ^ aren't ^.

5 ^ Very funny. ^ Instructor was angry.

6 What ^ about?

7 ^ Said I hadn't been practising. But I have ^!

8 Have you ^? When ^?

9 ^ Every day. ^ Been playing Formula 1 City Racer on the computer.

10 ^ Unbelievable!

B Match a statement from box 1 to a question in box 2 and a reply in box 3.

1

1 I've got to go.
2 I'm going dancing.
3 Have you heard the news?
4 I'm going to study in India.
5 I bought that DVD you were talking about.
6 I can't come to your house on Tuesday.
7 I managed to open the tin of beans.
8 I'm reading a fantastic book.

2

a How long for?
b Who by?
c Who with?
d What about?
e Why not?
f Where from?
g Where to?
h What with?

3

A The Internet. I ordered it last week.
B I've got to visit my aunt in hospital that day.
C Just one semester – about four months.
D Home. I'm late.
E A knife.
F I can't remember. Her name starts with P.
G The hospital. They're going to close it.
H My sister.

1 g D 2 .... 3 .... 4 ....
5 .... 6 .... 7 .... 8 ....

C Write full versions of the questions from box 2 in Exercise B.

1 a How long are you going for?
2 b Who ....?
3 c Who ....?
4 d What ....?
5 e Why ....?
6 f Where ....?
7 g Where ....?
8 h What ....?

D Complete the dialogues with short answers, echo statements and echo questions from the box (two if possible!).

Are you? Can't you? Hasn't she? Have you? Neither can I. Neither does mine. Neither have we. ~~Neither were we.~~ Nor would I. Should I? So am I. So did they. So does ours. So have I. So should you! Theirs doesn't. We didn't. ~~Weren't you?~~ Wouldn't you? Yes, he does!

1 A: I wasn't going to tell her.
B: Neither were we. / Weren't you?
2 A: My grandfather doesn't have a computer.
B: ....
3 A: I would never do something like that.
B: ....
4 A: You should have been more careful.
B: ....
5 A: I got lost on the way.
B: ....
6 A: I can't remember his name.
B: ....
7 A: Our car keeps breaking down.
B: ....
8 A: She's never flown before.
B: ....
9 A: I'm late. Got to go.
B: ....
10 A: Sorry about the accident.
B: ....

E Use ellipsis and substitution to make these sentences sound more natural.

1. I'm going to Mexico and she is ~~going to Mexico~~ too.
2. We've bought a new TV and we've bought a new digital camera.
3. He had a driving lesson today and I had a driving lesson yesterday.
4. I've never been to England and I've never met an English person.
5. I've never been to England and I never will go to England.
6. I am a 20-year-old university student and I would like to apply for the position of sales assistant in your shop.
7. Don't forget to take your passports and don't forget to take your tickets.
8. I've bought some new shoes. You can have my old shoes.
9. I didn't watch the film. I don't think you should watch the film either.
10. I don't want to take my driving test again, but I'll probably have to take my driving test again.

MY TURN!

Continue this online conversation, using your own ideas and language from this unit.

Your friend: Hi! Feeling good today!
You:
Your friend:
You:
Your friend:
You:
Your friend:
You:
Your friend:
You:

MY TEST!

Circle the correct option.

1. You should have slowed down or .... **a** have stopped **b** should have stopped **c** stopped
2. I wanted to tell a joke but I couldn't think of .... **a** a good **b** a one **c** a good one
3. I've never driven a car or .... a motorbike. **a** rode **b** ridden **c** have ridden
4. If .... doubt, ask someone for advice. **a** in **b** you **c** you're
5. A: We had a lovely day. B: .... **a** Neither have we **b** So did we **c** So have we

My Test! answers: 1c 2c 3b 4a 5b

44 Formal and academic English

The origins of human language present something of a mystery.

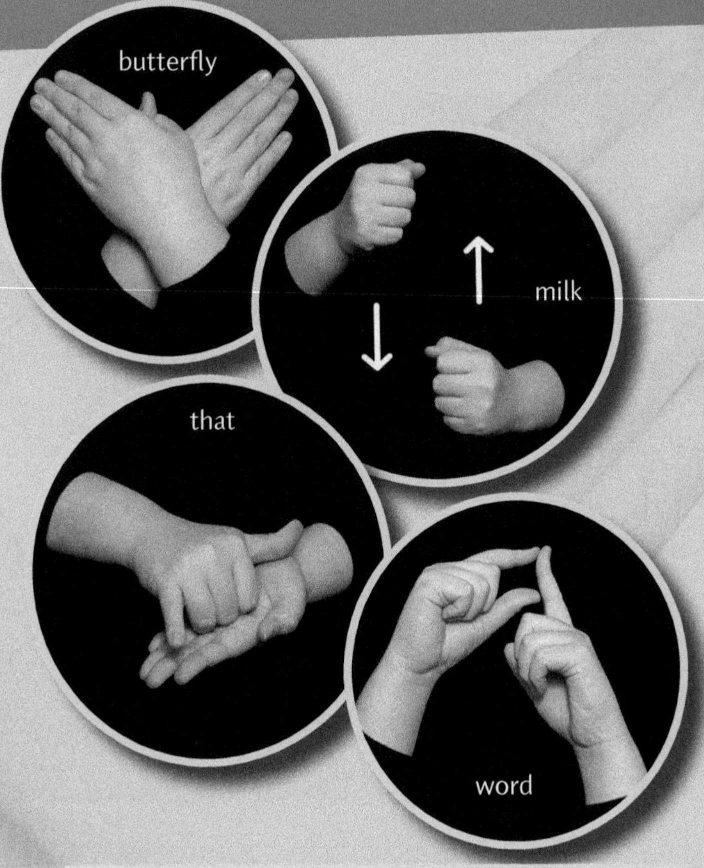

The origins of human language present something of a **mystery**. On the one hand, evidence suggests that **behaviour** such as **the habit of walking** on two legs, **the manufacture of** stone tools and **the use of** fire for **the cooking of** meat originated millions of years ago. **However, the characteristic that** most clearly sets humans apart from animals, language, **may** have **much more recent origins. There** is **fossil evidence to** suggest that the mouths and throats of early humans were physically **incapable of** speech in the modern sense until perhaps as little as 70,000 years ago.

One of the most interesting possibilities is that language **pre-dates** speech, perhaps by millions of years. The brain and hands **may have been used** to communicate long before **the development of spoken language**, a process that **may** date back to the time humans started walking on two legs. **As** modern sign languages demonstrate, **it** is perfectly possible **for** a non-spoken language **to** have a rich grammar and vocabulary.

In fact, modern sign languages may **offer an explanation for** another mystery of language: the **deeply fundamental** distinction between nouns and verbs, stored in separate parts of the brain. In sign languages, nouns tend to **be communicated** by forming shapes from the hands; verbs tend to involve **hand movements**. Perhaps the first sentence involved a shape **meaning** *monkey* and another meaning *tree*, **followed** by a movement meaning *climb*.

?

1. Why couldn't early humans speak like modern humans?
2. How are verbs usually expressed in sign languages?

Answers: 1 Their mouths and throats were physically incapable of speech. 2 With hand movements

Formal and academic English

Nouns and noun phrases

1 In academic English and formal English, we put a lot of information into noun phrases. In less formal English, we use verbs more often to give the same information.

Formal: *The **origins** of human language present something of a **mystery**.*

Less formal: *We don't really **know** how human language **started**.*

2 To make language more formal, we can change verbs and adjectives into nouns. This process is called *nominalisation*.

*The habit of **walking** on two legs, the **manufacture** of stone tools ...*

In academic and formal texts, we also sometimes change verbs (including modal verbs) into adjectives and adverbs.

*Early humans **couldn't** speak. → Early humans were **incapable** of speech.*

▶ See Unit 32 for more information on conversion.

When we change transitive verbs (= verbs with objects) into nouns, the object may become a possessive with *of*. We can include the subject of a transitive verb with *by*. We can include the subject of an intransitive verb (= a verb with no object) with *of*.

***The scientist** discovered **the fossil** ... → the discovery **of the** fossil **by the scientist** ...*

***The monkey** moved ... → the movement **of the monkey** ...*

Some nouns are followed by other prepositions, e.g. ***research into*** and ***explanation for***. (See Unit 19.)

Possessives with *'s* are possible for both subjects and objects in formal and academic English, but they are less common than possessives with *of*.

3 In formal and academic English, we often put a lot of information into noun phrases. Techniques include:
- nouns as adjectives (see Unit 21):
  fossil *evidence*, ***language*** *origins*
- participles as adjectives:
  interesting *possibilities*, ***non-spoken*** *language*
- adjectives with adverbs:
  the ***deeply fundamental*** *distinction*
- prepositions after nouns:
  the distinction ***between*** *nouns and verbs*
- clauses:
  the characteristic ***that most clearly sets humans apart***

Verbs

4 We use the present simple more than the continuous. In the future tense, ***will*** is more common than ***going to***; ***shall*** with ***I*** / ***we*** is also common.
The true story ***will*** *not be known for many years.*
In this paper, we ***shall*** *demonstrate that ...*

We often use ***may*** (***have***) rather than the adverbs ***maybe*** and ***perhaps***.
Modern speech ***may have*** *originated as recently as 70,000 years ago.*

We often use the present simple (even if the person is dead) or present perfect.
Stokoe (2001) ***claims*** / ***has claimed*** *that sign languages ...*

Impersonal subjects

5 We often avoid personal subjects in academic English. For example:
- passive voice (see Units 7 and 8):
  The brain and hands ***may have been used*** *to communicate ...*
- ***it*** and ***there*** as dummy subjects (see Unit 15):
  It *is believed that ...,* ***There*** *is evidence to suggest that ...*
- verbs that can be used with or without human subjects (see Unit 29):
  Language ***developed*** *from simpler forms of communication.*
- converting verbs into nouns (see above and Unit 32):
  This behaviour *originated millions of years ago.*
- other abstract nouns as subject:
  Modern sign languages *demonstrate that ...*
- ***to***-clauses (see Unit 26):
  It is important ***to*** *understand that ...*

We often use *As* to introduce an opinion that we agree with.
As *modern sign languages demonstrate, it is perfectly possible for ...*

Punctuation

6 Use colons (:) to introduce an explanation or an example.
... ***another mystery*** *of language: the distinction between ...*

We often use semi-colons (;) instead of linking words such as ***while*** / ***whereas*** to show the relationship between two separate ideas.
... nouns tend to be communicated by forming shapes from the hands; verbs tend to involve hand movements ...

We often use colons to introduce a list and semi-colons to separate the items in a list, especially when the items are long or complex.
There are three main ways of communicating: we may communicate using spoken language; we may write our message; or we may use hand signals and other visual clues.

In general, avoid contractions (e.g. ***it's*** or ***we're***) in formal English.

Vocabulary

7 Academic English uses verbs like ***believe, argue, claim*** and ***suggest***, rather than ***think***. We often use longer or more complicated words in formal English than in neutral and informal English.

neutral / informal : formal
help : assist
can / can't : be (un)able to
get : become
check : clarify
get in touch : contact
ask about : enquire about
tell : inform
have : possess
give : provide with
get : receive / obtain
ask for : request
need : require
want : would like

neutral / informal : formal
a lot of : a great deal of
about / on : concerning / regarding
much more : considerably more
very : extremely / most
because of : due to
more / extra : further / additional
a few : several
(not) enough : (in)sufficient

In general, avoid most phrasal verbs in formal English.

▶ See Unit 25 for some formal equivalents of phrasal verbs.

Practice

A Rewrite the sentences to make them more formal by changing the underlined words.

1 We couldn't get the same results as other researchers.
We were unable to obtain the same results as other researchers.

2 Maybe more evidence will be found soon.

3 In this paper, we're going to discuss our experiments.

4 It's been argued that there hasn't been enough time for language to develop.

5 We reckon the theory has a few weaknesses.

6 In his book, Winters was claiming that human language is much more complex.

7 It's important to remember that they've found no evidence for this.

8 We weren't given enough help.

9 Lots of research needs to be done because of the dangers of mistakes.

10 Maybe language started millions of years ago.

B Complete each sentence b by changing the underlined verbs in sentence a into nouns. Write *of* or *by* in the boxes.

1 a We analysed the results in the laboratory.
b The analysis [of] the results took place in the laboratory.

2 a Ancient humans produced stone tools.
b We are interested in the .... [ ] stone tools [ ] ancient humans.

3 a The experiment failed.
b After the .... [ ] the experiment, we decided to use a different approach.

4 a The researcher will present her findings.
b At 3 pm there will be a .... [ ] the researcher's findings.

5 a We will discuss the differences in part 2.
b There will be a .... [ ] the differences in part 2.

6 a The machine exploded before we could get any results.
b We were unable to get any results after the .... [ ] the machine.

7 a He discovered the location of the fossils by accident.
b The .... [ ] the location of the fossils was an accident.

8 a Stick (2009) observed this process in a series of famous experiments.
b The .... [ ] this process [ ] Stick in a series of experiments is now famous.

9 a New techniques have developed in recent years.
b The .... [ ] new techniques has continued in recent years.

10 a We understand the relationship much better these days.
b Our .... [ ] the relationship has improved dramatically recently.

C Rewrite these sentences without the human subjects (underlined). The clues in brackets will help you. Write in your notebook.

1 They may have identified the true causes.
(Clue: Use the passive.)
The true causes may have been identified.

2 They need to conduct more experiments.
(Clue: Change the verb into an adjective and use *it*.)

3 They didn't find any evidence for the theory.
(Clue: Use *there*.)

4 They began their experiments five years ago.
(Clue: *begin* doesn't need a human subject.)

5 When they researched the situation, it showed a link between the two events.
(Clue: Change the verb into a noun and use *into*.)

6 The researchers hoped that they would get a better understanding of the process.
(Clue: Use *to*.)

7 With their research, they have proved that this is impossible.
(Clue: Use an abstract concept as subject.)

Use the same techniques for these sentences:

8 They expect that they will find more evidence.

9 They conducted a series of tests because they wanted to investigate the theory.

10 They don't really understand the cause of this behaviour.

D Add colons (:) and semi-colons (;) to these sentences.

1 Some researchers have claimed that language developed from sign language; others believe that spoken language must have come first.
2 The experiment revealed an unexpected problem the process did not work at low temperatures.
3 We have identified three possible causes for the failure of the experiment the equipment may have been faulty the wrong chemical may have been used or the results may have been recorded incorrectly.
4 There are a number of possible interpretations of the sign it could mean the monkey is going into the tree it could simply refer to the fact that there is a monkey in the tree or it could say that this is a tree where monkeys often hide.
5 Early researchers believed this was impossible later researchers have shown that it is in fact possible, but only under specific conditions.
6 There is one final stage in our analysis we need to decide whether the behaviour caused the changes in the brain or whether the changes led to the new behaviour.

E Rewrite the sentences, adding the information in brackets.

1 There is a need.
(The need is desperately urgent. The need has existed for several years. Respected experts need to provide answers to the question. The question is hugely important. The question is whether this is good for society.)
There is a desperately urgent need, which has existed for several years, for respected experts to provide the answers to the hugely important question of whether this is good for society.

2 The decision was unpopular with experts.
(They decided to stop the experiments. The decision was taken last week. It was hugely unpopular. The experts were internationally respected. They were experts in chemistry.)

....

3 The failure caused disagreement.
(The operation failed. It failed as a result of insufficient time. Scientists disagreed among themselves. They disagreed deeply.)

....

4 The discovery changed understanding.
(Archaeologists discovered a fossil. The fossil was a bone. The bone had been used as a tool. The discovery was incredibly important. Scientists understand how early tools developed.)

....

5 The prediction led to demands.
(Experts predicted that a new form of life would be discovered. The prediction was extremely widely reported. Scientists demanded more money. They wanted the money to spend on research.)

....

MY TURN!

Choose a topic you know quite a lot about and write a brief explanation of it, using formal English, in your notebook. Present the information to your friends.

MY TEST!

Circle the correct option.

1 .... began a series of dramatic changes.
a The telephone's invention by Bell b Bell's telephone invention c The invention of the telephone by Bell
2 For years, he has been carrying out research .... the life cycle of butterflies. a of b into c for
3 The problem that led to the failure of the experiment .... caused by bad weather.
a may be b may been c may have been
4 To sum up, there .... evidence to support the case of the prosecution.
a isn't enough b is not a lot of c is insufficient
5 The sign languages used by deaf people are just as sophisticated as spoken languages .... the 'sign' languages that have been taught to chimpanzees are completely different in terms of sophistication. a : b , c ;

My Test! answers: 1c 2b 3c 4c 5c

45 Informal and spoken English

There's loads of great stuff on their website.

Hi Maggie

I've been thinking about that article **U R** writing for the student **mag** about **uni** exchange programmes. I **reckon it'd** be **great** if we could speak to someone **who's** actually **been on** one – to talk about their experiences **and things like that**. Can **U get in touch with** the university to **get** some **info**? **FYI, there's loads of** great **stuff** on their website, but no good stories. Maybe they could **put U in touch with a couple of** people **who've** done exchanges …

Thanks, Tom

Hi Maggie. **D'you** get my **mail**?

Yeah ... I was **gonna mail** you back. I called that **guy**. The one you told me about. He's **gonna** set up some meetings. With some students he knows. **They**'ve actually done exchanges.

Cool. **And**?

And he was **really** helpful. He's **like**, 'I'm **really** glad you called'.

Cos he wants us to write about his ...?

... exchange programme. **Yeah**, **so** he wants me to come **and**, **well**, **you know**, have **a bit of** a chat and **maybe**, **you know**, take some photos **or whatever**. At the **uni**.

Brilliant. **Good on you**.

Thanks. And he's, **like**, **gonna set up** some meetings. With **a couple of** students **who've** done exchanges. Two or three, maybe. **Nice people**, **he says**. **D'you wanna** come **too**?

If I can, **yeah**.

?

1 Who are Tom and Maggie?
2 Who are they going to meet?

Answers: 1 University students who work on a student magazine 2 Someone who organises student exchanges and some students who have done exchanges

Informal and spoken English

Vocabulary

1 **Many of the most informal words change with fashions. Some informal words are used in some English-speaking contexts but not others. However, some very common and permanent examples include:**

a bit of (a little)	*maybe* (perhaps)
chat (conversation)	*plenty of* / *loads of* (a lot of)
a couple of (a few)	*pretty* (rather / quite)
cool (nice, fashionable)	*really* (very, absolutely)
guy (man)	*reckon* / *guess* (think)
kid (child)	*yeah* (yes)

*I feel **pretty** awful. I **guess** I'd better go home.*

▶ See Unit 44 for formal vocabulary.

2 **Most phrasal verbs are informal.**

*He's gonna **set up** some meetings ...*

▶ See Unit 25 for some formal equivalents of phrasal verbs.

3 ***Get*** is much more common in informal English than in formal English.

*Can you **get** in touch with the university to **get** some info?*

▶ See Unit 8 for more information on uses of *get*.

TIP

In very informal spoken English, we can use ***be like*** to mean 'said'.

*He's **like**, 'I'm really glad you called.'*
OR *He **said**, 'I'm really ...'*

Contractions and abbreviations

4 We usually use contractions, e.g. ***isn't*** or ***there's***, in informal English. Some contractions, e.g. ***should've*** or ***who've***, are very informal.

***There's** some great stuff on their website, but I **can't** find any good stories.*
*... put you in touch with a couple of people **who've** done exchanges.*

TIP

We often use ***there's*** instead of ***there are*** with plural nouns in informal speech.

*Look, **there's** three cats playing in the garden!*
OR (more formal) *... **there are** three cats ...*

5 Some words have short informal and longer formal forms.

cell (cell phone)	*net / web (Internet)*
info (information)	*paper (newspaper)*
mag (magazine)	*phone (telephone)*
mail (email)	*TV / telly (television)*
mobile (mobile phone)	*uni (university)*

▶ See Unit 33 for more examples of words which are often shortened.

6 Some grammar structures have a short form that we often say, or write, in very informal situations, e.g. ***gotta*** (***[have] got to***), ***gonna*** (***[be] going to***), ***wanna*** (***[do you] want to***), ***d'you*** (***do / did you***), ***cos*** (***because***) and ***dunno*** (***[I] don't know***).

*I **gotta** be back by 10, **cos** I've got an exam tomorrow morning.*

7 Some common abbreviations used in emails, SMS texting, etc., include:

btw (by the way)	*TX (thanks)*
IMHO (in my humble opinion)	*CU (see you)*
FYI (for your information)	*R (are)*
asap (as soon as possible)	*4 (for)*
LOL ([I'm] laughing out loud)	*2 (too / to)*
BFN (bye for now)	*U (you)*

Punctuation

8 In informal writing, we often use dashes (–) to show pauses or connections between parts of a sentence. We don't normally use colons (:) or semi-colons (;).

I'm going to do some studying tonight – not because I want to, but because I have to.

We can use dots (...) to show we think the reader can guess the rest.

Can you buy some food for the party? You know, crisps, snacks, cakes ...

We can use rows of question marks (??), exclamation marks (!!) or both (?!).

I can't find your email!!! Where is it??? What's going on?!?

We can use capital letters in order to add emphasis, for example if we are angry.

WHERE R U? BEEN WAITING 2 HOURS!

Spoken English

9 In informal spoken English, we often use pronouns / simple noun phrases (usually with no more than one adjective), adding extra information piece by piece at the end.

*I called that **guy**. **The one** you told me about. **He's** gonna set up some **meetings**. With some **students** he knows. **They've** actually done the exchange.*

We often use simple linking words such as ***and, but, or, so, because*** (***cos***) and ***if***.

*He wants me to come **and** (= in order to) have a bit of a chat to him.*

We use fillers (words / phrases with no meaning) while we think what to say, e.g. ***OK, well, so, right, now, then, like, you know, I mean*** and (***you***) ***see***.

***So** he wants me to come and, **well, you know**, have a bit of a chat to him.*

We use many phrases to refer to things in general or avoid being too specific, e.g. ***... or something, things like ..., ... and stuff, ... or whatever*** and ***kind of***.

*... to take some photos **or whatever**.*
*There's loads of great info **and stuff**.*

10 In informal English, we also often use ellipsis (see Unit 43), question tags (see Unit 38) and human subjects (see Unit 44).

Practice

A Rewrite the sentences, using more formal English.

1. Wanna go to the café?
   Do you want to go to the café?
2. There's not enough people here.
   ....
3. D'you reckon they heard us?
   ....
4. Dunno if Kelly can go, cos she's busy.
   ....
5. I would've gone if I'd known it was so important.
   ....
6. Who's gonna pay for it?
   ....
7. Ruth wants to talk to you. Dunno what she wants.
   ....
   ....
   ....
   ....
8. D'you do anything nice last weekend?
   ....
9. You're not gonna like this.
   ....
10. It'll be the first time he's seen it.
    ....

B Replace *get* (or phrases with *get*) in these sentences with a more formal / neutral word.

1. If you need any more information, please ~~get in touch with~~ contact us.
2. How did that window get broken?
3. How long does it take you to get home?
4. Your hair's much too long. When are you going to get it cut?
5. Please stop talking and get on with your work.
6. I posted the card two weeks ago but she only got it this morning.
7. We were trying to find our way home but we got lost.
8. Do you know where I can get real mayonnaise?
9. I couldn't get anything done because my computer was broken.
10. You're getting really good at tennis. Have you been practising?

C Complete this online conversation. Put one of the words from box 1 in spaces 1–7 and one of the abbreviations from box 2 in spaces a–g.

1 1–7	2 a–g
cos dunno gonna gotta ~~gotta~~ wanna whatever	BFN BFN BTW BTW TX IMHO ~~LOL~~

A:	I hear you've passed all your exams. Well done. If you get any cleverer, you'll need some new friends!
B:	[a] ....LOL.... . You know you'll always be my best friend! [b] .... , did I tell you? I've [1] ....gotta.... talk to this guy from the uni tomorrow. It's an interview for the student mag. I'm really nervous.
A:	Nervous? Why?
B:	[2] .... Maybe it's [3] .... he's some kind of important guy and I'm just a first-year student or [4] ....
A:	You shouldn't be nervous. [c] .... , he's probably really happy that you're [5] .... interview him. He's probably more nervous than you are! I would be!!!
B:	Yeah, maybe.
A:	[d] .... , you could interview me if you like. You know I did a student exchange a couple of years ago.
B:	Yeah … I forgot. Brilliant. D'you [6] .... meet for a coffee one day this week? I'll pay.
A:	Yeah, sounds cool. [e] .... ! Anyway, [7] .... go. I'm late. [f] ....
B:	[g] ....

D Change the underlined words to make the sentences more informal.

1 She ~~thinks~~ reckons she's so ~~fashionable~~ cool, but she's not.

2 Can you help me look after the children this weekend?

3 A: I'm trying to find out what's on television tonight but there's nothing in the newspaper.

B: Maybe you'll find some information on the Internet.

4 It's rather late, so perhaps I'd better go soon.

5 I very much regret that I didn't manage to have a conversation with that man.

6 A: Have you got any cleaning chemicals for getting jewellery very clean?

B: Well, I've got a lot of odds and ends in the kitchen. See if you can find some.

7 We were just having a little fun when this woman came up to us and she said, 'What's going on?!?'

8 A: I've got a few tickets for the concert. Do you want them?

B: Yes. That'd be wonderful.

E Complete this email with punctuation: dashes –, dots ..., question marks ???, exclamation marks !!! and mixtures ?!?.

Hi Julia,

It was great talking to you last week [1] – really useful and interesting.

I've managed to write up my notes from the interview (attached). Sorry it's a bit long [2] ...... you had so much to say and I wanted to include everything. Well, not everything (I didn't include the stuff about your bad grades [3] ......). Not sure what my editor will say [4] ...... he told me to write 500 words max [5] ......

BTW, I feel a bit stupid asking, but what's your surname [6] ...... I know you wrote it down for me, but [7] ......

One last thing [8] ...... you mentioned that the exchange programme cost about £6,000 … but who pays [9] ...... It's not the poor student, is it [10] ......

Anyway, could you have a quick look at the interview and let me know if it's OK?

Cheers,

Maggie

MY TURN!

Find an informal email you have written in your language. Try to translate it into informal English in your notebook.

MY TEST!

Circle the correct option.

1 I found .... really good stuff on the Internet. a a couple of b loads of c bit of

2 I'm .... looking forward to having a chat later. a really b very c pretty

3 I told him to calm down and he's .... , 'Me? Calm down!?!' a I mean b like c you know

4 A: Here U R. B: .... ! a YW b JK c TX

5 Jess can't come out with us tonight .... she's got lots of work to do. a like b well c cos

My Test! answers: 1b 2a 3b 4c 5c

46 International English

As grammar plenty, na so trouble plenty.

Before before, the grammar was not plenty and everybody was happy. But now grammar began to be plenty and people were not happy. As grammar **plenty, na so trouble plenty**. And as trouble plenty, **na so plenty people** were dying.
(*grammar* = rules, government regulations)
(Ken Saro Wiwa, Nigerian poet and author)

If you **don't do nothing** but farm work, your social security **don't be nothing**.
(Speaker of a variety of American English)

Prices are lower than **what** they have been.
(John Howard, former Australian Prime Minister)

You must **be having** a lot of friends of your own age.
(Speaker of a variety of Indian English)

Though it may not be a direct translation, **but** it is more acceptable in English.
(Speaker of a variety of Singaporean English)

He was willing to stay surprised us all.
(Speaker of a variety of Hong Kong English)

The patient was **status post** cholecystectomy.
(Example of medical English)

The defendant was not informed **as to** the offence **whereof** he had been accused.
(Example of written legal English)

?
1 Which speaker / text is easiest to understand?
2 Which do you find difficult to understand?

International English

Variation in English

1 There are thousands of different varieties of English. Which you use depends on who and where you are, what your first language is, your job, your point in communicating. One variety is not in itself better or worse than another. All varieties (including all the samples of English above) are good for some purposes and bad for others.

When we choose which variety of English to use, we have to balance a) the need to communicate our message so that other people understand it, and b) the need to say something about ourselves (e.g. our nationality, our culture, our personality or our level of education).

2 Examples of variation include:
- present continuous instead of present simple: *You must* ***be having*** *a lot of friends ...* (instead of *... have ...*)
- double negatives: *If you* ***don't do nothing*** *but farm work, ...* (instead of *... don't do anything*)
- different uses of linking words: ***He was willing to stay*** *surprised us all.* (instead of *The fact that he was willing to stay ...*)

Standard English

3 When we are using English to speak with people whose mother tongue is different from ours, we need to use a standard form of English: one which is acceptable and understandable around the world.

There is no official standard English but an unofficial one is developing. It is not the same as standard British English (BrE), or mainstream American English (AmE), but it is quite similar to them.

Most speakers of English do not speak standard English all the time, but they generally understand a standard form and can use it when they need to.

Standards are changing, particularly in spoken language. Some grammar structures that were non-standard a few years ago have become (or are becoming) standard.

Accuracy in International English is important because it reduces the dangers of misunderstandings and it makes communication more fluent and efficient.

> TIP
>
> The varieties of English shown on the previous page are not standard international English. Apart from where we have indicated otherwise, all the other grammar in this book is based on standard English.

British, American and International English

4 Two important varieties of English are British English (BrE) and American English (AmE). The differences between them do not usually cause misunderstandings. In international English (IntE), you can mix the two.

In BrE, some nouns (e.g. ***team, committee, band, army, government, company***) and names of companies and organisations can be singular or plural. In AmE, the verb is often singular, but there is some flexibility.

The team ***was*** */* ***were*** *happy with* ***its*** */* ***their*** *performance.* (BrE)
The team ***was*** *happy with* ***its*** */* ***their*** *performance.* (AmE)

Verbs which can be irregular in BrE but regular in AmE include:

learn → *learnt* → *learnt* (AmE: *learned*)
smell → *smelt* → *smelt* (AmE: *smelled*)
burn → *burnt* → *burnt* (AmE: *burned*)

Fit is usually irregular in AmE (***fit*** → ***fit*** → ***fit***) but regular in BrE (***fitted***). In IntE, it is safest to use the regular forms (***learned, fitted***, etc.).

BrE usually uses ***get*** → ***got*** → ***got***; AmE usually uses ***get*** → ***got*** → ***gotten***.

> TIP
>
> In AmE, ***have got*** (for possession or obligation) is less common than in BrE. In IntE, ***have*** is more common.
>
> BrE: ***I've got*** *to go now.*
> AmE: *I* ***have to*** *go now.*

In AmE, it is becoming common to use the past simple with ***yet, already*** and ***just***. In BrE, we usually use the present perfect. Both are acceptable in IntE.

A: Did you finish yet? / Have you finished yet?
B: No. I('ve) just started.

In AmE, it is normal to use an infinitive without *to* after verbs like ***suggest, recommend*** and ***demand***. In BrE, we often use ***should*** or another structure. Both are acceptable in IntE.

AmE: *I suggest that he* ***be*** *thanked.*
BrE: *I suggest that he* ***should be*** *thanked.*
OR *I suggest thanking him.*

5 Differences in vocabulary are much bigger and more likely to cause misunderstandings. In general, American vocabulary is more widely understood. Here is a list of BrE items that are not widely used outside the UK, together with their more generally understood equivalents.

biscuit : cookie | *lorry : truck*
cheers : thanks / goodbye | *pram : stroller*
fancy : want | *sweets : candy*
fortnight : two weeks | *queue : line*

> The American meaning of ***billion*** (= a thousand million) is also now used in Britain, but may cause confusion with speakers of languages where ***billion*** means ***a million million***. In international communication, it is safer to say ***a thousand million***.

6 Differences in spelling generally do not cause misunderstandings. American spellings (especially *-**ize***) are becoming popular in many other varieties of English, including BrE.

BrE: ***organise*** */* ***organize*** | AmE: ***organize***
BrE: *col****our****, behavi****our*** | AmE: *col****or****, behavi****or***
BrE: *theat****re****, cent****re*** | AmE: *theat****er****, cent****er***

Using clearer grammar to help others to understand

7 In international communication, we may need to be careful about how we express ourselves so that other people can more easily understand us. This means using clearer (sometimes slightly longer) grammatical forms.

Use relative pronouns (e.g. ***that***) in relative clauses:
Here's an example of language ***that*** *people struggle with.* (instead of *Here's an example of language people struggle with.*)

Split a sentence with a relative clause into two sentences:
People sometimes struggle with language. Here's an example.

Use full clauses instead of participle clauses:
Before ***you study*** *abroad, learn the language.*
(instead of *Before* ***studying*** *abroad, learn the language.*)

Avoid unusual grammar structures:
You've almost certainly heard *about this.*
(instead of ***You're bound to have heard*** *about this.*)

Practice

A Imagine you are in each of the situations below. Decide which variety of English to use:

- International English (IntE)
- British English (BrE)
- American English (AmE)
- Another variety (say which)

1. You attend a business meeting in your country with colleagues from around the world. IntE
2. You become an expert in a particular subject (e.g. a lawyer or an engineer) and you have to explain something technical to another expert in the same subject. ....
3. You go on holiday and make friends with some people from another non-English speaking country. ....
4. You have an interview for a job with an international company in your country. ....
5. You join an online chat with teenagers from around the world. ....
6. You join an online discussion group with a wide range of people from around the world. ....
7. You are on holiday in London and you need to visit the doctor. ....
8. You go to university in the USA and you want to make friends with American students. ....
9. You go to university in a non-English-speaking country and you want to make friends with other international students. ....
10. You are on holiday in a non-English-speaking country. You buy some fruit in the market. ....

Which of the situations might really happen in your life? In what other situations might you need to speak English? Will you need International English or a different variety?

B Mark these statements True or False based on the advice in this unit. Do you agree with the advice?

1	It is important to speak like a native English speaker.	False
2	It doesn't matter if I use bad grammar.	
3	I should adapt my grammar and vocabulary when I speak to people from different backgrounds.	
4	Standard English is better than non-standard varieties.	
5	Non-standard varieties are important ways to express your culture, but are less useful for international communication.	
6	International English may include a mixture of British and American standards.	
7	I need to think about the person I'm speaking to when I decide how to speak.	
8	All native speakers use standard English.	
9	There are much bigger problems with international vocabulary than international grammar.	
10	It is acceptable to mix British and American grammar or spelling in the same sentence.	

C Match the British English (BrE) and American English (AmE) words in the box to the correct pictures. Then underline the word in each pair which you think is more common in International English.

a biscuit candy a cookie curtains a diaper drapes a faucet ~~football~~ a fortnight a line a lorry a nappy a pram a queue a restroom sneakers ~~soccer~~ a stroller sweets a tap a toilet trainers a truck two weeks

1	BrE football	AmE soccer	2	BrE	AmE ....
3	BrE	AmE	4	BrE	AmE ....
5	BrE	AmE	6	BrE	AmE ....
7	BrE	AmE	8	BrE	AmE ....
9	BrE	AmE	10	BrE	AmE ....
11	BrE	AmE	12	BrE	AmE ....

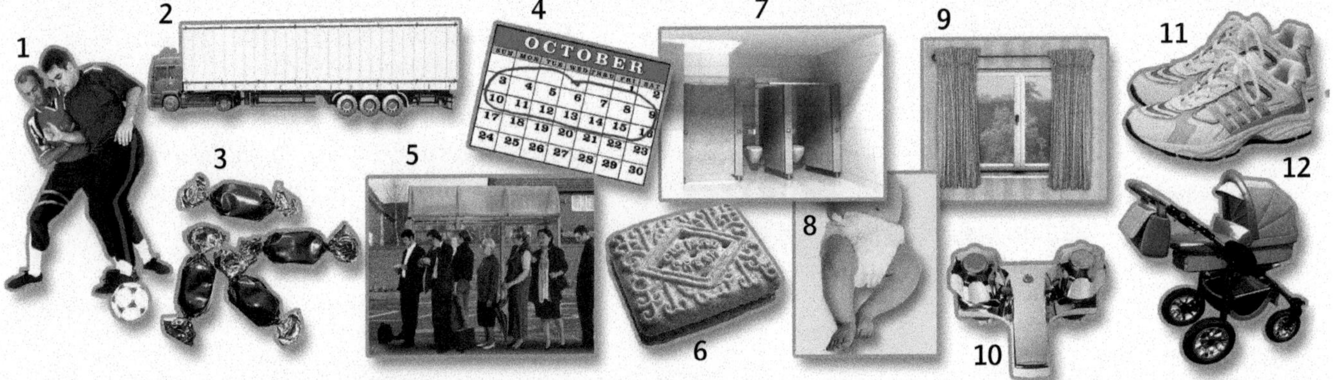

D Decide if these sentences use typical British English (BrE), typical American English (AmE) or a mixture. Underline the words that helped you decide. What (if anything) would you change to make them more international?

1 I just remembered that I didn't write that email yet.
AmE – No need to change

2 The rock band have decided to split up after 20 years together.

3 They recommended that she change her behavior.

4 I'm sorry – I shouldn't have got so angry when you burnt my toast.

5 A: Have you tried on your new shirt yet?
B: Yes, it fit me perfectly.

6 It's better to put the baby in the stroller while you're waiting in line.

7 The committee plans to organize its next meeting in a fortnight.

8 A: Do you fancy trying one of these biscuits?
B: Oh, yes please. Cheers.

E Rewrite these sentences to make them clearer and simpler.

1 They're thought to have stolen the money.
Some people think they stole the money.

2 You're sure to make lots of friends.

3 In our group, women outnumber men by a wide margin.

4 If you hadn't put in too much paper, the machine wouldn't have got broken.

5 The children left in the playground were too noisy.

6 She uses strange words no one else understands.

7 You're unlikely to pick up new words unless you pay close attention.

8 No sooner had we sorted out the first problem than another three appeared.

MY TURN!

Think of three words in your language that are difficult to translate into English. How would you explain the words in simple international English to someone who doesn't know anything about your country? Write in your notebook.

MY TEST!

All the options below might be considered correct in some varieties of English, but which of the following would be most acceptable in International English?

1 I didn't say .... a nothing to nobody b anything to nobody c anything to anybody
2 A: Did you like the sweater I bought you? B: Yes, it .... perfectly. a fitted b has fit c fit
3 Do you .... ? a biscuit b fancy a cookie c want a cookie
4 There is not one single variety of English .... around the world.
a people speak b that people speak c spoken by people
5 .... I went straight to bed.
a Having arrived home very late, b Arriving home very late, c I arrived home very late so

My Test! answers: 1c 2a 3c 4b 5c

R6 Review: linking and reference words; ellipsis and substitution; formal and academic English; informal and spoken English

A Circle the correct option.

1 a as long as (b) until c as soon as
2 a Even though b In case c In fact
3 a as well b instead c therefore
4 a due to b rather than c according to
5 a as a result b on the other hand c in spite of
6 a yet b but c or
7 a as b so c both
8 a therefore b however c in case
9 a rather than b because of c even though
10 a Instead of b Even though c In spite of
11 a yet b until c instead

Dinosaurs ruled the Earth for over 100 million years [1]… the end of the so-called Cretaceous Period, about 65 million years ago, when they suddenly disappeared. [2]… , the dinosaurs were not the only animals to suddenly die out; many other species did [3]… . What was the reason for this?

Scientists believe that the extinction of the dinosaurs and other animals was mainly [4]… climate change. Temperatures at the end of the Cretaceous Period dropped significantly. These environmental changes reduced the food available to the dinosaurs and, [5]… , they were unable to survive.

One theory about why the climate changed is based on the discovery that about 65 million years ago the Earth was hit by a huge asteroid [6]… meteor coming from outer space. The impact of this was [7]… great that it caused massive forest fires, tidal waves and dust clouds which blocked out sunlight and led to environmental change.

Some scientists, [8]… , believe that many species died out [9]… environmental changes well before the asteroid hit the Earth. This may have been caused by a series of volcanic eruptions.

[10]… the fact that both of these theories have a lot of evidence to support them, neither of them can explain why some animals, like dinosaurs, died out, [11]… others, like frogs, survived.

B Underline the correct option.

1 I saw Jack at a party three months ago. *There* / *That* was the last time we spoke.
2 These apples look nice but they're not the tastiest *ones* / *those* I've ever had.
3 When my cousin *went* / *came* to visit us last week, she *took* / *brought* a huge fruit cake for us.
4 It's not a good idea to use a computer for hours on end without taking breaks. I know *it* / *this* but I don't always do the right thing.
5 Most scientists nowadays believe that human activity is causing climate change but there are *these* / *those* who disagree with this idea.
6 After *he* / *they* had asked the shop assistant what the thief had taken, the police officers interviewed some customers who'd been in the shop.
7 My aunt's got two plum trees which always give her lots of fruit. She's really proud of *those* / *them* and I can understand why.
8 My flight details are *in the same way* / *as follows*: Depart: Madrid 12.20; Arrive: London Gatwick 14.30.
9 Asma told me about a course she was doing but *it* / *this* didn't sound very interesting.
10 Don Quixote and Sancho Panza are two of the greatest characters in European literature. The former is a romantic idealist and *the following* / *the latter* is down-to-earth and realistic.

C Match the sentences to the correct short answers.

1 Our front room gets very warm.
2 We had the best seats in the theatre.
3 Pietro was really impressed by the concert.
4 My dad never has his mobile phone on.
5 I haven't had anything to eat yet.
6 I'm sorry you have to leave so soon.
7 My teachers have suggested I apply for university.
8 I can never remember all my passwords.
9 We can learn a new language at school next year.
10 My school has no swimming pool or tennis courts.

a Neither do I.
b So are we.
c Mine haven't.
d Nor can I.
e Can you?
f So does mine.
g Doesn't it?
h Nor have I.
i Did you?
j So were we.

1 …f… 2 ……… 3 ……… 4 ……… 5 ………
6 ……… 7 ……… 8 ……… 9 ……… 10 ………

D Cross out all the words that can be omitted without changing the meaning.

1 The film was so boring ~~that~~ I fell asleep.
2 I've been to the chemist's and I've been to the post office.
3 If it's possible, go to bed early before an exam.
4 Put the knives and the forks on the table.
5 I don't want to have a drink but you may want to have a drink.
6 I saw the programme and I found it very interesting.

Replace the underlined words with ONE word only.

7 Izzie had a party on her birthday and she really enjoyed ~~the party~~ it.
8 No one else knew the answer but I knew the answer.
9 I love small, sweet tomatoes but I also like larger, sharper-tasting tomatoes.
10 Our neighbours were being very noisy, so we went to talk to our neighbours.
11 There's a big spider in the kitchen and there's another big spider in the bathroom too.
12 It's not my fault and it's not your fault either.

E Rewrite the sentences to make them more formal. Include the words in brackets in the correct form.

1 She wants to get in touch with Neelam.
(like / contact)
She .... would like to contact .... Neelam
2 The way they behave is getting more and more difficult.
(behaviour / become / increasingly)
Their .... difficult.
3 They expect more evidence to come out later.
(expect / further / emerge)
It ....
later.
4 We're going to talk about the problem.
(shall / discuss / issue)
We ....
5 We know a lot more about dinosaurs than we did.
(knowledge / increase / greatly)
Our ....
6 They couldn't help us last week. (unable / provide / assistance)
They ....
last week.
7 Perhaps she asked for extra information.
(may / request / additional)
She ....
information.
8 Plenty of evidence shows that global warming is affecting the Arctic.
(deal / demonstrate / by)
There ....
.... global warming.
9 No one has explained why the project director isn't here.
(no / explanation / absence)
There ....
.... the project director.
10 We need to check this point before we go on.
(important / clarify / continue)
It ....
....

F Match the pairs (formal to formal and informal to informal).

1	What's on TV tonight?	a	I'm afraid I don't know.
2	What's on television this evening?	b	I dunno really.
3	What are those children doing?	a	I think they're just playing.
4	What're those kids up to?	b	I reckon they're just playing.
5	Would you like to use my mobile phone?	a	Oh, thanks a lot.
6	D'you wanna use my mobile?	b	Oh, thank you very much.
7	Why d'you like that guy?	a	Cos he's really nice.
8	Why do you like that man?	b	Because he's very friendly.
9	I sent that information to you last week.	a	But I only got it today.
10	I sent you that info last week.	b	But I only received it today.
11	What's in the paper today?	a	Some stuff about the economy.
12	What's in the newspaper today?	b	An article about the economy.
13	What problem does Blanca have?	a	She's just got the sack.
14	What's up with Blanca?	b	She's recently lost her job.
15	Do you think it's time for us to go?	a	Yeah, we'd better get going.
16	Time to go, d'you reckon?	b	Yes, we should leave now.

Irregular verbs

infinitive	past simple	past participle
awake	awoke	awoken
be	was / were	been
beat	beat	beaten
become	became	become
begin	began	begun
bet	bet	bet
bite	bit	bitten
bleed	bled	bled
blow	blew	blown
break	broke	broken
bring	brought	brought
build	built	built
burn	burnt / burned	burnt / burned
burst	burst	burst
buy	bought	bought
cast	cast	cast
catch	caught	caught
choose	chose	chosen
come	came	come
cost	cost	cost
cut	cut	cut
deal	dealt	dealt
dig	dug	dug
dive	dived	dived
do	did	done
draw	drew	drawn
dream	dreamt / dreamed	dreamt / dreamed
drink	drank	drunk
drive	drove	driven
eat	ate	eaten
fall	fell	fallen
feel	felt	felt
fight	fought	fought
find	found	found
fit	fit / fitted	fit / fitted
flee	fled	fled
fly	flew	flown
forbid	forbade / forbad	forbidden
forecast	forecast / forecasted	forecast / forecasted
forget	forgot	forgotten
forgive	forgave	forgiven
get	got	got
give	gave	given
go	went	gone
grow	grew	grown
have	had	had
hear	heard	heard
hide	hid	hidden
hit	hit	hit
hold	held	held
hurt	hurt	hurt
keep	kept	kept
know	knew	known
lay	laid	laid
lead	led	led
lean	leant / leaned	leant / leaned
learn	learnt / learned	learnt / learned
leave	left	left

infinitive	past simple	past participle
lend	lent	lent
let	let	let
lie	lay / lied	lain / lied
light	lit / lighted	lit / lighted
lose	lost	lost
make	made	made
mean	meant	meant
meet	met	met
pay	paid	paid
put	put	put
quit	quit	quit
read	read	read
ride	rode	ridden
rise	rose	risen
run	ran	run
say	said	said
see	saw	seen
seek	sought	sought
sell	sold	sold
send	sent	sent
set	set	set
shake	shook	shaken
shine	shone	shone
shoot	shot	shot
show	showed	shown
shut	shut	shut
sing	sang	sung
sink	sank	sunk
sit	sat	sat
sleep	slept	slept
smell	smelt / smelled	smelt / smelled
speak	spoke	spoken
spell	spelt / spelled	spelt / spelled
spend	spent	spent
spill	spilt / spilled	spilt / spilled
spin	spun	spun / span
spoil	spoilt / spoiled	spoilt / spoiled
stand	stood	stood
steal	stole	stolen
stick	stuck	stuck
sting	stung	stung
strike	struck	struck
swear	swore	sworn
sweep	swept	swept
swell	swelled	swollen / swelled
swim	swam	swum
take	took	taken
teach	taught	taught
tell	told	told
think	thought	thought
throw	threw	thrown
understand	understood	understood
wake	woke	woken
wear	wore	worn
win	won	won
write	wrote	written

Verb patterns

Verbs followed by *to*-infinitive

These verbs are followed by the *to*-infinitive.

afford	expect	prepare
agree	fail	pretend
appear	guarantee	promise
aim	happen	refuse
arrange	help (also with infinitive without to)	seem
ask	hesitate	tend
attempt	hope	threaten
choose	intend	train
claim	learn	want
decide	long	wish
decline	manage	would like / love / hate / prefer
demand	neglect	
deserve	offer	
	plan	

Verbs + object + *to*-infinitive

These verbs are followed by an object and the *to*-infinitive.

advise	forbid	remind
allow	force	request
ask	get (persuade)	teach
challenge	help	tell
command	instruct	urge
direct	invite	want
enable	mean (intend)	warn
encourage	order	would like / love / prefer / hate
expect	persuade	

Verbs followed by *-ing*

These verbs are followed by *-ing*.

admit	feel like	mind
avoid	finish	miss
can't help	hate	postpone
consider	imagine	recommend
delay	involve	risk
deny	justify	sit
detest	keep	spend time
dislike	lie	stand
dread	love	suggest
enjoy	like (enjoy)	
fancy	mention	

Verbs with prepositions and most phrasal verbs are followed by *-ing*.

carry on	get around to	look into
decide on	get into	put off
end up	get on with	put up with
	give up	talk about
	insist on	think about
	keep on	work on
	look forward to	worry about

Verbs followed by *-ing* or *to*-infinitive

These verbs can be followed by *-ing* or the *to*-infinitive with no change in meaning.

begin	intend
bother	like
can't bear	love
can't stand	prefer
continue	start
hate	

These verbs can be followed by *-ing* or the *to*-infinitive with a change in meaning.

continue	remember
forget	stop
go on	try
mean	want
regret	

Verbs + infinitive without *to*

These verbs are followed by the infinitive without *to*.

modal verbs (*can, could, may, might, must, ought to, should*)
help (also with *to*-infinitive)
had better
would rather

Verbs + object + infinitive without *to*

These verbs are followed by an object and the infinitive without *to*.

have (= to cause someone to do something)
help
let
make (= to tell or to force; with *to*-infinitive in passive form)
sense verbs (*feel, hear, listen to, notice, see, watch*) when they describe complete events (with *-ing* when they describe an unfinished process)

Glossary

advert	a picture, short film, text, etc. which tries to persuade people to buy a product or service 19
agony	very bad pain 31
alien	relating to creatures from another planet 8
appeal	a request especially to a court of law to change a previous decision 34
artificial	not natural, but made by people 13
baking soda	a mixture of powders used to make cakes rise and become light when they are baked 38
beetroot	a round, dark red vegetable, that is usually cooked and eaten cold 16
beggar	someone who is very poor and lives by asking people for money or food 18
blood vessels	tubes through which blood flows in the body 31
bubble	a ball of air or gas with liquid around it 38
campus	an area of land containing all the main buildings of a university 23
carbon dioxide	a gas that is produced when people and animals breathe out, or when carbon is burned (formula CO_2) 38
carbon footprint	Someone's carbon footprint is a measurement of the amount of carbon dioxide that their activities produce. 23
cliff	an area of high rocks next to the sea 12
climate change	the way the Earth's weather is changing 3
coastline	the part of the land along the edge of the sea 36
collide	When two objects collide, they hit each other with force, usually while moving. 41
comet	an object in space that leaves a bright line behind it in the sky 8
convinced	completely certain about something 41
curve	to move in a gradual, smooth bend 24
customer	a person or organisation that buys things or services from a shop or business 19
decade	a period of ten years, especially a period such as 1860 to 1869, or 1990 to 1999 13
drill	to make a hole in something, e.g. the ground, using a special tool 36
expedition	an organised journey, especially a long one for a particular purpose 4
exploit	to use or develop something for your advantage 10
famine	when people living in an area do not have enough food 14
fertile plain	a large area of flat land that can produce a large number of good quality crops 36
fine-tune	to make very small changes to something in order to make it work as well as possible 32
fjord	a long strip of sea between steep hills, found especially in Norway 33
foam	a substance like cream which is filled with bubbles of air 16
food colouring	a substance that is added to food to change its colour artificially 38
forehead	the part of your face between your eyes and your hair 31
fossil	part of an animal or plant from thousands of years ago, preserved in rock 44
fossil fuels	fuels such as gas, coal and oil, which were formed underground from plant and animal remains millions of years ago 23
gravity	the force that makes objects fall to the ground 24
greenhouse gases	gases which stop heat escaping from the Earth's atmosphere so that temperatures rise (the greenhouse effect), especially carbon dioxide 3
grin	a wide smile 1
groan	to make a long, low sound because you are sad or in pain 31
hibernate	If an animal hibernates, it goes to sleep for the winter. 18
horizontally	in a flat or level position or direction 24
hugging	holding someone or something close to your body with your arms, usually to show that you like, love or value them 17
indefinitely	for a period of time for which no end has been fixed 24
ingredient	one of the foods or liquids you use to make a particular meal or mixture 38
magnificent	very good or very beautiful 2

manipulate	to control someone or something in a clever way 32
manufacture	the process of producing goods 44
mask	to prevent something from being seen or noticed 32
mole	a small animal that digs underground and cannot see well 31
monument	something that is built to make people remember a famous person or something important that happened 2
moth	an insect with large wings that often flies at night 12
necklace	a piece of jewellery that you wear around your neck 20
nodding your head	moving your head down and then up, sometimes several times 17
omelette	a food made with eggs that have been mixed and fried 16
orientate	to learn about a new place that you are in 32
ornamental	beautiful rather than useful 21
out of breath	unable to breathe very well, for example because you have been running or doing some type of energetic exercise 18
paralysed	unable to move all or part of your body because of an injury or illness 42
parmesan cheese	a hard dry Italian cheese used especially in cooking and for putting on particular types of Italian food, such as pasta 16
please	to make someone happy 37
pre-date	to exist or happen before something else 44
procession	a line of people or cars that moves forward slowly as part of a ceremony or public event 2
prosperity	the state of being successful and having a lot of money 36
receipt	a piece of paper that proves that you have received goods or money 35
refund	an amount of money that is given back to you, especially because you are not happy with something you have bought 35
rift	a very large hole that separates parts of the Earth's surface 41
set sth / sb back	to delay an event, process or person 39
shatter	to break suddenly into a lot of small pieces 29
slam	to close quickly with a loud noise 29
sofa	a large, comfortable seat for more than one person 6
soft palate	the soft part that forms the top of the mouth at the back, separating the nose from the throat 31
squawk	If a bird squawks, it makes a loud, unpleasant noise. 34
squeak	to make a short, high sound 33
steering wheel	a wheel that you turn to control the direction of a vehicle 12
stove	a piece of equipment that you cook on 29
stroll	a slow and relaxed walk 32
stunning	very beautiful 21
sustainability	development that causes little or no damage to the environment and therefore is able to continue for a long time 23
theoretically	in a way that obeys some rules but is not likely 24
thermos	a container that keeps hot liquids hot or cold liquids cold 16
throat	the back part of your mouth and the part inside your neck 44
tippex	a white liquid used for painting over mistakes in a piece of writing 16
trapped	If someone or something is trapped, they are unable to move or escape from a place or situation. 4
trip	to hit your foot on something and sometimes fall down 29
twist	to injure part of your body by bending it in the wrong direction 29
UFO	unidentified flying object: something strange that you see in the sky that could be from another part of the universe 8
utterly	completely 21
view	the things that you can see from a place 3
volcano	a mountain with a large hole at the top which sometimes explodes 38
washing-up liquid	a thick liquid soap used to wash pans, plates, knives and forks, etc. 38
zip	a thing for fastening clothes, bags, etc. consisting of two rows of very small parts that connect together 41

Grammar index

Thanks and Acknowledgements

Mark Lloyd would like to thank Rosa for being so supportive and understanding of the demands placed on a writer, Jeremy for being such an accommodating and insightful co-author, Penny for opening my eyes to countless aspects of the language of which I had previously been ignorant even after nearly 20 years of teaching, and Robert Vernon for heroically holding the whole process together. A special 'thank you', too, to Matthew Duffy, who was courageous enough to invite me to join the *Active Grammar* project in the first place.

Jeremy Day would like to thank Penny and Mark for their energy and inspiration. It's been a pleasure spending a year discussing the intricacies of advanced English grammar with such experts. Tom Bradbury has done an excellent job as writer of the Review units. Robert Vernon has been great as editor, keeping us on track and making the whole process as smooth as possible. Thanks also to Lynn Townsend and Lynn Dunlop, who got me involved in this project in the first place. Many amazing people influenced and inspired the texts in this book, most memorably the artists Lisa Fittipaldi and Michael Monaco. Above all, huge thanks to my wife Ania and our children, Emilia and Tom, for their patience and support while I was working on this project.

The authors and publishers would like to thank the following individuals who commented on the materials during the development stage:
Nella Burnett-Stuart, Mónica Martina Carrera García, Christopher Douloff, Dany Etienne, Ludmila Kozhevnikova, Adrian McDermott, Aisha Osman, Irma Piña and Seda Toprak.

The publishers are grateful to the following for permission to reproduce copyright photographs and materials:
Key: l = left, c = centre, r = right, t = top, b = bottom
Alamy /©PCN Photography for p. 9, /©Joe Sohm/Visions of America, LLC for p. 42, /©North Wind Picture Archives for p. 60, /©Derya Duzen for p. 66, /©Odilon Dimier/PhotoAlto for p. 72(b), /©Dennis Cox for p. 92, /©Cindy Miller Hopkins/Danita Delimont, Agent for p. 100, /©Vicki Beaver for p. 120, /©Art Kowalsky for p. 142(fjord), /©Reinhard Dirscherl for p. 176(Rift valley), /©Matthew Antonino for p. 188(tl), /©Matthew Antonino for p. 188(tr), /©Matthew Antonino for p. 188(bl), /©Matthew Antonino for p. 188(br), /©Magdalena Rehova for p. 196(tl), /©Rob Crandall for p. 196(tr), /©Melba Photo Agency for p. 196(c), /©Deborah Benbrook for p. 196(bl); The Art Archive for p. 56; Corbis /©Nora Feller for p. 18, /©HO/Reuters for p. 21, /©Galen Rowell/Encyclopedia for p. 112, /©Jerry Cooke for p. 166; Courtesy of elBulli, www.elbulli.com for p. 68(r); Courtesy of ETH Zürich for p. 98; Courtesy of Lisa Fittipaldi, www.lisafittipaldi.com for p. 180(l) and p. 182; Getty Images /©Roger Fenton/Hulton Archive for p. 13, /©Marco Simoni/Robert Harding World Imagery for p. 14(bl), /©Echo/Cultura for p. 26, /©Betsie Van der Meer/Stone for p. 44, /©Lluis Gene/AFP for p. 68(l), /©Holos/Stone for p. 72(t), /©Image Source for p. 116, /©Justin Sullivan for p. 130, /©Thomas Kokta/Radius Images for p. 196(br); iStockphoto.com /©Loretta Hostettler for p. 6, /©Holger Mette for p. 10, /©ralf mitsch for p. 14(tr), /©Jonathan Barton for p. 142(rucksack), /©directphotoorg for p. 142(sushi), /©Radoslaw Kostka for p. 142(jacuzzi), /©Richard Gillard for p. 179; By courtesy of the Association of Mouth and Foot Painting Artists Worldwide and of Michael Monaco, who is a student member of the Association, www.vdmfk.com for p. 180(r); Photolibrary.com /©Philip Wallick/age fotostock for p. 14(br), /©Robert Harding Travel for p. 90, /©age fotostock for p. 146(r), /©age fotostock for p. 154; Press Association Images /©Dario Lopez-Mills/AP for p. 64, /©Federico Gambarini/DPA for p. 71, /©John Giles/PA Archive for p. 146(l); Science Photo Library /©Ria Novosti for p. 34 and p. 102
While every effort has been made, it has not always been possible to identify the sources of all the material used, or to trace all copyright holders. If any omissions are brought to our notice, we will be happy to include the appropriate acknowledgements on reprinting.

Review units written by Tom Bradbury.
Picture research by Suzanne Williams/Pictureresearch.co.uk
Illustrations by David Shephard, Humberto Blanco, Julian Mosedale, Leo Brown, Mark Draisey, Mark Duffin, Roger Penwill, Rory Walker and Tom Croft.

Notes